NO MAN'S LAND

'George Monbiot investigates what could be the final struggles of Africa's surviving pastoral peoples. He also tells his own story, of a perilous journey through one of the world's harshest environments, writing with humour and a refreshing lightness of touch'
– Oliver Tickell, *Daily Telegraph*

'This is a fascinating book that occasionally blossoms with haunting prose . . . The future of East Africa's nomads is a cause worth fighting for. They are fortunate to have Monbiot on their side'
– Mary Anne Fitzgerald, *Independent on Sunday*

'I found the book moving, compassionate, bristling with rage, in tone both exhilarating and depressing. What I found really great about *No Man's Land* was the fact that George took the nomads of Kenya and Tanzania on their own terms'
– Biyi Bandele Thomas, *Kaleidoscope*, Radio 4

'He is extremely perceptive on the hopelessness, the loss of identity, that nomads feel when turned out of their traditional grazing-grounds and robbed of their cattle, whose care is their only skill and their sole means of life . . . But his tale is always readable because it is told by means of talks with people. As to style, he hits the reader a smack now and then with a phrase that is sharply right' – The *Tablet*
'Monbiot's book has some disturbing sections, of beatings, killings, starvation and famine. But it also has passages describing great beauty, of landscapes, birds, weather and atmosphere . . . An inquiring book by a sensitive man' – *Africa Analysis*

'Monbiot's lucid, unhysterical prose holds the dispassionate analysis of conviction . . . Recently, Monbiot spoke to the Royal Geographical Society whilst on crutches, because of injuries sustained during peaceful protest (defending Solsbury Hill from the Department of Transport). The rich irony is, the abuse of power that he took personal risks to expose in East Africa has injured him in our own back yard' – *Amnesty Magazine*

'Monbiot, still only thirty, has written a splendid book, deserving of a prize and one that makes one pause in the lemming-like rush of life in the West to ponder the fate of fellow human beings whose dignity in the face of adversity leaves us with a lot to be desired. The blood-soaked plains of Africa have shaken the West but it has not stirred. Monbiot's book should prod us all into action'
– *Western Morning News*

GEORGE MONBIOT was born in 1963. He studied zoology at Oxford, then worked for the BBC, where he won a Sony Award and the Lloyds National Screenwriting Competition. He is the author of *Poisoned Arrows* and *Amazon Watershed*, which won the Sir Peter Kent Award. In the course of his travels he has been shot at, beaten up by military police, shipwrecked, stung almost to death by hornets and swept away down a mountain river. He is *persona non grata* in seven countries and has a life sentence *in absentia* in Indonesia. He is a Visiting Fellow of Green College, Oxford.

Also by George Monbiot

Poisoned Arrows

Amazon Watershed

George Monbiot

NO MAN'S LAND

AN INVESTIGATIVE JOURNEY
through KENYA AND TANZANIA

PICADOR

First published 1994 by Macmillan London

This edition published 1995 by Picador
an imprint of Macmillan General Books
Cavaye Place London SW10 9PG
and Basingstoke

Associated companies throughout the world

ISBN 0 330 34123 5

Copyright © George Monbiot 1994

1 3 5 7 9 8 6 4 2

A CIP catalogue record for this book is available from
the British Library

Photoset by Parker Typesetting Service, Leicester
Printed by Cox & Wyman Ltd, Reading, Berkshire

CONTENTS

ACKNOWLEDGEMENTS

My great thanks to Adrian Arbib, Ruth McCoy, Karen Twining, Moses Mpoke, Stephen Natiang, Dismas Ekeno, Toronkei ole Pose, John Munyes, Jonathon Kamumon, Rose Etemesi, Jane Wambui, the doctors and nurses of the Lodwar District Hospital, Ian Leggatt, Kate Geary, David Presswell, Mike Hamblett, Shelley Braithwaite, John French, Alois Lesuan, Jock Conyngham, Ntoros ole Baari, Brian Nugent, Daniel Juma, Daniel Somoire, Joseph Simel, Ander McIntyre, Helen Lawrence, Guy Horton, Charles Lane, Oliver Tickell, Sir Crispin Tickell, Casper Henderson, Rachel Duncan, Jan Dean and the staff of Green College, Antony Harwood, Roland Philipps, Tanya Stobbs, Emil Brugman, Peter Kisopia, Paul Baxter, Christopher Thouless, Thomas Harding, Matayo Kalimapus, Akale and the people of Ngilukumong, Esther, Dismas Karenga, Pius Chuchu, Loparikoi Nataana, Apetet and the people of Naramam, Stephen Ewano, Daniel Edapal, Father Seamus, Pastor Nicholas, Nasha, Samson and the people of Enkaroni, Olurie and the people of Loibor Serrit, Paul Ntiati, the staff of GREP, Ben Koissaba, Metoe ole Loombaa, Moringe Parkipuny, Mr arap Kipkeo, the people of Ilkimpa, Gidamwaghwela Gidaweda, Duncan Getakanod and family, Rosemary Benzina, Patrick, Gabriel Lenyakopiro, Peter and Julius, George Lekamario, Wilfred Thesiger, Ntalon, Ledumen and the people of Leseven, Archer's Post Health Centre, Father Lino, my friends in Wajir district, Joyce Mbogo, Daudi and Margaret Limlim, William Eipa, Paul Symonds, Geoff Sayer, the staff of Oxfam Nairobi, Eliud Ngunjiri, Roger Short, Virginia Luling, Anna Piussi, Eve Rogers, Killian Holland, Douglas Johnson, Henry Fossebrook, Olivia Graham, Tracy Worcester, David and Emma Marrian, Marcus Colchester, Adrian Cullis, Richard Harrison, Chris Gerrard, Vernon Reynolds, Richard Bradley, Hannah Scrase, Danielle Seif, Koi Thomson, John Hemming, Jean Bagnall-Smith, John Ruthven, Grant Sonnex, Kevin Watkins, Alex de Waal, Monica Kathina, Dhyani

Berger, Ed Barrow, Angelo Bonfiglioli.

Unfortunately I do not have the space to list the hundreds of books and papers I found invaluable.

LIST OF ILLUSTRATIONS

1. Matayo
2. The desert around Ngilukumong
3. Herdsman in the Lokwanomoru mountains
4. Waiting for the Toposa
5. After the rain at Ngilukumong
6. The massacre at Kokuro
7. Fleeing the Pokot
8. Maasai herds
9. Amboseli: torn apart by tourists
10. Narok: after the flood
11. Tourists haggling with the Maasai
12. Catching the white ox
13. Toronkei losing his moranhood
14. Canada comes to Tanzania
15. Ntalon and the Nkunono outcasts
16. The water that kept the Samburu alive, in the Sarova Shaba Hotel
17. Waiting for the rain in Samburu district
18. Fugitives in Nachola
19. The civil servants among those murdered by the army in Wajir
20. Drawing water in Wajir
21. Two identity cards: the Somalis are registered twice
22. On the streets in Kitale . . .
23. . . . and on the trash heap
24. Daudi and Margaret in Kibera
25. Moses leaving the wilderness

All the photographs are reproduced by kind permission of the photographer, Adrian Arbib

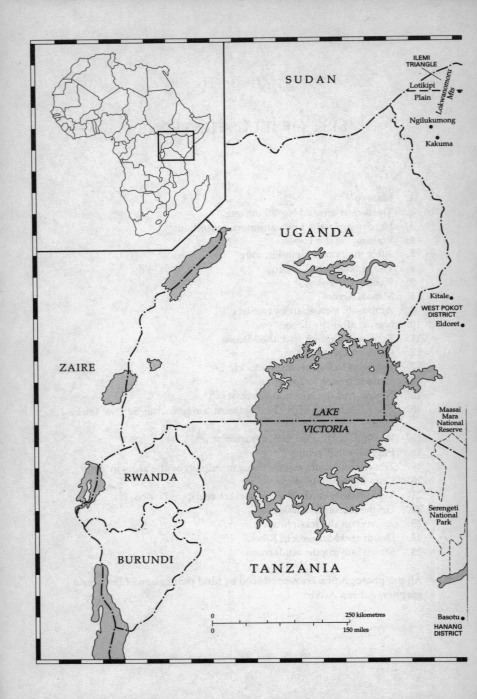

SUDAN

ILEMI
TRIANGLE

Lotikipi
Plain

*Lokvyanomoru
Mts*

Ngilukumong

Kakuma

UGANDA

Kitale

WEST POKOT
DISTRICT

Eldoret

ZAIRE

*LAKE
VICTORIA*

Maasai
Mara
National
Reserve

RWANDA

Serengeti
National
Park

BURUNDI

TANZANIA

| 0 | | 250 kilometres |
| 0 | | 150 miles |

Basotu

HANANG
DISTRICT

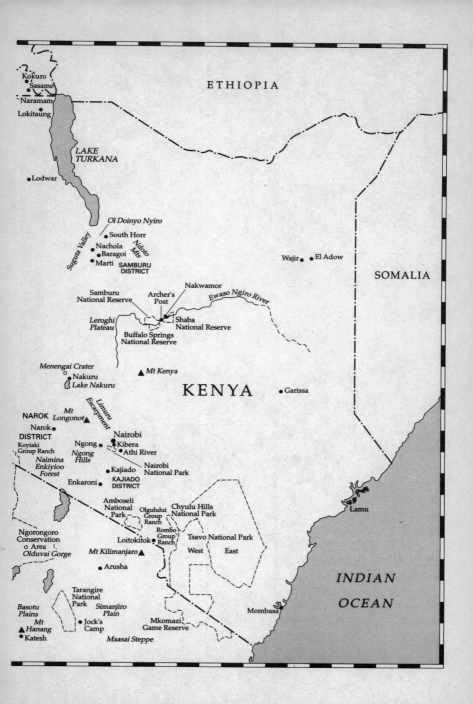

ETHIOPIA

Kokuro
Sasame
Naramam
Lokitaung

LAKE
TURKANA

Lodwar

Ol Doinyo Nyiro
South Horr
Nachola
Baragoi
Marti
SAMBURU
DISTRICT

Sugata Valley

Ndoto Mts

Wajir   El Adow

SOMALIA

Nakwamor

Samburu
National Reserve

Archer's
Post

Ewaso Ngiro River

Leroghi
Plateau

Shaba
National Reserve

Buffalo Springs
National Reserve

Menengai Crater
Nakuru
Lake Nakuru

Mt Kenya

KENYA

Garissa

NAROK
DISTRICT
Narok

Mt
Longonot

Limuru Escarpment

Nairobi
Kibera
Athi River

Koyiaki
Group Ranch

Naimina
Enkiyioo
Forest

Ngong
Ngong
Hills

Kajiado

Nairobi
National Park

Enkaroni

KAJIADO
DISTRICT

Ngorongoro
Conservation
o Area
Olduvai Gorge

Amboseli
National
Park

Olgulului
Group
Ranch

Chyulu Hills
National Park

Lamu

Rombo
Group
Ranch

Loitokitok

Tsavo National Park

Mt Kilimanjaro

West   East

Arusha

Basotu
Plains
Mt
Hanang
Katesh

Tarangire
National
Park

Jock's
Camp

Simanjiro
Plain

Maasai Steppe

Mkomazi
Game Reserve

Mombasa

INDIAN

OCEAN

INTRODUCTION

Cain slew Abel because Abel was the beloved of God. Abel was a herder of sheep, one of God's people, while Cain, as a tiller of the ground, was an infidel. Their conflict, the conflict between nomads and settled society, is fundamental to humankind. Civilization, from the Latin *civis*, a townsperson, means the culture of those whose homes do not move. The horde, from the Turkish *ordu*, a camp and its people, is its antithesis, which both defines civilization and threatens it. We, the stayers, detest the movers, be they Huns, Mongols, Kurds or Gypsies. This is partly because we feel that they threaten us or our property. But I have come to believe that there are more substantial reasons for our disdain. We hate them because they remind us of who we are.

Humankind was born on the road. Our brains, our physique, our emotional identity are those of the migrant. The restlessness which, in one corrupted form or another, is felt by every human being on earth, is incurable, for it is fundamental to our nature. In the African savannahs in which humankind evolved, the land and the seasons were too variable for our ancestors to have stayed in one place. When the wild animals and the patches of edible plants shifted with the rains, the people were forced to follow. Their journeys must have taken them vast distances across the Rift Valley, through its grasslands and its woods, around its mineral lakes and volcano fields.

We evolved the characteristics that make us human – our two-leggedness, our complex brains, our enhanced ability to communicate, our use of sight as the primary sense – partly as a response to this need to travel. With them came emotions –

1

our great capacity for anger, fear, excitement, curiosity and wonder – without which our ancestors could not have negotiated the wild beasts, the human friends or enemies, the open wastes and the oases of fabulous abundance through which they passed. Like our two-leggedness, these emotional characteristics have stayed with us long after the lifestyle that gave rise to them has gone. While once they kept us alive, now they torment us. They beat against the inside of our skulls, demanding consummation, threatening us with insanity if we do not heed them. But there are no appropriate means by which they can be fully expressed.

We invent occasions, such as a football match or a war game, in which we symbolically hunt, fight or flee, express our anger, terror or excitement. We may use literature, the cinema or computer games to excite our curiosity, our wonder or our fear. Television tries to provide us with a substitute for the variety encountered by our ancestors, travelling across the most varied environment on earth. Ambition allows us to make symbolic conquests and provides us with the means to exploit and defend the symbols deemed to be resources. But these substitutes will never fully satisfy our urges. Our 'culture of violence' is the product of our culture of non-violence, in which arbitrary, meaningless acts of depravity – in life or on film – replace our ancestors' response to the dangers of the savannah.

The remaining migrants are utterly different from those who gave rise to us. They are sophisticated, specialized peoples, whose lives have changed perhaps as swiftly as those of any groups on earth. The first humans were hunters and gatherers or scavengers, while today's foot travellers may be traders, entertainers, bandits or true nomads. But the very fact that they travel means that we can see enough of the other, unappeased side of our nature in them to hate them with the passion with which two estranged brothers may hate. We want to break the mirror of the past, so that we may no longer see what we cannot be. We want, like Cain, to rise up and slay our brother, so that we no longer have to acknowledge that the hordes, not the civilized, are the beloved of the God of our creation.

2

Deliberately in some cases, accidentally in others, we are wiping out the last migrants. The Gypsies of Europe, having survived the Holocaust, are threatened by the age-old prejudices with which settled society confronts them. Even in the most liberal nations they are finding their right to travel restricted. The Kurds are struggling against the governments of every country in which they exist: at least one of these governments wants to exterminate them. Many of the Bedouin are succumbing to the promises of easy living proffered by the civilized around whom they travel. As these migrants disappear it is not only they but we who are diminished, for with them we lose what they may have to teach us about who we really are.

Of all the migratory peoples remaining on earth, none can show us more than the true nomads: the herders of animals, who live by driving their beasts from one place to another in search of good grazing. Like the first human beings, they depend on the natural environment in which they travel. Of the nomads, those who can tell us most about ourselves are surely the people following the trails of our ancestors: the migrants crossing the grasslands, the woods and the volcano fields in the savannahs of East Africa.

This book tells the story of my journeys among some of the most extraordinary peoples on earth. It shows how they are confronting the forces which threaten to deprive both them and us of the life that civilization has tried to suppress. Travelling in the savannahs with the Turkana, the Maasai, the Barabaig, Samburu and Somalis, I have seen astonishing and terrible things. In northern Kenya I saw how bandits, equipped by the corrupt governments of both Kenya itself and some of its neighbours, have been massacring the nomads, driving the survivors into famine zones where first the cattle and then the humans die. Further south I watched the open savannahs upon which the nomads rely being divided up and reduced by ploughing; I have seen the local people curtail their own culture and prepare to kill the outsiders threatening to dispossess them.

Among the Maasai and Samburu I found, controversially, that one of the greatest threats to their existence and to their environment is conservation. This, by taking their best lands and confining them to areas too small to support their herds, forces the nomads to destroy the resources that keep them alive. I have found evidence of systematic beatings and false imprisonment carried out by people purporting to be protecting wildlife. I have followed the victims of government policies, government neglect and corrupt foreign interests to the slums around the big cities, where I found them living in conditions of the most appalling brutality.

But, most significantly, I have seen that the nomads of East Africa are finding ways to survive. All nomads are opportunists, and the adaptability and cultural flexibility that opportunism demands means that they are possibly better equipped than any other of the world's traditional peoples to withstand dramatic change. Even in the most frightful slums I have found what appear to be the first stirrings of hope.

To help me cover these stories I turned to my best friend, Adrian Arbib, a professional photographer and a superb mechanic, who had twice saved my life on a previous expedition. Reliable, unflinching, quietly aware of the difficulties and frustrations of what we set out to do, he was an excellent travelling companion. In September 1992 I succumbed to my own restlessness, and we began our journey through East Africa.

CHAPTER ONE

The Travelling Star

To the Turkana of northern Kenya, God and the sky are the same. They possess the same name – Akuj – and the will of God can be divined by reading the sky. For these nomads, as for many others, no one place on earth is important enough for a god or a spirit to make its own: there are no home gods because there is no home. Instead there is a unifying principle, stretching over all the lands the people cross: one sky and one God.

If the horns of a sickle moon point towards heaven, the tribes below will suffer hunger. If they point towards the earth then rain will fall. If the moon stands upright in the sky, God and the earth are in harmony and all will be well for the Turkana. But if the moon rises red, there will be war.

Rain follows the dark shadow of a camel appearing in the eastern sky, or a red planet which stays close to the horizon. But of all the potent messengers of fortune, none is greater than a travelling star. The Turkana, like the shepherds attending the birth of Christ, will follow one to their destiny, wherever it might go. In the first week of my journeys among them, a comet crossed the western sky. The herdsmen dropped their plans and chased it over the mountains. To them, as to their ancestors, the only hope of survival in these arid lands is movement. The nomads and their herds will die if they are left behind by the rain.

But for the elders of Ngilukumong, where my story begins, the great migrations have come to an end. They are too old to move and have settled around an oasis in the semi-desert to end their days with story-telling, prophecy and games. These men, who have lived a life of murder, theft, flight and concealment, who have run on occasions one hundred miles without a rest, who have crossed the regions known as Beyond Urine, for the only way to reach them is to drink one's own urine, are gentle in their old age. Leaning on the trunk of the tree in whose shade they gather are fighting sticks, spears and a Kalashnikov. Once the weapons of warriors, these are now used by the elders only for defence against their enemies the Toposa and Dodoth, who stalk the margins of their lands. Somehow, in the harshest of all the arid places of East Africa, they have found a balance in life, a contentment denied to the people of the richest lands on earth.

There were, of course, discontents among them, quarrelsome, greedy or irritable people, but it soon became clear to me that this was a tribe subject to the therapy of constant movement, that the old men had fulfilled their human destiny through a lifetime of travel. Besides their weapons and their animals they owned next to nothing. They coveted my possessions, the extravagances of the civilized, but were more concerned to relieve me of my money, with which they could buy tobacco and food. As nomads they owned nothing which they or their donkeys could not carry. Their lives had been as hard, as sparse as those of any people on earth, but the constraint to move had been a double freedom: freedom from both the trauma of possessiveness and the misery of introspection. A sufferer from both, I found in my own travels a release from the decay to which I had succumbed at home.

Like anyone softened by civilization, I found the lands of the Turkana almost unendurable. I have never been anywhere as hot as those deserts, waiting, at that time, for the late autumn rains. If, on my first days there, I got to my feet abruptly, I would stagger for a second, lose my vision and almost pass out, then have to stand still for a minute or two until the horizon stopped dancing and swirling around me and levelled out once more to an obdurate grey line. I found no energy for anything but drinking water and stumbling from my day shelter to the hide on which I slept at night.

Even then, under a sky as open and unrelenting as the land, I lay face upwards, tickled by the trails of sweat that ran

down my forehead and over my chest. The air snapped and
rustled with mosquitoes. In the glow of the fires I saw the
translucent tails of white scorpions, held high as they pranced
past my hide. The Turkana told me of camel spiders – known to
some as wind scorpions on account of their inordinate speed –
which came in the night, reputedly paralysed the limb or flank
of an animal or man, and chewed away a chunk of flesh the
size of a child's fist. On the plains beyond the thorn compound
I heard the song of a lone hyena; on the sand one morning I
found the track of a snake, sidling around my feet. The aridity,
the inflexibility of this land, the flies by day and the mosquitoes
by night, made nothing seem so appealing as a ragged wet day
in England, the ditches flushed with black water and dead
leaves, the rain spattering against the windows of dogged
civilization. But after a day or two, I began, slowly, to uncurl
and enjoy the place. I started to explore first the settlement
itself, then the wide savannahs that surround it.

Ngilukumong is one of the camps where the old men, the
children and some of the women stay while the young men
and their sisters take the cattle into the mountains. During the
long dry seasons there is no grass on the surrounding plains –
so cattle could not survive there – but there are, in some places,
hardy and mildly toxic green shrubs. Along the banks of the
empty river that twists past the camp is a narrow and winding
forest. On the trees and bushes there the inhabitants graze
their camels and goats, whose milk, blood and meat keep them
alive until the rains return. Then, amid great excitement, the
herders come back with their cattle and stay until the grass
brought up by the rain is exhausted, whereupon they leave the
hard pan of the plains once more and drive their beasts back to
the hills.

While the herders move every day, building themselves no
houses and knowing no home, the people of Ngilukumong
may stay on one spot for years and move, when they do, just
short distances up and down the seasonal river. But this does
not mean that theirs is a permanent village. The inhabitants are
ready to flee at any time if that is what their enemies, disease or
a devastating drought demand. When I stayed among them,

the Toposa, armed with AK47s and G3s, were moving south from the Sudanese border, and ripples of anxiety were running through the Turkana population. Some of the elders of the camp spoke of abandoning Ngilukumong and moving further into the centre of the district.

This lack of permanence is reflected in the architecture of their camp. From a distance their houses look like birds' nests turned upside down. Coming closer, but for the increasing scale, the impression is hardly dispelled. They are domes of woven twigs, thatched with grass and leaves, about eight feet high and ten feet wide, entered by a hole through which one has to crawl. Nothing on or in them is irreplaceable and the whole camp can be packed and loaded onto donkeys in the space of an hour or two, abandoning the houses. They surround a thorn corral, where the goats are kept at night to protect them from hyenas. Each clump of houses is itself surrounded by another thorn fence, to protect the people from the same predators. Up and down the course of the river there are stories of infants, children, even adults, being carried away or consumed in the night.

On my third day at Ngilukumong, I left the huts and walked out across the savannahs. It felt as if the ground and the sky, as hard, as hot, as monotonous as each other, conspired to clap me flat between their two planes. At my feet the ground was level grey, with nothing to arrest the eye but stones and dried goats' droppings rolled in the dust. In places I saw the tracks of scarab beetles, or the skeleton trail of a twig skidded across the dust by the wind. I found the bones of goats and a herd of ghostly cattle, their skulls tilted back, jaws open, as if waiting to catch the rain. Raising my eyes, I saw that the plain was broken by single trees and infrequent bright shrubs. They were oddly dispersed, as if, in that heat, none could bear to be jostling its neighbour. They shimmered and shifted in the mirage lakes that preceded me across the plain. It seemed as if the sun were melting the earth. Black, shiny, labile, it hardened again to dull grey as I approached.

Drifting above the mirage I saw the top half of a man, head bowed, his spear across his shoulders, crossing the plain in search of his lost camel. Beyond him was a wavering haze of grey mountains. The half-man in the mirage and I were the only people on the plain. The landscape swirling around my head, I turned and walked towards the forest.

Under the trees, the great corrugated acacias and the thin and twisted *Ziziphus*, my head stopped spinning and the sweat, held back while I was walking, started from my skin. I sat on a low branch, listened and watched. The old trees soughed and creaked in the wind funnelled along the river bed. A gust would bring a patter of pods and dried leaves to the ground, followed immediately by the rustle of small feet, as the goats browsing in the forest rushed in to sweep them up. In the treetops birds called. I heard the harsh swozzle of a go-away bird, the tumbling laughter of a black-headed oriole, the unnerving strumming of mourning doves, like fingers rubbed across a drum.

Each way I turned was a portrait of the Turkana and their animals, framed by the trunks of the trees. I saw an old man, standing straight on one straight leg, his other bent before him as if he were about to start walking, speaking in a haze of yellow light to a boy carrying a herding switch. In the next frame I saw camels, stretching their necks into the canopy of the trees, their flat feet planted in the sand. A woman in a knotty bower used a stick to beat yellow berries, as hard and dry as hunza apricots, from a thorn bush. Beside her, in a plain frame of two straight-trunked trees, a boy bounced on the low branch of an acacia, bringing it close enough to the ground, as it dipped, for his herd of many-coloured goats to reach. Shoving, climbing over each other, they tore away mouthfuls of leaves as the branch swung down to them, then craned and reared up as it flicked out of reach. Beside me, on the trunk of the tree upon which I sat, were the skins of hatched cicadas, split down the back, their front claws raised as if in prayer.

I stepped out into the bed of the empty river. Its last coat of clay, now baked, split and curled, tinkled at my feet like broken china. The wind, gusting heat, dried out my throat, threw dust into my eyes, and carried snatches of laughter and screams from the clump of women gathered around a waterhole.

Stiff-legged, pompous, a ground hornbill strutted among the bushes on the far bank, black as the devil, cravatted with a shocking red wattle like coagulated blood.

As I walked down the river bed, across the far levee and over the level ground beyond, I found myself looking for bones. I had convinced myself that I would be the one to discover that critical fragment, those two deep orbits staring across three million years. I pored over the river gravels, the pebbles of the plain, the stones of the trails leading from Ngilukumong to the nearest trading settlement, hunting for the first human being.

The earliest of all human or pre-human remains were found just one hundred miles from where I now walked. On the eastern shores of Lake Turkana the excavation team led by the famous palaeontologist and conservationist Richard Leakey discovered the remains of upright pre-humans around three million years old. They lived in a land wetter than the Turkana's is today, but subject like theirs to long dry seasons and irregular rains. In certain places and at certain times the rains would have brought flushes of food: migrating animals, nesting birds, hatching insects and edible plants. In between , as today, there would have been wastes where nothing could be eaten. The only means of survival would have been migration, following the game herds, trekking from one patch of fruiting trees to another, chasing the rain.

Life in the savannahs required abilities our more distant forest ancestors did not possess. The savannah apes needed to be able to eat anything, and this meant both changes to the hands and teeth and the use of new tools, for cracking bones and nuts, cutting animal hides or digging for roots. On the open plains smell and hearing would have been of less use than sight. The need to cover great distances, perhaps also to carry food and infants, would have encouraged a shift from four legs to two. The variability of the environment, the predators that stalked it and the need to exploit everything that could be exploited would have required communication, planning and speculation: the demands that shaped the human mind. We are what we are because of the savannahs, and our ancestral need to move across them.

When human beings left East Africa, they chose to live in places as similar as possible to those in which they had evolved. Palaeontology suggests that humankind moved even into the frozen tundra before it moved into forests, and our abiding fear and folklore of the forest may be an echo of our ancestral propensity for open spaces. Open spaces, whether savannah, desert, steppe or tundra, mean movement, for in all cases short bursts of abundance are followed by long lean periods, and concentrations of animals or edible plants are surrounded by emptiness. Only much later, through force of circumstance or force of numbers, did humans move into more constant environments. Our brains, hands, limbs and senses, our social life and patterns of thought are those of the migrant.

I found not a skull or even a fragment of bone (except the remains of dismembered livestock) but a perfect stone arrowhead. An inch and a half long, with a short haft, it was chipped from a fine-grained, maroon stone. I suspected that this was not the work of our ancestors, but that of the nomads crossing the same savannahs in historical times. The iron age in Turkana district did not begin until around 500 AD.

It would be tempting to think that there had been a simple progression in East Africa from the world's first migrant peoples to some of its last, but nothing could be further from the truth. In Africa, as in Europe and Asia, Cain preceded Abel. The herders of beasts could not have survived without the tillers of the ground, for they have always depended, in the harshest seasons, on grain they purchase with meat or milk. There have probably always been migrant peoples on the savannahs, but before the emergence of agriculture they would have survived by hunting, scavenging and gathering. Herders – or nomads – did not take over until four or five thousand years ago.

The herders occupied the open regions of the world while the farmers stayed in the closed ones, the steady and reliable forest zones which, through both need and fear, they had cleared for fields. In these places they built the settlements that were in time to become the world's great cities. Nomads could not survive in this environment as there was not enough grass for their animals. While the Black Huns, the nomad invaders from the central Asian steppes, found good grazing for their horses on the Russian and Hungarian plains, and were thus able to overrun eastern Europe with comparative ease, the closed lands of western Europe forced them to break up in search of small pockets of grass. This was their undoing: the resulting disarray and debilitation contributed to Attila's defeat in northern France.

While the hordes sacked civilization, civilization coveted the lands of the hordes. As settled peoples outgrew their closed places, they started fighting for control of the nomads' best grazing lands, places wet enough for planting crops. Over centuries the nomads were pushed back, and those whose lands were richest were the first to fall. Only the herders in some of the driest places on earth were left alone; it was for this reason that I began my journeys among the Turkana. In the parched and isolated north-western corner of Kenya, they had remained their own masters. Change was working its way across their lands, but it was still possible to see something of how they lived before the most intrusive settled people in history – the modern Europeans – arrived in East Africa. At Ngilukumong, before investigating the threats to the Turkana's existence, I could find out what it was that the world risked losing if the last of its nomads were to disappear.

The East African nomads' mobility and their capacity to push aside or assimilate the earlier inhabitants of their lands were comparable to the powers of the migrant forces of Central Asia. As the Huns, who may have originated as the Hsiung-Nu of northern China, hammered on the doors of Rome, and the Turks, arising just to the west of the Gobi Desert, soon colonized the Mediterranean coast, the Maasai swept from southern Sudan to northern Tanzania in three centuries. The Turkana, emerging in what is now Uganda, drove the competing nomads from the lands they now occupy in Kenya in as many decades.

During the late seventeenth or early eighteenth century the elders of the Jie tribe, in the eastern Ugandan mountains, sent their young people eastwards to find new pastures. The grazing they encountered there was so good and the inhabitants so easy to rout that the scouts decided to keep the land for themselves. They refused to report back to their parents. When the elders threatened them, they denied that they were Jie any more, and named themselves after a holy mountain they had found in their new land called Aturkan. When the elders pressed their case, they declared war.

Holding back their parents on their western flank, the Turkana, like Joshua advancing over Canaan, stormed south and east through the savannahs, routing the Samburu, Gabbra, Toposa, Dodoth and Merille peoples, stopping only at the mountain wall of West Pokot and the eastern edge of the dry Suguta Valley. By the time the British arrived in their lands the Turkana had become so accustomed to military success that they refused to compromise, even in the face of the King's African Rifles. Trying simultaneously to crush the Turkana and to supply their own troops with free meat, the British organized punitive raids, stealing from the nomads 250,000 cattle between 1916 and 1918. Thousands of Turkana were killed, but in 1918 they surrounded and defeated one of the biggest expeditions the British sent against them.

Using their notorious Witchcraft and Collective Punishment ordinances, the authorities killed or exiled the Turkana's spiritual leaders and continued to loot vast numbers of cattle, bringing the Turkana to the verge of starvation, but they never succeeded in establishing full control. Convinced that the Turkana were beyond redemption, the British declared their district closed and, with the exception of an occasional bloody attempt to impose some incomprehensible law, left them to their own devices.

Although roads, two vicious droughts and automatic weapons have, since Independence, begun to twist the pattern of their lives, most Turkana remain as uncivilized – as mobile – as the rebellious Jie. Their migrations over the savannahs recapitulate those of the early humans. No one, to my knowledge, knows how old the tracks of the Turkana are, but the topography of parts of their land forces the traveller into a network of gullies and gorges. If the pre-humans followed the rains into the mountains, they would have had to have taken exactly the same routes as the Turkana. This means, astonishingly, that the trails established three million years ago by our earliest ancestors are likely still to be in use.

But the Turkana have evolved a more efficient means of surviving in the savannahs than that of the pre-humans. While our ancestors had to rely on what they could consume themselves, the Turkana use their animals to convert inedible vegetation into meat and milk. Herding can thus support a far higher population than hunting and gathering alone. To find the best grazing, the young men may trek with their animals for hundreds of miles, into the mountains of Ethiopia, Sudan or Uganda, or down to the acacia woodlands of the southern ranges. Their survival depends upon the experience and predictions of the elders. One mistake, one misdirected journey, could destroy all the animals a man possesses.

Every day at Ngilukumong the old men gathered beneath a tree to play *ajua*, the Turkana version of the oldest board game on earth. Sitting on tiny wooden stools, wrapped in their blankets, they shifted pebbles along two lines of cavities scooped from the dust, frowning with concentration. As they considered their moves, they discussed the prospects in the mountains. Every few days a scout would run into the camp with news of the rains, the grass that had been found, the movements of their enemies. The old men would absorb this intelligence, watch the sky at night and decide, as they played, what should be done. In placing their pebbles in the holes, it was as if they were placing their herds around the mountains. Indeed, ajua is a herders' game, which follows a flock of stones around a district in the dirt and requires the skill of checking numbers without having to count. No herder could survive in the savannahs if he could not scan his beasts and know immediately that every one was there.

At night, silent, sitting outside their houses on their stools, the old men would watch the sky. They tracked the movement of the planets, noted the colour of the stars, judged the depth of the haze around the moon, sought shadows in the air.

Certain, discrete signs they could explain to me. But there were others they could not describe, the invisible manifestations of Akuj, the God of the Sky. Their divination was a matter of survival. Growth and desiccation are so rapid in those savannahs that the Turkana must anticipate the rain: the herders must start moving towards it before it falls. Somehow, working with elemental signs unrecognized by Western meteorologists, with a sensitivity that may be inseparable from spiritual enlightenment, the old men were nearly always right.

Most of the elders at Ngilukumong were tall, lean and very dark. But for a blanket flung across one shoulder, sandals, and a few beads around the neck, they were naked. They wore circular blades as bracelets; some wore a steel hook on one finger. Traditionalists had covered their scalps with domes of blue and orange clay. They carried staves with sharp heads and tiny stools. Tied up in the corners of their blankets were wads of a heavy black tobacco, so strong that when I copied them by sucking some I nearly passed out.

At first I was nervous of these old men. Their self-possession illuminated my own insecurity. Unsettled, impatient, alarmed that I might be offending, I said too much, apologized too much, shifted around too much. Never embarrassed by silence, they watched me with bemusement and said nothing. But after two or three days, as something of the stillness of Ngilukumong settled over me, the old men gradually became more intelligible.

The man in whose enclosure I was sleeping, Dismas Ekeno, seldom spoke. He sang, to his absent cattle, every night. At dusk I watched him standing in the goat corral, amid the wailing kids, the thud of young rams fighting, the groans of the old nannies, as still and silent as a heron in a pond, watching and assessing. He would dart forward and seize a goat that needed treatment, drawing a thorn from a foot or spitting tobacco juice into an infected eye.

Dismas never raised his voice, never showed his teeth, and never lost his stillness or intensity. He became expansive only when talking of his animals. He was a brilliant craftsman. On luminous nights he used the blade he wore on his wrist to

15

carve logs into wooden urns, singing in a low cracked voice about his cows. Although Dismas had two wives, a large herd and the respect of the other elders, he still deferred to his father. Natiang was a handsome, grey-bearded dandy who wore a wooden comb in his hair and must have been twice the age he looked. He was the clown of Ngilukumong, who disconcertingly smirked with repressed laughter whenever he laid eyes on me, admonished me at length in Turkana – which I could not understand – and put his hands over his ears and howled in mock horror when I asked my translator what was going on. But it was he who gave me the most precious gift I ever received in East Africa, a ring carved by his great grandfather from fossil ivory.

No one at Ngilukumong fascinated me as much as Matayo. He had a long, gentle face, with sad folds of skin pulling down the corners of his eyes and a twisted scar on the bridge of his nose. When he spoke he spread out his hands and brought them together, drew circles in the air, pushed his arguments away to the horizon, holding my gaze with eyes that seemed sadly aware of all the weaknesses of humankind. He had killed more than three hundred men, and from central Kenya to southern Sudan his name was used to frighten little children.

Matayo had acquired the third of his twelve names on killing his first Toposa. As a souvenir of the event, his chest and stomach were decorated with chains of scars. With a borrowed rifle he started cattle-raiding, stealing from the Toposa, Dodoth, Dongiro, Karamojong, Merille and Samburu peoples. He became known as a man who never wasted a bullet, and in 1940 was recruited into the British Army. He was taken all over the world and collected bullets in his thigh and shoulder from the Italians in Abyssinia, shrapnel in his foot from the Japanese in Burma, and a long shallow dent in his skull from the Germans in the Western Desert. When the war ended he went home, but soon found that for him its attractions had faded. He slipped away one morning and started walking. He walked into the Ethiopian Highlands, crossed into Sudan, followed the Nile into Uganda, walked round Lake Victoria to Tanzania and returned through the Rift Valley to Turkana district, keeping himself alive on the way by hunting. Back home he started raiding again and defending his own community from counter raids: in one attack he fired twelve bullets and killed all twelve of the raiders. This life came to an end when he lent his brother his gun for a battle with the Toposa and the brother never returned. Now he felt sorry he had killed so many people: he saw that all those men had parents, just like his own sons.

'In the old days,' he told me, 'I felt no remorse. Now I know it does not please God.'

He had watched East Africa falling apart, and blamed the civil wars he had seen for the droughts that were becoming longer and longer in Turkana district.

'God and the angels reject us now. When I was a young man, this land was rich, the cattle were fat and the grass was high. Rain fell every year. But since then the nations have begun to fight, and all has been conflict and destruction. Because everyone wants to be in charge, God wants none of us.'

Matayo himself appeared to be indestructible. At seventy-five he walked with a long, stiff stride, ate nothing and vanished into the desert for weeks at a time, appearing again without explanation to settle on his stool in front of his hut and call his wives for a mug of tea.

The women at Ngilukumong had small flat breasts and hard, determined faces. They shaved the sides of their heads and wore their hair in tight greasy plaits. Beads were piled from their collarbones to their chins. Some of them wore copper plugs in holes in their lower lips. Among them were the most rapacious people I have ever met, who harried me like skuas when they discovered that I had brought money, food and tobacco to the camp.

Dismas's first wife, Akale, looked like one of Hollywood's malevolent Red Indians. Her cheekbones were sharp and shiny, her chin jutted, she kept her eyelids screwed half shut to discipline her wandering left eye, and when she saw something she wanted she never gave up. She was utterly unscrupulous. If I asked her for a cup of water she would pick up her jerrycan as if about to pour one for me, then disappear

17

behind her hut. She would wait until I was croaking with thirst, then ask what I would give her in return. Several times when I refused to hand over my penknife, my tape recorder or my watch she tried to hit me; once she threatened me with a stick. But I soon discovered that behind her ferocious stare she was trying hard not to laugh: if I made to hit her back she would cackle and run away.

Dismas's second wife was still a child, a shy, grave twelve-year-old who would retreat from me with an expression of solemn piety, slip behind a hut and then break into sniggers. Dismas was not allowed to sleep with her until she was old enough to bear children. Too young to own a house, she lived with Dismas's mother, a silent, bitter old woman who watched me with steady loathing and flicked indoors at my approach.

Attached to Dismas's enclosure were the huts belonging to Mary Akutang, or Mary Blowing Wind. Like the North American Indians, the Turkana are named after something visible or sensible at the time of their birth. The child is held to its mother's breast, and the names of the surrounding phenomena are called out. When it begins to suckle it signals that it accepts the last name called. Thus Dismas Ekeno was named after his mother's kitchen, the man who lived next door had the name of a tree. Mary was a tough but occasionally melancholy woman who said she had loved her husband so much that she still mourned him every day. He had beaten her, but used to beg her forgiveness the next day by slaughtering a camel or an ox. She was gruff, considerate and frank, and one of the few women who did not come round to my shelter to tease me. The others were merciless, simultaneously flirting and pretending to be horrified by my appearance, laughing at everything I said, pitiful when asking for tobacco, implacable when refusing me water. As a *mzungu* – a European – and therefore a rich, clumsy and above all sedentary man, I was fair game.

Their children were quiet and capable. All of them possessed their own animals and soon after they were weaned from their mothers they started suckling from their allotted goats, squirting the milk into their hands and lapping it up as the nanny's kid shoved and nuzzled at the other udder. By the time they were three they could recognize every animal in their father's herd and count them at a glance. By the time they were six they were herding the young goats themselves.

For the Turkana to survive in one of the harshest human environments in the world, they must understand the animals and their needs as if they were their own kind. They must know what to allow them to eat and when, be sensitive to the slightest signs of change, be able to diagnose and treat disease themselves. Only when I tried to drive a herd myself, and within half an hour was yelling, swearing, soaked in sweat, exhausted and close to despair, the desert dotted with stray animals, did I realize how skilled the Turkana were in seeming to get their beasts from one place to another without doing a thing.

As I talked to the elders and watched them at work, I began to realize that their survival depended on far more than the control of animals, veterinary medicine and meteorology. Every day several people I had never seen before arrived in the camp, stayed for a few hours, sometimes a few days, talking with one of the elders there, then wandered away again. I was told they were brothers, which I soon discovered meant anything from a natural brother to a distant relative of someone's wife.

All these men had come to trade, not goods, but names and obligations. They were there to keep in touch with anyone who might be persuaded to give them something if, in the future, they were to fall on hard times. Some had walked 200 miles for no other purpose. In an environment as inconstant as the Turkana's, no one is assured of his prosperity. A man with hundreds of beasts can within a season find himself with none, if he misjudges his migrations or runs into raiders. His only means of survival, in that case, is to fall back on his relatives or friends, and borrow animals from them with which he can rebuild his herd. He needs, therefore, to keep people well disposed towards him, especially in areas far from his own, in case a disaster affects everyone close to home. For these reasons, rich men are always inclined to give or lend an animal to a deserving relative or friend, in the hope that they can call in the debt if the tables are turned. This means, incidentally, that no one among the traditional Turkana is likely to starve if other people are wealthy.

One of the best ways to build up networks of friends is to marry as many women as possible. With every wife a man is introduced to an extended family in another clan: the best insurance against future disaster. More wives means more sons, and more sons means that he can split his herds among them and send them in different directions, so that if one herd dies he can fall back on the others. The bridepiece of cattle, camels and goats he hands over to his father-in-law serves less to buy the bride than to buy a new list of contacts, all of whom, by sharing the payment, become indebted to him.

Polygamy is a troublesome and expensive way of managing one's affairs. In Turkana district it means that the men, whose wives tend to gang up on them, are remorselessly henpecked; in other regions, as the men strive to retain control, it has led to the brutal repression of women. But for many herding peoples it is the only way of keeping a family alive. This is why polygamy is acceptable in the Old Testament, where the nomadic Israelites are wandering the desert in search of their promised land. This is why it is unacceptable in the New Testament, where they have settled down as farmers in a fertile and well watered place, where life is more predictable. Monogamy is the luxury of static peoples.

Turkana life, like ajua, is a board game of the most astonishing complexity. The board is a land whose squares keep shifting from place to place as the rains come and go and alliances rise and collapse. The counters are the herds, whose numbers rise and fall, which can move anywhere in two dimensions. On the faces of the die are rain, sun, raiders, war, disease and luck. To stay in the game a man must know and be known to several thousand other players. Without written records he must remember how they are related to him, what they owe and what they are owed. He must know every species of plant and its properties, every animal he owns and its genealogy. He must be able to read the sky and navigate by the stars. He must keep his herds moving around the board for as long as seventy or eighty years, for to lose the game is to die. It is perhaps not entirely surprising that in 1992 the educated Turkana came top of the Kenyan school league.

While all Turkana must know a great deal about their world, it is the elders whose minds, in their quiet oases, shift and whirr with the most critical calculations. Much of the knowledge they share and pass down to their descendants is encoded in stories, poetry and songs. This is their literature, their art, their law and their science: books and paintings are of no value to nomadic peoples who must move with little more than what they stand in; their libraries and their museums are in their heads. But their power over the younger men is not just a matter of knowledge, for the elders, like the Old Testament patriarchs, are holy.

On starry nights I would watch them mumbling their prayers, their faces upturned to the heavens as Akuj, the God of the Sky, winked and flashed at them from across the cosmos. They told me that if they were to lose touch with God they would immediately run into misfortune. A man becomes more holy as he ages, and God invests him with greater powers. His final sanction over younger men is his curse, and this, if justified, is said by the Turkana invariably to be fatal. There has been much written on how people, knowing that they have been cursed, will lose interest in life and fade away, but the Turkana have stories of curses laid upon people without their knowledge which have resulted no less surely in a swift and unpleasant death.

When Christian missionaries arrived in the district they had little difficulty in evangelizing the Turkana, for they were half-way there already. It was not hard for them to associate themselves with the Old Testament herders, who smote their enemies and stole their stock, made alliances, sold daughters, fought over waterholes. There were some striking congruities between their religion and that of the ancient Israelites: both peoples, for instance, believed that God rejected a sacrifice if the smoke fell flat. But in truth, while the Turkana were happy to call themselves Christians to get the missionaries off their backs, they ignored the inconvenient teachings of the Bible,

21

and got on with what they had been doing anyway. When the priests remonstrated with them they found the Turkana frustratingly pragmatic. Why, they argued, should they desist, as Leviticus demanded, from drinking blood, when the same chapter instructed people neither to round the corners of their hair nor to eat of a tree they had possessed for less than five years, both of which the missionaries conspicuously ignored?

The irony of the Turkana's evangelization is that the God of the Middle Eastern nomads was introduced to them by sedentary Europeans, whose ancestors were woodland spirit worshippers. Every significant monotheistic religion arose among peoples who were or had recently been nomadic, and nomadic tribes at opposite ends of the world have held startlingly similar monotheistic beliefs. Even the Huns, described as godless by their sedentary (and largely animist) victims, worshipped Tengri, God of the Blue Sky. Judaism, Christianity and Islam took root among nomads who had recently settled, and all three characterize nomadic traits – the shepherd, the pilgrim, the wanderer in the wilderness – as godly, and the life of the city as degenerate. All three have immodestly been reintroduced by their sedentary apostles to the people from whom they came. In Turkana district one missionary, a German, has acknowledged the illogicality of this inversion: finding in the Turkana's religion more truth than in his own, he converted, and now lives with his herds in a camp near the Ugandan border.

I spent a week visiting the people of Ngilukumong and the surrounding camps, talking to the elders and, with less success, their wives, exchanging gifts, drinking milk flavoured with charcoal and cows' urine. I found that the long drought in the district had devastated the herds: some of the Turkana had survived for sixty days on nothing but wild berries. Threatened by famine and rumours of the approaching Toposa, people had contemplated driving their camels and goats towards the hills to join the young men in the cattle camps, but while I was with them news arrived of the most terrible massacres in those places. So many herders were now being killed by the Toposa that some of the survivors were fleeing with their cattle to the lowlands, even though there was no grass. If this were to continue, the elders said, the depletion of their herds could be so catastrophic that the Turkana as a people would never recover.

I was astonished by the energy and stamina of the Turkana. Women who had eaten nothing at all – not even berries – for a week would be up at dawn driving out the goats, building new houses or fetching water, laughing, shouting, scolding their children. They seemed indefatigable. I knew that the Turkana, like many desert peoples, have adaptations that allow them to survive famine and thirst better than other humans, but though fit and well nourished, I could not keep up with them; whom any Western doctor would have described as starving. We shared the food we had brought with the people of Ngilukumong and confined ourselves to half a meal a day, and I soon began to feel so weak and sapped that I almost became convinced it was I who was starving, not they.

On my visits I noticed that many of the people were blind, some suffered from swollen bellies caused by malnutrition, others had chains of fresh scars across their stomachs, where traditional healers had tried to release their bad humours. I watched boys pursue a giant monitor lizard, hissing and scrabbling over the desert, kill it with sticks and then feed it to their dogs: lizards, like monkeys, cannot be eaten by people on account of their fingers, which the Turkana say make them almost human. While I wandered around and talked, Adrian set up his tripod under the trees at Ngilukumong, where the backdrops of huts on one side, desert and forest on the other, made a perfect studio. At first suspicious of him, the Turkana women, delighted though not astonished by Polaroids of themselves, began neglecting their work and mooning around the trees in the hope of having their portraits taken.

Throughout this period I felt that I was learning not only about the Turkana but also about ourselves. It seemed to me that we in the West lose something by living so far, historically and geographically, from our God, that the inseparability of religion and ordinary life among the Turkana lends their existence a resonance and depth that ours lacks. I saw how hard it is for our own society ever to become wise while old people are ostracized. I speculated about how our savannah ancestors might have lived, and whether the conditions that determine Turkana life might not have exerted similar effects on theirs.

It seemed likely that the first humans, like the Turkana, would have needed to solve the most complex environmental and social equations to survive. They did not herd domestic animals, but they would have had to follow and anticipate the movements of wild game, which would surely have been just as difficult. Unable to make use of most of the leafy plants on the savannahs, they must have concentrated on the patches of food found in their midst: forests of edible fruit, for example, or colonies of nesting birds.

It is not inconceivable that people would have tried, in the course of a season, to secure these valuable patches for themselves and their groups; if so, it is plausible that complex social networks would have evolved as people tried to negotiate access to each other's resources, knowing that when their own were exhausted they could survive only by falling back on someone else's. This might also have meant that – for the same reasons as the Turkana – the early humans were polygamous, spreading their risks in that uncertain environment among as many families as possible. The fact that human males are larger than females, the exaggeration of human genitalia and the distribution of bodily hair suggest that this may have been the case, because such secondary sexual characteristics tend to be most clearly expressed in polygamous animals. But what, I wondered, would all these ideas, if correct, tell us about ourselves?

I felt that they might help to explain why we have such astoundingly complex brains: why, in our settled societies, we can get by with the use of just a fraction of our intellect, and why, though there seems to be no earthly need, human beings are capable of learning thirty languages, recalling pi to the thousandth place, speculating on the most arcane astrophysical conundrums. If the early human beings were indeed subject to the conditions faced by the Turkana, they may, by complete contrast to our common assumptions, have had the richest of intellectual lives. Our need for intellectual activity may have declined ever since. If we evolved to immerse ourselves in labyrinthine social networks, this could explain why so many of us feel isolated and lonely, why we strive so hard to define ourselves as part of a social group. And if, as some of the evidence suggests, our common ancestors were polygamous, this could account for why monogamy, which would otherwise make so much sense in civilized societies, manifestly fails to satisfy the human male's most fundamental urges.

On my eighth night at Ngilukumong, I heard music coming from the desert and walked out to investigate. I found the women of the camp sitting on the ground, clapping and chanting a high forlorn song. They were praying for rain, to both Jesus and His Father, Akuj.

The clouds broke with a rustle of settling dust. Falling from the hot night air, raindrops sizzled in the sand and stung my face. I ran back to the enclosure, picked up my cow hide and plunged into an empty hut. With a sharp crack and a rushing sound the roof caved in, and I was drenched. I ran to another hut, passed my torch across the floor and saw both a scorpion and the track of a snake. I sat outside, the cow hide wrapped around my shoulders, feeling the dust in my hair run down my face in muddy trails. Someone in one of the houses began to sing. The short rains, so long awaited, had at last begun.

The man who claimed credit for their inception lived in a filthy hut on the other side of the river. Like all Turkana rainmakers, Loktelej had to remain apart from the other people of his community. He sat outside his house in a red beret and safari jacket, scowling across at Ngilukumong, drawing shapes in the dust with his stick. The next day, when I crossed the muddy waters of the rejuvenated river, he received me with a sour grace and refused to tell me anything until I gave him money and tobacco. He explained, in the clipped, patronizing tone with which one might address an imbecile, that God had appeared to him three nights ago, in the shape of a blue man. He had been instructed to gather together the elders of

25

Ngilukumong, slaughter a goat and then pray from dusk to dawn. The process would inevitably make the rain fall, and anyone who said otherwise was a jealous fraud. Only he, Loktelej, had the power to make rain, though there were those at Ngilukumong who were determined to steal it from him.

I wondered whether it might have been the case that Loktelej was simply a little better at divining the intentions of the clouds than the other men. If he reached the same conclusion as the other elders a day before they did, called them together and announced that he would make rain, he might occasionally have been able to convince them, when they saw the signs the next day, that it had been his doing. From what the other elders, who were at least as sceptical as me, told me later, this appeared to be close to the truth.

But I was interested in testing the prophetic powers of the men who professed them. After leaving Loktelej I visited the fortune-teller, who lived in a camp a short walk across the desert. I told him who I was and where I had come from. He stared at me for a second, stepped into his hut and re-emerged with a goat's skin and two hide sandals. He beat the sandals on the skin, then hurled them down. They bounced into the air and thudded into the dust a few inches from the hide. One of them was upside down. The fortune-teller shook his head, muttered rapidly and shook his head again. He looked up at me.

'You are in the most imminent danger. Your life is in danger. I warn you that you may very soon die.'

On the following day I took my binoculars out of my bag and, having extracted them an hour later from the greasy hands of everyone at Ngilukumong, I walked up the river to look for birds. Driven from the desert by the drought, they had concentrated in the bankside forest. Like the Turkana, they sang when the rain had fallen. I saw six species of yellow weaver birds, a paradise flycatcher, orioles, rollers, curly-crested helmet shrikes, woodpeckers, starlings, buffalo weavers, mousebirds, drongos, go-away birds, hornbills, hoopoes, scimitar bills, hawks and cut-throats. Swaying in the top of a thorn tree was a martial eagle, one of the largest birds of prey in the world, and said by the Turkana to subsist on goats and the occasional human child.

Back in the camp, I discussed the birds I had seen with the elders. They knew the calls, the food and habits of every one, and there was scarcely a bird to whom they did not attach a story or a song. They told me that bad luck would befall the family of any man who ate a bird with a raucous voice, for harsh words meant curses, and curses meant certain misfortune. Looking through the pictures in my bird book they pointed out the nightjars, which brought rain if they landed inside a goat corral, and the stone curlew, which brought raiders to a camp and had to be driven away with flaming brands.

They told me that if you blocked up the nest of a ground hornbill the bird would produce a magical white powder which would cause the blockage to fall away. If a man gathered this powder, he needed only to walk into a shop and money would fall into his bag. They cackled over the hideous marabou stork, which they described as an old widow whose gonorrhoea had made her head swell and her hair fall out. When I turned to the black-and-white drawing of a pair of ostriches, everyone started talking at once. Ostriches were the most sought-after game: an old man in the next camp had spent a whole day in his youth running one down, chasing it on foot for 150 miles before he cornered it in a gorge on the other side of the district. Not only were ostriches excellent to eat, but they provided the feathers worn by the men in their clay headdresses and by dancing women in their hair. Their eggshells were ground down to make the flat beads used by warriors to commemorate men they had killed.

When the old men began to talk of owls I felt the hairs prickle on my spine. The elders told me that if an owl called from the top of a house, someone within would fall sick and die. I remembered having heard the same superstition in Britain. An owl calling from the roof or falling down a chimney presaged for some rural people, as late as the 1930s, the certain death of an inhabitant. I felt that perhaps this concordance should not be altogether surprising: the owl, with its almost human calls, its silent visitations in the night, is the bird of death in many parts of the world. Lilith, Sumerian goddess of the underworld, built her home in a hollow tree, and on friezes is attended by the watchful face of the screech owl. Her winged, claw-footed figure is shadowed by the Nightmare of the ancient Greeks, the bird woman who swept down on men in their dreams.

But when they told me about woodpeckers a cold tremor passed through my body. They said that if a woodpecker called from behind a man at the beginning of a journey, something terrible would happen in his home. If it called from in front he should follow it, as it would lead him to good fortune: he would find his lost animals or secure the loan he was seeking. It was, I knew, a woodpecker which led the Sabines to Picenum, which translates as Woodpecker City. In medieval Germany, if a woodpecker called from the right at the beginning of a journey it meant that the quest would be a successful one. Horace and Plautus describe it as a bird of omen which must be followed if a man is to meet with good fortune.

It seemed impossible to me that this belief could have reached the Turkana by diffusion, across such wastes of land and sea. Discounting the reports of some Irish missionaries that Turkana and Gaelic are mutually intelligible, and the extraordinary and none too credible implication that the Turkana and the Gaels had a recent common origin, I could only imagine that what I had been told was a manifestation of a collective unconscious, more congruent than I could have believed possible. It served to bolster my impression that by looking at the lives of the nomads I could learn something about my own, that we should be foolish to neglect what they may have to teach us about what it means to be human.

On my last night at Ngilukumong, Natiang, who lived in a nearby camp, slaughtered a fat-tailed sheep. By the light of a half moon we crossed the desert to his house, our shadows crisp on the sand, unintelligible shapes scuttling and whispering among the thorn twigs. The mountains were dark against a luminous sky.

Natiang and his friends sat on the sand of his enclosure, talking and watching the sky. Every part of the sheep had been cooked, and they passed me pieces of meat, sections of colon, and slabs of roasted white fat, which to the Turkana were the animal's best cuts. Before the sheep had been cooked they had read its intestines and found that light showers, but no substantial rains, would be coming from the north-west; that there were raiders in the western mountains and the threat of a new epidemic in the centre of the district. They told me that such divination was never wrong.

We sat for while in silence. In the corral a young ram, kept away from the she-goats, was moaning. Cicadas sounded like the breathing of the desert. From across the dry lands came the sad, descending cry of the long-tailed nightjar.

'We! Listen to the river!' said Natiang at last.

Carried across the plains by gusts of wind, I heard a low dull roar. From far off, echoing over the desert, came the thud and boom of a collapsing bank. The rains had started in the western mountains and the rivers there had burst into spate.

When we returned to Dismas's enclosure, we found Matayo waiting for us. He lowered himself slowly onto his stool, and waited until everyone had fallen silent.

'There was once a famous prophet, who was closer to God than any other. If a drought came he would say to God "Send us rain" and rain would come the next day. He would ask "Give us grass" and grass would come the next day.

'People believed in him absolutely; anything he said was believed. His curses were very powerful. He would send messages all over the district, telling people a drought or a raid was coming and what they needed to do about it. He used to call all the young men together to warn them of the hardships coming and tell them where to migrate to. This man was named Lukokoi.

'The prophets who are alive today are not like him. Most like to cheat; they do not know God well. They dream the

29

wrong dreams and they don't come true. They pray to God and nothing happens.

'In the colonial times the white settlers came here and asked the Turkana if they had a leader. They said yes: Lukokoi. When they heard this, the British captured him and took him to Eldoret. They told the Turkana that they were taking him there so he could teach them his skills. But instead they threw him in prison. They tricked the Turkana.

'He soon died. They buried him at a junction where every road in Kenya meets. They never told the Turkana he had died; they kept saying he was still alive and would return. It was only ten years later that we heard he was dead.

'Since then we have faced many hardships: droughts, raids, disease and hunger. The grass hasn't been as it was before. It was because of his death that the district has become so dry. That is the story of that man.'

He stopped abruptly, and in the eyes that looked straight past me at the glittering horizon, I felt I could see an unfathomable regret, as if he were certain that all he had known and spoken of was past. On the horizon, among the cold stars creeping over the edge of the earth, I fancied he could see what was to come. He rose to his feet.

'I, Matayo, as well as Dismas and the others here, send our greetings to all the mzungus.'

CHAPTER TWO

Popcorn Republic

In Lodwar, the capital of Turkana district, men with metal sticks and red badges patrolled the sandy streets, extorting money from the starving. Goats picked among the rubbish for cabbage leaves and newspaper. A blacksmith hammered wrist blades out of six-inch nails. Adrian had left for Nairobi to pick up our Land-Rover. When he returned we would drive into the mountains to see a cattle camp where a Turkana friend named John had promised to show us how the herders were coping with an invasion by their enemies.

I had decided to stay and speak to the officials there about the famine now progressing in the district. On a morning of blinding light I walked past the Turkana women sitting in the sand, weaving mats out of doum palm leaves; past the low concrete buildings, where hides were bought or sugar was sold, where unblinking Somalis lounged against their doorposts chewing narcotic herbs; past the shabby restaurant selling *Assorted Caks* and *Harmburgers*; past the beggars hopping or crawling with outstretched hands among homeless fugitives no richer than themselves, towards the hill where the Kenyan flag sagged among radio masts and air-conditioning units. I felt light-footed, elated and sick. At the foot of the hill I paused and leant against a telegraph pole. I could hear the blood rumbling in my temples. A woman stopped and asked if I were all right. I said I was fine. I slid down the pole and my head hit the ground with a thud.

In Lodwar District Hospital I lay on the springs of an iron bedstead with my eyes closed. At the other end of the ward a man with his skull cleft by a fighting stick sat on his bed and shouted to an imaginary friend. Men in crude traction sighed

31

and groaned. Beneath me, on the concrete floor under my bed, was the tormenting drip-drip of a leaky tap. I was going to ask the nurse to turn it off until I realized I was listening to the sound of my own sweat.

When the doctor took my temperature I heard him whisper 'Cerebral' to the nurse, and almost as if he had repeated them I remembered the words of the fortune-teller at Ngilukumong. I tried to open my eyes. Every part of my body felt so heavy I could scarcely shift it. In the dark, listening to the moans of the injured and the shouts of the brain-damaged warrior, I clung to the bed springs as if they could stop me from slipping away. I felt lonelier that I had ever been before. Nothing could have convinced me then that this illness and the change to my plans it necessitated would save my life.

I lay that way for two days and a night. Flies tickled my flesh, but I was too weak to brush them away. The nurses, struggling with hundreds of patients and moribund equipment, nevertheless did all they could, and the drugs they administered slowly began to work. When, on the second day, I opened my eyes, I was so delighted to be alive that I tried to spring up from my bed. When the doctor discharged me, he said he thought he had lost me three times.

Released into Lodwar, I took leave of my senses. No one had told me that cerebral malaria unhinges the mind, and I soon became convinced that I had gone permanently mad. I could not understand anything said to me and it was clear that nothing I said in reply made any sense. I was still jabbering and hallucinating when Adrian returned to Lodwar. He took one look at me and, almost as frightened as I was, put me into the Land Rover and took me back to Nairobi. There the hallucinations, the voices and the confusion soon faded away, but it has taken me almost a year to regain my self-confidence.

We returned to Turkana district a few weeks later to find that the rains that had begun with the storm at Ngilukumong had ended with a trickle: in the centre of the district just a fraction of what the people had hoped for had fallen. In the mountains, however, the storms had lasted longer. We wanted, first, to see how the young men survived while driving their cattle herds through the highlands, before moving on to investigate the stories we had heard of an intensification of raiding by tribes from Sudan and Ethiopia and the flight of many of their victims to the famine zones. We visited John, the man who had promised to take us to his relatives' cattle camp before I became ill. We found him incoherent with wretchedness. Soon after Adrian had driven me back to Nairobi, the camp had been encircled by Toposa raiders. All but two of its ninety-eight people had been killed.

We decided to travel to the eastern edge of the Lokwanomoru Mountains, which both Sudan and Kenya claim as their territory. Hidden somewhere in the thorn scrub at their feet was a camp where, John believed, the herders were hospitable and might allow us to stay with them. He warned us to leave as soon as we had found what we wanted to know, for the area swarmed with Toposa and Dongiro spies, and mzungus were considered to be rich pickings.

At first we drove across a region that might have been an industrial wasteland. The trees were black and leafless. The stony desert had been oxidized oil-brown and, beyond the crumbling towers of the termite hills, volcanoes rose from the plains like conical slag heaps. But, as we approached the mountains, the land became greener. Abyssinian rollers fluttered from tree to tree like gigantic blue butterflies. In our wake a swallow-tailed kite roiled the air, swooping and swerving at the insects we disturbed.

One hundred miles north of Lodwar we parked the Land-Rover beside a trading post at the end of the track, the last permanent settlement before the badlands where people never stayed still. A few derelict Turkana huts were clustered around the thorn shelter belonging to a Somali trader, who sold grain, tea and sugar to passing nomads. Half a dozen Turkana men in tattered shirts and nylon trousers stood around and stared. One man sat on the ground, mending the butt of a rifle that the British had captured from the Italians in the Second World War.

I hired two of the spectators to carry the sack of tobacco and the food we had brought and we set off towards the mountains

33

in the west. The plain was scored with cattle paths, but for the first hour or two of our journey I saw neither cows nor human beings. The ground glittered with quartzite and chalcedony. As we approached the mountains, the bush became denser and greener. In the beds of dry streams I saw human footprints. Birds hissed in the foliage. I caught a glimpse of passing cattle, and the pale blanket of a herder. A mile or two short of the mountain wall one of the ragged men stopped and abruptly sat down. At the foot of a flowering tree the wind stirred the ashes of a bonfire.

We sat for some minutes without speaking, brushing away flies, and I slowly became aware that we were surrounded. People stepped silently from the bush and sat down in front of us. No one smiled or uttered a word. I could only imagine that someone had run on ahead to tell them we were coming. By the time forty or fifty people had gathered, I began to feel nervous: if I smiled at someone his stare merely hardened to a frown. They were the toughest-looking people I have ever seen. The men scowled into the sun, showing their broken teeth. The women leant forwards in a predatory manner, their eyes flicking between us as if sizing us up.

Guessing that I should explain what we were doing, I stood up and made a short speech. I told them that we were hoping to find out how the Turkana there lived, what their problems were and what they were doing to confront them. I said that we would like to stay with a cattle camp for a few days and had brought food and tobacco to share with our hosts. We would feel honoured if anyone were able to look after us, but we would understand if they wanted us to go away. I sat down. Nobody spoke. The Turkana continued to stare at us. Then a woman at the back leant across to her neighbour and, in a whisper loud enough for everyone to hear, said, 'Why can't he just give us the tobacco and go away?'

All but three of the Turkana stood up and dispersed. The three men who remained continued to sit and stare at us. They looked like the models for an illustration of the criminal physiognomy. Each one had either a broken nose or a torn ear. The man in the middle had a low forehead, a huge jaw, a nose almost flattened against his face. His narrow red eyes were surrounded by a grid of inflexible lines. His chest and stomach were covered in killing scars.

'These,' said our translator, 'are your hosts.'

I cannot believe that any of the world's rural people live in conditions harsher than those of the Turkana of Naramam, the camp to which the three men led us. On the lower slopes of the first of the mountains, it consisted of no more than a few thorn windbreaks scattered among the rocks. The inhabitants slept on cow hides, using rocks as both mattresses and pillows. The flies, which followed the cattle, crowded into the corners of my eyes and crawled into my nostrils. When I yawned they flew in before I had a chance to close my mouth. There was just one waterhole, two miles away, and this was used by both humans and animals. Floating in the jerrycans carried back to the camp by the women were flecks of dung and green algae. There was no food. The drought had depleted their herds, so the Turkana here could rarely afford either to slaughter an animal or to trade one for grain. They subsisted on a few mouthfuls of milk a day.

I was surprised to see old people, young children, even nursing mothers at Naramam, and I asked Loparikoi, the man with the flattened nose, why they had not been left behind in an oasis camp. He told me that the forests in which these weaker people had been living had now become too dangerous to inhabit without the protection of the younger men; here they were closer to the Toposa, but stood a better chance of surviving a raid, as the young men had all the community's guns. They slowed the herders down, and the camels they had brought were ill-suited to the mountains, but had they been left where they were they would certainly have died.

Loparikoi was as unyielding as he looked. In raiding the Toposa he played full back, remaining behind to waylay the enemy as they pursued the people who had stolen their cattle. He never smiled and he barked curt instructions to his four wives. But he looked after us well and neglected no measure that would help to defend his community.

A new moon rose that night, and was quickly blotted out by

clouds. Sand rattled over the rocks. I lay down and found myself too nervous and uncomfortable to sleep. On the other side of the compound a fire spurted and flared in the wind. I sat up and shifted around on the rocks. Then, beyond the camp, I heard a hoarse shout and the clank of metal. I sprang to my feet, convinced we were under attack. But the shout settled into a chant, and I realized that the women were dancing.

A line of fifteen or twenty were converging on a group of seated men, then easing back just before they trampled them. They were chanting so fiercely that, had the men not appeared so calm, I might have imagined the women were preparing to assault them. The iron rings on their ankles clattered as they stamped their feet in time to the song. The noise vibrated through my chest. Even the warriors, sitting in studied non-chalance on the ground, seemed to be affected. Later I discovered that the women were exhorting the men to raid the Toposa and steal back the cattle that had been taken from them.

The women broke up and a line of young men left the ground and began to clap. Five girls came forward and started dancing in front of them. By turns the men leapt at the dancers, who sprang away deftly and laughed. When the rain came rustling down from the mountains the women ran to the wind-breaks and covered them with hides to keep the children sleeping in their lee from getting wet. Everyone else huddled beneath the bushes.

Soaked by a succession of showers, numbed by jagged rocks whichever way I turned, I lay awake all night. Two or three hours before dawn I got up in the middle of a storm and stumbled out into the darkness. On the edge of the camp I found Loparikoi sitting on a rock, with a Kalashnikov wrapped in a cow hide. I asked him if he were waiting for anyone. He turned towards me, the rain spattering against his face.

'These are the nights when the Toposa come. They wait for this darkness. It is always during the rain that they appear.'

The flies awoke even before the sun had risen, and crept over my face. I tried to eat some of the food we had brought, but every time I took it out of the polythene bag the flies clustered over it before I could get it into my mouth. Half an hour after dawn I heard the herdboys whistling and clucking to their cows and I followed them out of the camp towards the mountains. The bush became thicker and thicker, until all I could see of the cows were horns moving through the crowns of the shrubs. We descended into a gully and, following the bed of an empty stream, entered a cleft in the mountains. As we stepped between the walls of orange rock, we passed into another world. The flies deserted us, the air became cool and still, sound trembled and reverberated up the gorge. Crossing the narrow band of sky above us were sandgrouse and redwing starlings, their wings translucent against the brightening sky.

The cattle climbed one wall of the gorge by a narrow trail, but with a couple of boys we carried on into the mountains. We came to the watering-hole, a tiny concrete pond built by the British when they used this passage as a supply line for their troops in Ethiopia. The boys told me that they still found, scattered all over the mountains, the bullet casings left behind by those men. They brushed the scum aside, bent down and drank the black water. They told me that this was the best time to drink: in an hour the pool would be frothing with livestock and even fouler than it was now. We walked up the fissure into which the gorge disappeared, where we found the skeleton of a hyena, shot by a herder a few weeks before. On the rocks above it, painted in cow dung, was the silhouette of a Kalashnikov.

Every day the elders of the cattle camps gathered beneath a wild olive tree in the widest part of the gorge to talk and watch their herds go by. Its roots, clutching the bare rocks, were polished black by generations of herders' feet and elders' backsides: the boys said it had been used by the Turkana for hundreds of years. Its leaves flared yellow against the shadows of the gorge. We sat beneath it and waited for the elders to arrive.

They came in threes and fours, stalking cautiously up the chasm with spears or cocked rifles. As they arrived at the tree they nodded to us. The boys stood up and walked away. The elders sat on the roots or the rocks, cradling their guns. Most of these were Winchesters, Lee Enfields, Italian Mk 3s and 4s, their stocks bound up with cloth or leather where they had split, rags stuffed into their muzzles to keep the dirt out. One man appeared with a submachine gun, which he hid behind a rock when he saw us. They wore home-made leather bandoliers across their shoulders, blankets, sandals and either clay headdresses or plastic homburg hats. A young man arrived with a sack of bullets and started bargaining with the elders. He had bought them from their enemies the Toposa: it seemed like the global arms trade in miniature.

Animals began converging on the waterhole from all directions, tripping down the steep paths of the mountains, clattering over the rocks of the gorge. The walls echoed with bleats, brays, the groans of camels, the lowing of cows. They waited, with their herders, in orderly groups while the animals ahead of them drank, each clustered according to its kind. While the camels waded and bellowed in the pool, donkeys stood pressed into the shade of a projecting bluff with lowered heads. The cows that had run in, excited by the smell of water, their ears raised, bells clanging, now stood in the early sun, huffing through their nostrils. Fat-tailed sheep, whose breeding seems to have taken from their brains what it has added to their tails, got themselves wedged together between the rocks and wailed pathetically. Only the goats were undisciplined, bounding around the walls of the gorge, taking flying leaps as they scattered from their herders. One goat misjudged its jump and landed with a crash in the murky pool, panicking the camels.

With aluminium pots balanced on their heads, women straightened up from the pool, and slowly lilted, lithe and steady, back to their camps. Boys stood on the high rocks and threw stones into the water. I looked up and saw, fringing the gorge like guards on the battlements of a fort, Turkana men, standing watch against the light with their spears.

Among the elders was a domineering old man named Esuron. He had a smashed mouth and a bullet scar on his forearm. He spoke in staccato shouts, turning around to check that the others were listening, as he explained why the Toposa had become such a threat to his people.

'In the old days those people had honour. They would fight us in daylight, with spears, and they came only to steal our cattle. No women were killed, no children were killed. If they killed men they speared them honourably in battle. When we raided the Toposa, we did the same.

'Now all that has changed. Every Toposa has a gun. Not guns like these, but real guns, guns from the government, G3s, Kalashnikovs, HK11s. Now it's just war. They come here at night and shoot everyone, men, women, children. Sometimes they don't even bother to steal the animals. We are their enemies, and they are trying to wipe us out.'

There were two reasons, I knew, for the arming of the Toposa by the Sudanese. The first was the government's hope that the Toposa would fight the rebels of the Dinka tribe: the Sudanese People's Liberation Army or SPLA. The Toposa, less concerned with the government's wars than their own, had been turning up at army barracks, training for a few days, then sloping off with the guns and rocket launchers they were given. The second related to the deal that the Kenyan government had struck with the SPLA. In return for assistance from Nairobi and a new road, the Sudanese rebels had allowed Kenyan troops to patrol the Ilemi Triangle: the land in which the mountains lay. This was claimed by both countries, as they had both administered it before Independence. The Kenyan government had hoped to find oil and alluvial gold there: it had so far been disappointed. The Sudanese government hoped that the Toposa would drive out people it considered Kenyan, and reclaim the territory for Sudan.

'How can we defend ourselves against these people? The guns we have hardly work, and when they do we have only a handful of bullets. The point of having a gun is to put bullets in.' Esuron opened and shut his rifle's empty breech. 'Otherwise it might as well be a toothbrush.' He wheezed with laughter. 'Their spies are everywhere. Up there, in the mountains, even watching us now, there are spies. They know we are here. They know you are here. They know just when to strike. Every day someone along these mountains is raided. Every month there is a massacre.

'We can't go to where the best grazing is. Even here, where the grass is poor, is not safe, and if the Toposa keep coming we will have to go south, where there is nothing. How can you keep one cow alive down there? We either die up here from the Toposa, or die down there from starvation.'

The Turkana, armed with spears and old rifles, were trying to raid the Toposa back. Sometimes they managed to steal a few cows, sometimes they killed a Toposa fighter and took his gun, but these inconsequential gains did nothing to restore the balance of power. In the mountains, as in the plains, the snakes were now longer than the ladders.

The next day we left Naramam and drove south-east, to the settlement of Lokitaung. There we met John, the man who was to have taken us to his cattle camp. Though he had scarcely recovered from the shock of the killings, he agreed to show us what had become of his people. The land we crossed on our way to Kokuro was better watered than any other I had seen in the far north. The low hills were covered with a gauze of young grass and the trees were in flower. Yet for mile after mile I saw neither a cow nor a human being. We passed deserted camps, an empty trading centre, wells overgrown with creepers and grass. Only after half an hour of driving did we see another person. We stopped to pick him up. He was a stooped old man with a grey beard, who looked up at us with vacant eyes. He carried a stick and a tin, in which he had been collecting gum arabic from the acacia bushes. He said that everyone else had been killed or had fled, but that the raiders had no interest in him as he was old and without animals. In the hills he had seen the spies of the Merille people, who melted away as he approached.

After thirty miles we came to the settlement of Sasame, the last inhabited village in the north-east of the district. Fifty or sixty Turkana had crowded around a police post inside a thorn corral ten feet high. Policemen in camouflage walked around the perimeter with submachine guns. We asked three of them to travel with us, in case we ran into trouble. Twenty miles further on, we left the road and drove across the desert. We stopped at a clump of empty huts. For as far as I could see, scattered over the ground like puffballs, were the skulls of the inhabitants.

The Turkana do not bury people who are violently killed, in case, by acknowledging misfortune, they encourage it to reappear. So the remains of all the people of the cattle camp still lay where the hyenas had dragged them. At my feet was the jawbone of a child. Beyond it was the skull, the cranium stoved in. A little further off I saw the ribcage and part of the spine. Beside the Land Rover was an old man's skull and, rolled beside it, upside down, the head of a woman. When I noticed the broken strings of beads scattered where her neck had been, the significance of what I saw struck me for the first time. These bleached fragments had been human beings, people like Matayo, Dismas, Akale and the serious, attentive children who herded the goats at Ngilukumong. Now only the wind moved round the camp.

As I walked between the houses, metal cartridge cases tinkled at my feet. I found cooking pots, a half-burnt fire, the iron rings that women wore around their ankles. Skirts, sandals, the panniers carried by donkeys, all made of leather, had been torn apart by the hyenas. A faint smell still lingered around the skulls. But for the rustling of the empty huts in the wind, there was no sound. Even the three policemen, who had talked excitedly all the way to Kokuro, had fallen silent. No one but the beasts had been here since the massacre.

This was the camp of a group of old people, women and children, who had been left by the young men in a place considered safe from raiders. The Toposa spies who spotted them saw that they were weak and poorly defended. With their allies the Dongiro, an Ethiopian tribe that had also persuaded the Sudanese government to give it weapons, they decided to attack. At midnight they surrounded every group of huts, refraining from firing a shot until they were all in position. The shooting lasted for two hours. One woman escaped, one boy was left unnoticed under a pile of bodies. The other ninety-six were all shot dead. The boy, wandering alone in the savannahs two weeks later, was caught and killed by Toposa spies. Looking around the field of skulls I remembered that, had I not fallen ill, we would have been there too.

A mile from the camp was the local police post: ten metal huts in a barbed-wire compound, on a high exposed knoll

41

where the wind shrieked in the wires of the radio mast. The chief of police, a soft, plump, amiable man from central Kenya, was delighted to see us. He lay on his bed, which was stained grey with sweat, fanning his stomach. He hated this place. There was nothing, he said, but dust and heat and flies. Through the door I saw his men sitting on benches outside their huts, fat, vacant and irritable. A vulture rose on a thermal lifting off the hill and slid away across the savannah. I asked him what the police had done on the night of the raid.

'Us? We hid under our beds. It was dangerous out there.'

Lodwar was packed with people who had fled from the Toposa. Too frightened to stay in the highlands, they had taken their cattle down to the plains, to regions where no rain had fallen for four or five years. Their animals had died and now they came as mendicants to Lodwar, with nothing but the clothes they wore. They built themselves huts of sticks and dried grass in the hills outside the town. By day they came down to the streets, to beg, to sell their beads or their weapons, to stare at the civil servants eating steaks on the verandah of the smart hotel.

I soon discovered that these northerners were not the only fugitives to reach the town. Toiling up the road from the southern savannahs I saw a caravan of twenty donkeys and perhaps sixty grim-faced men and women. On the backs of the donkeys little children sat in howdahs, shaded from the sun by leather canopies. They made no effort to brush away the flies crowded round the mucus on their faces. In their eyes was the dull, abstracted aspect of starvation.

The men told me that they had come from the most fertile place in Turkana district, the riverine forests close to the southern mountains. The grass was thick there and the trees were in leaf, but, like the refugees from the northern savannahs, they dared not stay where they could have kept their animals alive. In their case the Pokot, the hill people of the south, had driven them out of their homes, and the carnage they had wrought was, if anything, worse than what the Toposa had accomplished in the north.

The story was sickeningly similar to that of the people of Naramam, except that the Pokot had been armed not by the government of Sudan but by the government of Kenya. They were a part of the Kalenjin group of tribes, to which the Kenyan President and many of his ministers belonged. They had been given automatic weapons in order to drive people of other tribes from the regions in which they lived and, it was rumoured, to secede from the rest of Kenya if President Moi lost the forthcoming election. Like the Toposa, they were more interested in raiding the Turkana than becoming involved in national politics, but in this case their motivation was more a matter of money than enmity. All the evidence suggested that people at the highest levels of government were profiting from their activities.

The men in the caravan told me that when they tried to follow the raiders, to recapture their animals, they found the Kenyan army in their way. They were machine-gunned by uniformed soldiers and strafed by air force helicopters. While better and better weapons were reaching the Pokot, the Home Guards in south Turkana district – local men equipped with old rifles by the government – were being disarmed. On the admission of an MP from West Pokot district, the raids were discussed and sanctioned by officials there before they took place. Cattle trucks were waiting in Pokot villages even before the raiders left their homes. The Pokot would storm into Turkana district, round up as many animals as they could, shooting anyone they came across, and drive them back to the waiting lorries. On the way to Nairobi the convoys were waved through the police posts without being checked. They drove straight to the abattoirs of the Kenya Meat Commission.

The scale of this racket could scarcely be exaggerated. The Pokot raiders, whose numbers were sometimes great enough to encircle a region of many square miles, escaped on some occasions with ten or fifteen thousand cattle. One raid alone brought so much meat onto the Nairobi market that the price of beef there dropped overnight from seventy shillings a kilo to twenty. Several hundred Turkana had been killed in these attacks and almost all the rest had fled.

The Pokot, in the south, and the Toposa, in the north, had made most of Turkana district a no man's land. The population had concentrated into the only safe places in the region: the central deserts, all of which were stricken by drought. As a result, most of the 350,000 Turkana were threatened with starvation. Hundreds had died already, and without help the crisis would become a catastrophe.

Walking around Lodwar, I met some of the victims of the famine. Old men walked up to me and, with a gaze of the most pitiful distress, touched their lips and ran a hand over their throats and down onto their bellies, to show that they were starving. People hung around the back entrances of the restaurants and hotels in the hope of picking up some scraps: as often as not the dogs or the goats got there first. Adrian asked some of these Turkana if he could take their pictures, to show people what was happening in the district, but when he raised his camera one of the men I had seen before, with a red badge and a metal stick, came running out into the street. He raised the stick over Adrian's head.

'No pictures of thin people.'

We remonstrated with him and another man, similarly equipped, emerged from the shade. They told us to get out of Lodwar. We argued that we had every right to be there. They said that if we stayed we would have to pay them a fine. These men – though they were both in their fifties – were members of KANU Youth, a band of unpaid vigilantes accountable only to the head of the KANU party, the President. Everyone, I later discovered, even the district commissioner and the local MP, was afraid of them. Like the privileged members of Hitler Youth, they could do whatever they pleased. They used their ill-founded authority to extort money and favours from the people of Lodwar, forcing some of the starving to hand over everything they possessed.

To find out what other government departments were doing for the fugitives, I retraced the short walk to the compound of government offices which I had failed to complete a few weeks before. I was passed through a succession of dapper, well-fed men from central Kenya, mildly irritated at being interrupted in their conversations, woken up, or distracted from their perusal of the newspapers. After meeting five or six people who denied all responsibility for anything relating to the district, I was finally introduced to a man who claimed to be solving the Turkana's problems. He turned the air-conditioning up and sat back in his revolving chair.

The government, he said, was doing everything in its powers to help the hungry people there. I asked him exactly what that meant. It meant, he assured me, everything. Did it include, I asked, providing food relief?

'The food relief is definitely, I will say definitely, on its way.'

'But there were warnings of this famine in January. It's now October. Why hasn't the food relief arrived?'

'I must repeat to you that the government, even myself, is doing everything within its powers to assist the people here.'

I later discovered that local officials, fearful of losing face if they admitted that they could not cope with what was happening in their regions, had not informed their superiors that something was going wrong. This delayed any action for several months. When, at last, the news did reach Nairobi, the government, loath to admit that it could not look after the people of Kenya, refused to make a request to the World Food Programme for assistance. Yet there was nothing Kenya could do by itself, for the World Bank, whose representatives in Nairobi were obsessed with balancing the country's budget, had advised the country to sell its strategic food reserves. Only when reports in the Kenyan papers revealed that Turkana men and women were taking their children down to the town of Eldoret to give them away to strangers as the only means of keeping them alive did the government resolve to do something. It seemed, in October, as if a famine relief effort were just about to begin.

Then, however, the officials realized that they had a prior commitment. They had decided to hold an agriculture show in Lodwar, to demonstrate to the desert people the techniques of mechanized farming, as practised in the wet highlands of central Kenya. All staff and resources in the district were requisitioned to prepare for the show, which the district commissioner determined would be a roaring success. Ploughs, combine harvesters, seed drills and sprayers were brought up in convoys of lorries from Nairobi. Cattle and sheep had been fattened up for months in special stalls and were displayed as the ideals to which the Turkana herders should aspire. There were discos, beer tents and stand-up comedians. It was, as the DC had hoped, a roaring success. But the Turkana, unable to pay the entrance fee, were not allowed in, and stood on the other side of the barbed-wire fence gawping at the incomprehensible machines, watching with starving eyes as the civil servants inside ate hot dogs, candyfloss and popcorn. Only in November, ten months after the Turkana had first asked their local officials for help, did food aid arrive in the district. Even then, only a fraction of what they required was received, and had it not been for a frantic reorganization of the food relief effort by the charity Oxfam, thousands more Turkana would undoubtedly have died.

I had promised the people of Ngilukumong that, before we left Turkana district, we would return to their camp to buy some of their possessions for an exhibition of Turkana life which we wanted to stage in England. Leaving behind the misery in Lodwar, we passed through the town of Kakuma and took the familiar track over the savannahs to the river. On the way I saw a tall stiff figure, striding along the track ahead of us, that I immediately recognized as Matayo. We stopped beside him, and he came to the window with a smile, shook hands and, still without speaking, climbed into the back of the Land Rover. I watched him in the mirror, calm and dignified, looking straight ahead. As we approached Ngilukumong, he leant forward and asked, 'Did George and Adrian bring me the bag they promised?'

I told him we had.

'Ah. Matayo is glad.'

The feeble rains had brought up a sprinkling of green seedlings, which cracked the earth under the acacia trees. In the desert there were patches of white flowers, and the faintest tinge of pale green. Women drew water from a brown pool trapped in a meander of the river bed. On the bank two old men sat hidden behind a bush, in the hope that the women would take off their skirts. We parked by the camp, and everyone stopped what they were doing and clustered round the Land Rover. The women did their best not to look pleased to see us, twisting their involuntary smiles into grimaces. Dismas's mother came out of her hut, glanced at us and, scorn twisting the tight knots in her face, spat on the ground and went back in.

I sat with Dismas in his enclosure, while he polished a new stool he had carved with a piece of broken glass. For half an hour he said nothing, then he asked me my news. He told me his news: the rains had been so poor that he had sent half his goats away to his brother in the mountains. In a month or two the winter rains – the long rains – were due to begin. He hoped enough would fall to allow the herders to bring their cattle back to the plains: he missed the young men and feared for their safety.

The Turkana needed no reminding that we intended to buy some of their handicrafts, and a crowd soon gathered outside the enclosure, holding pots, troughs, spears, sticks, jewellery and stools. Akale, unsurprisingly, stood at their head, waving some moth-eaten object and angrily demanding that I buy it from her. Some of the work was exquisite. There were milk containers carved from soft wood into perfect hollow spheres, little wooden urns with carved handles, salt containers made from the hollow wingbones of ostriches, with neat caps of lizard skin, leather bands decorated with fossil cowrie shells from the ancient lake that once covered the Lotikipi Plains, strings of ceramic beads bought from Arab traders in the seventeenth century, leaf-shaped earrings of beaten brass, slipped into the soft tail skins of mice where they pierced the ear, necklaces made from electric flex, bits of indicator lens and a speedometer cable scavenged from wrecked cars. There was a thief's bracelet, strung with pieces of soft wood, little bits of which could be bitten off and surreptitiously spat towards the

47

man from whom one wished to steal, with the aim of magically blinding the victim to one's intentions. Natiang brought a furious little girl, twisting and kicking.

'What'll you give me for this one? One hundred? Two hundred?'

The girl sunk her teeth into his hand and, howling with pain and laughter, Natiang released her and hopped around, clutching the wound, while she hid behind the corral, watching us with horrified eyes.

The prices the women demanded were outrageous. If I paid someone even half of what she asked, she would run off sniggering gleefully, while the others danced around and hit each other with delight. If I refused to buy something, they shouted, swore and stamped their feet, accusing me of hoarding my wealth and trying to steal the milk from their breasts. For two days I sat under a tree, bargaining, arguing, turning away items I had already bought, asking for those I did not have. The women went back to their houses and returned with cowbells, axes, donkey panniers, fighting rings and lip plugs.

When I had spent all my money I tried to persuade the women that I wanted no more, but they pursued me everywhere I went. When I locked myself in the Land Rover, Akale shoved a sharp stick through the window, jabbing me in the arm, and insisted I bought her skirt. When I refused she told me that because of my meanness her baby would die of starvation. She persisted with this line of argument until I reminded her that she did not have a baby. As the sun went down, the women gave up and went away. The elders, driven into their huts by the racket, came out and settled on their stools. I left them tracking the stars across the heavens, waiting for the rain.

CHAPTER THREE

God's Land

*The land shall not be sold for ever: for the land is mine; for ye
are strangers and sojourners with me.*

Leviticus 25:23

Written across the face of Nairobi was the history of
modern Kenya, from the first colonial adventures to
the present. The railway station, around which the
city had been built, had suffered little more than a coat of paint
since its construction in 1900. Wandering the platforms, I
should not have been greatly surprised if a steam train had
pulled in and discharged a cargo of men with pith helmets and
walrus moustaches, and women in long dresses with parasols.
Only Diana Ross, crooning over the intercom, woke me from
my retrospection, with a song that seemed to be addressed to
me, but may simply have been a convenient substitute for
station announcements.

> *'Do you know where you're going to,*
> *Do you like the things that life is showing you?*
> *Where are you going to?*
> *Do you know? . . .'*

Casting their shadows over the classical façades built to
glorify the Empire were the monuments which the modern
rulers of Kenya had dedicated to themselves. The Kenyatta
Conference Centre, monstrous by the standards of any city,
was to be dwarfed by a tower built in honour of President Moi,
with one storey for every year of his life. As the project was
constantly delayed by the mysterious disappearance of funds,

49

it promised, eventually, to be a stupendous construction.

On the streets, beneath the office blocks and towering hotels, seven- and eight-year-olds jostled blindly among trousers and skirts, sucking on plastic bags. Among the men and women pushing past them were business people in suits or silk blouses; relaxed civil servants with KANU badges on their lapels; market women in headscarves and wrap-around skirts carrying stacks of empty baskets on their heads; ragged men selling flowers, asking for money or trying to thrust leaflets into people's hands.

I noticed that perhaps one-third of the cars going past were driven by white people, and I remembered that the whites had retained a good deal of their economic power in Kenya. But I never noticed any overt hostility towards them or towards me. Instead, mzungus still appeared to be treated with deference: I saw black Kenyans stepping into the street to make way for Europeans on the pavement. I found this hard to understand, until I realized that much of Kenya's bitterness about colonization had been directed not at the whites but at the Asians. The Asians had often found themselves to be the intermediaries between the Kenyans and the Europeans, and appear to have been blamed for most of the excesses of empire.

Everywhere I went in Nairobi I saw images of the nomads I was preparing to visit. They appeared on postcards, on the covers of glossy books, on the logos of safari companies, on batiks for sale in the tourist shops, as carvings in the foyers of the smart hotels. The men in the pictures were young, long-limbed and beautiful, with smooth cheeks and girlish lashes. Gazing at the camera, dancing, standing on one leg, they looked calm and arrogant. They had adorned themselves with earrings, necklaces and pendants of beads. Their long hair was braided and rubbed with red ochre. Like Roman centurions, they carried spears and dressed in red togas. The women in the photographs seemed to combine a remote and self-assured grace with the challenging stare of sexual competence. Like the young men, they were long and limber, the European ideal, with small breasts and clean, grave, finely cut faces. Some were bare-chested. The Maasai seemed to embody all the promise and the challenge of Africa.

I soon began to suspect that these images might have more to do with the way the Maasai were seen than the way they were. There was a consistency about the faces and the figures which seemed unnatural, and did not correspond to the shapes of the Maasai people I saw wandering around Nairobi. It seemed as if the photographers and the artists had been selecting something that the buyers wanted to see. Watching the foreign visitors in shops buying spears, postcards, safari suits, beads and wooden carvings, I tried to imagine what this might be. It seemed to me that they were looking for something as different from themselves as possible, for the essence of wild Africa. The images which the photographers had chosen seemed to be those of the remote and independent nomad. I came to believe that the tourists were seeking an antidote to a surfeit of civilization.

But then I began to suspect that I was projecting my own motives onto the other mzungus. What drew me to the nomads? Why was I here? For the last six years I had been visiting the remotest tribal peoples in the world, travelling to the places where people were least affected by the ethics of industrial society, and writing and campaigning on behalf of those among them who were resisting the destruction of their lands or their forcible assimilation into the global economy. While it could sometimes be thrilling, in some respects this was the most dangerous, uncomfortable and psychologically damaging occupation I could have chosen.

Having given up an excellent job and spent more and more money on ever more expensive journeys, I was close to bankruptcy. I had made innumerable enemies, been banned from seven countries in Asia and Latin America, and faced life imprisonment if I were ever foolish enough to return to Indonesia. I had been threatened with lawsuits, survived two attempts on my life, been followed and monitored, on one occasion even in Britain. I had argued with most of my friends, lost one girlfriend after another, and spent every moment I possessed learning languages, reading papers on obscure subjects, travelling, writing and campaigning. I found it hard to see what I had gained. I had published two books and made some radio and television programmes, but they had earned me neither fame nor fortune. Yet here I was, in the middle of another investigation, and no less enthusiastic than I had been when I began this strange career.

Why did traditional peoples attract me? Why did I want to travel among the Maasai, the Turkana or the Samburu, rather than the agricultural peoples of the Kenyan Highlands, who seemed to be closer in outlook and lifestyle to me? Why was I even less interested in the lives of the civil servants in their suits and KANU badges? Or, for that matter, in the affairs of the people of my own country, the tourists wandering in and out of the gigantic hotels? I had no immediate answers, but I was reminded, as I sat behind the plate glass of a ground-floor café, watching the many different peoples of that remarkable city go by, that a world without diversity – a diversity of cultures, beliefs and approaches to the many problems besetting us – would be a world without a future.

It was to discover what was happening to the best known of the distinctive peoples of East Africa that we set to work in Nairobi, to learn something about the Maasai's recent history and to find out how their lives were changing now. They were, I knew, changing fast. A glance along those crowded streets made that quite clear, for there I saw long-ragged people with holes in their ears, guarding not their herds but other people's buildings, or foraging in the rubbish tips. But why, I wondered, had these people left the savannahs? What was happening to those who remained? Could they, did they want to, keep out of the shadow of civilization which now hung over their lands like the great glass towers of Nairobi?

Before the British arrived in East Africa, the Maasai prophet Mbatian predicted the arrival of an iron rhinoceros, on the back of which a strange pink people would be riding. In this, he said, 'I see the end for my children and the land. The strangers will come and kick my people down and keep them under their feet . . . however strong and brave our warriors are.'

The first Europeans to reach the Maasai's territory were so

struck by their fine features and their proud disdain for other races that they decided they could not be Africans at all, but one of the lost tribes of Israel, or the descendants of a Roman legion lost in Africa. They could not suppress their admiration for a tribe which had driven its enemies out of most of East Africa: the Maasai ranged all the way from north-central Kenya to northern Tanzania and occupied most of the land between Lake Victoria and the coast. At the same time, however, they recognized in the Maasai a threat to all they sought to implant in East Africa. These people, who ran down lions and killed them with spears, moved over vast distances, fought other tribes and other sections of their own tribe, stole cattle and wives and refused to till the ground, were the antithesis of the British concept of a decent and well-ordered society. They were also one of Africa's most effective fighting forces: were it not for the terrible misfortunes which soon befell them, they could well have made colonization impossible.

During the second half of the nineteenth century, busy trade routes developed between what is now Kenya to the Horn of Africa and the Arabian peninsula. It was down these trails that rinderpest, the deadly cattle disease, came to East Africa. In the 1890s it wiped out ninety per cent of the Maasai's herds. It was immediately followed by epidemics of smallpox, and by the time both these bovine and human plagues were spent, only forty per cent of the Maasai remained. They were a broken, ragged shadow of what they had been.

Yet the British still saw in them a threat to their ambitions. They regarded their warlike nomadism as a regressive characteristic, which would have to be stamped out if a morally superior society were to be established in Africa. In 1904 Sir Charles Eliot, the first colonial governor of Kenya, wrote, 'There can be no doubt that the Maasai and many other tribes must go under. It is a prospect which I view with equanimity and a clear conscience.' He and his successors set to work to accelerate the process.

Eliot and his colleagues did not want to destroy the people themselves, they wanted to destroy the tribal structures and traditions which encouraged them to remain uncivilized. They

believed they had a duty to turn East Africa into a law-abiding
and God-fearing place. They also needed to make it pay. The
only way in which these objectives could be met was to settle
people down and expose them to the redeeming influences of
religion, education and the market economy. This process,
while releasing the people of Kenya from the constraints of
superstition, illiteracy and barter, would also have the effect
of releasing much of their land for white settlement: The
British and white South African farmers who would take their
place would both show the natives the way forward and, by
means of the crops they would produce, help to make the
colony economically viable.

Responding to pressure from white settlers, the British
authorities made the Maasai promises they had no intention
of keeping, and fooled them into giving away the greater part
of their lands. The Maasai were confined to the least productive corner, the area to the south of Nairobi, and their old
lands were distributed to the settlers. The authorities then
began the task which the Kenyan government still pursues to
this day: to change the way the Maasai live.

To the Maasai, as to the Turkana, land cannot be permanently owned, divided up or sold. The land does not
belong to them but to God, and they are there by His grace
alone. Maasai elders can claim rights to use certain parts of
the land and, for a while, to keep other people out of them,
but everything is open to negotiation with other elders. The
British saw in this a prescription for disaster. They argued that
if no one owned the land, everyone would exploit it as heavily
as he could, because he would lose nothing by so doing. This
was why, they said, the Maasai owned so many cattle: no one
cared whether or not he overgrazed places which did not
belong to him. To prevent the land from being destroyed, the
British planned first to settle the Maasai and control their
grazing, and later to start privatizing the land, making every
herder responsible for his own patch.

The British failed to settle the majority of the Maasai, and
they left East Africa before they had time to make any progress with privatization. But when the Independent Kenyan

government took over, it continued the programmes they began. Like the departing colonists, the new government believed that the way forward for Kenya was to follow the route to development taken by the world's richest nations: the privatization of land and resources, the monetarization of the economy and the development of manufacturing industry. The nomads, though they were responsible for an extensive but largely unrecognized barter trade, appeared to produce very little for Kenya. They were, the government believed, primitive and undisciplined. Settling the Maasai and breaking up their land would be good for them and good for the country. It would discourage them from over-grazing the savannahs and turn them into potential money earners, allowing them, for the first time, to play a part in the consumer economy. Their land could be made productive: in other words, start to generate money, to help Kenya build up its industrial base.

The land over which the Maasai roamed would be divided up into private ranches. The government realized that it could not make this conversion all at once so, with help from the World Bank, it started with an intermediate stage, called group ranches. Every community of Maasai would be responsible for one piece of land and should not let its cattle leave that area. This would encourage the communities to look after their land and, the government hoped, to cull more of their cattle, easing pressure on the grazing and helping to feed Kenya's hungry people. But the plan was deeply flawed.

The government put a small committee of elders in charge of every group ranch. These people soon discovered that they did not have to obey what the other Maasai elders wanted. Within a few years, the committee members of most group ranches began to grab the best land, forbidding the other people in their communities to make use of it. Soon the ordinary Maasai realized that if they did not take land for themselves, the greedy committee members would seize the lot. The people of several of the group ranches had little option but to do as the government wanted and start to divide their savannahs into private farms. This process, I now discovered, was threatening the very existence of the Maasai.

As the lands were divided up, the most powerful elders took for themselves ranches large enough and wet enough to support their herds throughout the year. The remainder of the Maasai in these areas were left with small patches, well-watered only during the wet season. When the rains passed on, their herds, trapped in one place, were left behind, and swiftly died of starvation. All the people could do was to sell their pieces of land and hope to make a living in some other way. Unused to buying and selling in cash, they were conned by rich businessmen, some of whom, disgracefully, were their own elders. Buying up enormous areas for a pittance, these people set to work to make them profitable.

Some of them realized that they could make the most money by growing wheat and barley. Wheat (though not barley, which is used for making people drunk) is becoming an important food crop in East Africa. In the cities many people are now dependent on bread. The government has tried to reduce its imports of wheat by encouraging Kenyans to grow more themselves. Unfortunately most of the areas in which wheat can be farmed sustainably have already been ploughed. The majority of the new places, the savannahs where the Maasai lived, appear to be unsuitable for ploughing, and this use of the land seems to exhaust the soil within three or four years. So, while I shuffled through the libraries in Nairobi, the rich grass swards, the forests, the dew-ponds, the flowering shrub lands of Maasailand were going under the plough, perhaps never to emerge again.

Looking back over the history of Maasailand, it seems that the British misunderstood how the Maasai traditionally used and controlled their land. It was true that no one owned the savannahs, but this did not mean that their use was not controlled. Every group of elders regulated the areas they grazed: they decided who should be allowed in and for how long. If people abused the land they were punished. If they persisted, they could be tied to a tree and beaten to death. The elders knew that if someone over-exploited the land he was exploiting them.

The Maasai kept large herds of cattle not only because it

was prestigious to do so, but also because they needed enough animals to be sure that part of their herd would get through a drought. The savannahs may be the richest environment one year and the poorest the next, and the only means of survival there is to allow the numbers of your animals to fluctuate with these changes. If, as the British desired, Maasai herders had tried to keep a constant number of cows on a single patch of ground, the people would soon have died of starvation. Traditional nomadism supported more people on the savannahs than modern farming does today, while causing less damage.

At the end of November we left Nairobi to find out what was happening to the people of the southern savannahs. By great good fortune, we arrived in the region we had chosen to visit on the first day of the warriors' graduation. As we walked through the lands belonging to the community of Enkaroni, I could see a ribbon of scarlet threaded between the people's houses. From a distance, blazing against the greens and blues of the savannah, it looked as if a Chinese dragon had wound itself around the village. I saw smoke and heard what appeared to be a low roar. Coming closer, I saw that the scarlet was the cloaks of hundreds of Maasai elders. The roar was the sound of the Maasai dancing.

In the middle of the ring of huts a phalanx of young men was bobbing up and down, making a noise between their teeth like sand being sifted. They were dressed like the people whose photos I had seen in Nairobi, in red cloaks, stained maroon by red ochre, with bead jewellery and braided hair. A few resembled the people in the pictures, others were ugly or short and squat. Their village looked like a ring of gigantic weather-stained toadstools. Beyond the thorn fence, long grass and climbing flowers twisted up the trunks of the thorn trees, whose canopies were flat and distended, like wind-blown clouds. In the wind, while the sun was only halfway up the sky, it could have been a warm day in England: it was ten degrees cooler than Turkana district. To my amazement, three Grant's gazelles grazed just fifty yards from the houses, raising their heads from time to time to watch the dancing.

I did not have long to look around. We were soon surrounded by Maasai, speaking in their own language, English
and Swahili. Most of the people in the crowd were women, the
mothers of the young men. Their heads were shaven. They had
fine, tight lips and large curving black eyes, in which I noticed
the hard glint of derision. Yet, while there were some clear
themes, what struck me most about the Maasai was their diversity. There were people of every size and shape, every skin
colour from caramel to blue-black, an odd collection of noses,
mouths and ears which did not seem to belong either to the
tribe or to the individual. I remembered that the Maasai had, in
their conquests and migrations, assimilated people from an
enormous expanse of East Africa.

While the women and some of the young men – the
warriors – jostled round us, the elders kept to themselves.
They were drinking heavily, from buffalo horns, gourds and
cooking fat tins: one man swigged from a bottle labelled 'Perfumed JIK Bleach. Whitens, Removes Stains, Kills Germs'.
Some of them sat beneath the trees in the village compound,
others stood, unsteadily, talking and waving their sticks. A
man with mad red eyes raved around the enclosure shaking his
stick at the children, who scattered with little screams, then
crept out from behind the houses to follow him. The elders
were dressed simply, in scarlet cloaks and sandals. One or two
wore trousers underneath. They all carried sticks or short polished clubs, which confirmed their status as the decision-
makers of Enkaroni.

The warriors who had come to see us returned to their
dance: this time two of the young men stepped into the midst
of the dancers, jumped several times three or four feet into the
air then fell back with self-conscious smiles, making way for
two more. The other warriors uttered a cacophony of grunts,
yelps and roars. One boy crept up behind me and made a noise
like a lion grunting. I spun round. His hand shot under his
cloak, as if he were about to seize his knife, then he laughed
and shook my hand. I noticed that the warriors, when they
were not dancing, touched each other repeatedly, standing
with one arm around a friend's waist, or a hand on the back of

someone's neck. They strutted about like heroes, but when an argument flared up and they pulled out their knives, their mothers rushed from their houses, confiscated the weapons and scolded them.

They feigned disinterest in us, our car and our possessions, but when I unlocked the Land Rover to get something, turned round when someone called me and turned back, I found seven warriors sitting inside, twisting the rear-view mirror around to catch a glimpse of themselves, turning the wheel, hooting the horn, smearing sheep's fat and red ochre all over the seats. When I recorded one of their songs and played it back to them, they whooped and stamped with pleasure, snatching the headphones from each other and laughing at the people whose voices they recognized. They were monstrously vain, constantly adjusting their jewellery in my wing mirrors or asking their friends to tell them how they looked. But, perhaps because I recognized so much of myself in them, I felt comfortable in their presence, and as safe as if I had been among my friends. They were no closer to being noble savages than I was, but I soon began to discover that they had been shaped by forces utterly different from any to which I had been exposed.

One of the warriors, a serious, intelligent nineteen-year-old called Toronkei, with an innocent face but a low conspiratorial voice, took it upon himself to explain what was happening. On his thighs were smooth circular scars where he had pressed glowing embers into his flesh to test his courage. He had completed primary school and spoke excellent English, but had returned to Enkaroni when he became a warrior.

The village, he said, had been built just a few weeks ago, for the graduation ceremonies that would take place over the next four months. The warriors, as tradition demanded, had kidnapped their mothers from their fathers' corrals and stolen several of their fathers' cattle. They instructed the women to build them a village, or *manyatta*, as the ceremonial settlements are called. The events that would take place here would be the most important in a man's life, for this was where he would make the transition from a youth to an adult. On leaving the manyatta, as junior elders, they would be allowed to marry and to set up homes of their own, with the cattle their fathers had kept for them.

This, Toronkei explained, was the day on which the manyatta would be blessed. He showed me the three blessing rings the women had just completed, encircling the village. One, made of cow-dung, represented the warriors' attachment to their animals. The second, made of stones, showed the unity between the warriors. The third, a rope of plaited bark, invoked the blessing of the natural world. The elders, Toronkei told me, had to get drunk on a day like this to make their blessing effective. They were drinking mead, fermented from the honey of wild bees. The ceremony that was just about to begin had to be performed before the sun reached its zenith: this would ensure that the graduating warriors would go up in life rather than down.

Four elders started pacing around the manyatta, looking for the centre. When they were satisfied that they had found it, their wives brought them leather mantles and tied them over the elders' shoulders. The men told them to dig a hole on the spot they had chosen. When the hole was ready, the elders spat mouthfuls of mead into it – Toronkei said this represented God's blessing of rain – then planted a rock and two sprigs of an evergreen shrub. These were buried by the women in a cone of cow dung. The old men mumbled their blessings and the warriors responded with a murmur.

The elders went back to their mead and the young men to their dancing. Toronkei took me to his hut, a low box of woven sticks plastered with cow dung. But for a white beam of light from a hole in the wall, swirling with dust and smoke, the hut was dark. It smelt of leather, milk and the perfumed resin of the wood on the hearth. I watched Toronkei's mother making tea, her face sketched in a few smooth lines by the glow of the fire. As my eyes accommodated to the darkness, I realized that five or six warriors were sitting around me, drinking coagulated milk.

Toronkei told me that a boy could not qualify as a warrior, a *moran*, until he had been circumcised. When he reached the age of thirteen or fourteen, the circumciser visited his home and cut away his foreskin with a steel razor. The operation took five minutes, during which the boy had to stare calmly into the eyes of an elder, without twitching or blinking. If he succeeded he would be rewarded with a gift of cattle; if he flinched, he would be chased, ridiculed and ostracized. Yet the circumciser had an interest in causing him pain: it was said that if no boy flinched in a season of circumcision, the surgeon would meet an early death.

When the boy had recovered, he joined the others who were to become warriors, and they wandered around the savannahs, shooting birds with bows and arrows, getting into trouble, making the friends on whom they would depend for the rest of their lives. Among the Maasai, loyalty to one's age group – one's own generation of warriors – was the supreme principle that overrode all others. Without age groups, Toronkei told me, there would be no society, no organization, no Maasai.

The ethics of the moran seemed to combine those of monks, soldiers and juvenile delinquents. They were not allowed to drink or to take tobacco. They would starve themselves for days, and allow the elders to set them tests of stamina and restraint, such as driving cattle over the seventy miles to Nairobi and back, without eating, drinking or sleeping, within three days. At other times they would scorn such honourable behaviour, beg or steal a couple of oxen, drive them into the bush, slaughter them and for two weeks eat and carouse. In the past they might have attacked other tribes or other sections of the Maasai, coming together with several hundred or even several thousand other men, marshalled and deployed with the discipline of a modern army. In battle, honour demanded that they never abandoned a fellow warrior, even if hopelessly outnumbered.

At other times three or four moran would sneak off together to raid an enemy, stealing cattle to add to their fathers' herds. Maasai caught raiding could now be imprisoned for several years in Kenya, and the practice had largely stopped, but one of the warriors at Enkaroni admitted to having made off with a couple of heifers from a farm belonging to some

Kikuyu settlers, escaping under a hail of bullets.

The warriors were allowed to have sex with unmarried girls, but not to make them pregnant: there were various traditional methods of contraception, not all of them successful. They were expected to share their lovers, as they shared everything, with the other people in their age group. This continued beyond marriage: theoretically any man could arrive at the home of another in his age group and expect his host to leave for the night while he slept with one of the man's wives. This custom was now dying out, but not before AIDS had become well-established among the Maasai.

It was their sharing of both possessions and decision-making that held the age groups together, and it was the age groups which held the community together. The bond between the Maasai men was stronger than that of the Turkana, whose alliances shifted with the demands of their harsher environment and who, unlike all but one of the other tribes of Kenya, remained uncircumcised. The cohesion of the Maasai age groups allowed them to control the way their savannahs were grazed.

The elders, like the warriors, deferred to each other. There were no leaders, merely men who chaired discussions and sought to identify a consensus. Like many nomads, the Maasai typically abhorred authoritarianism, and elders who tried to impose their views would lose respect and influence. One result was that no one was able to monopolize the land: everyone kept everyone else in check. A system similar to the Turkana's, where rich men lent some of their animals to the poor, meant that no one went hungry while others prospered.

When the warriors had drunk their milk they began to sing what Toronkei called 'happiness songs', rocking backwards and forwards, lifting their heads then sinking back. The hoarse, growling noise they made was almost hypnotic. I had begun to sing with them when the faint light from the doorway was blotted out and everyone fell silent. A tall emaciated man, clearly suffering from an attempt to make his blessing of the manyatta especially powerful, stalked into the hut. He turned his head slowly, taking in the figures sitting round the fire with a scowl.

'Who are you?' he demanded.

I introduced myself. He stared at me without speaking. I asked him who he was, and he said he was Samson, the father of Toronkei. I asked if he had any other children. He frowned.

'I am drinking alcohol, so I am not in full sense. But I will address myself to your question. I am possessed of ten children and two wives. I am a polygamist.'

He sank back onto a bed of cattle hides, put a hand over his eyes and was immediately asleep.

We returned to Enkaroni three weeks later, to see the second of the graduation ceremonies, the blessing of the spokesman of the moran. He would, when the warriors had graduated, chair the age group's meetings and represent their views to other people. An ox had been slaughtered and divided among the age groups and the sexes. Each group sat in its own circle and ate. We were invited to join every one of them, and I was soon so full of meat that I could scarcely stand. It was in this state that I was caught by a party of women who, having possessed themselves of some of the elders' mead, had been selflessly blessing the manyatta behind the huts.

They were dancing. As I tried to pass, my arms were seized and I was dragged into their midst. I was surrounded by handsome, jeering faces. Hands darted through the crowd and tugged at my sleeves. A small, imperious woman of about forty, with dark glittering eyes, commanded me to start dancing. I shook my head, but she whacked me on the arm and told me again to dance. I did my best. The women choked with laughter, bending over and wheezing as if it hurt. The small woman moved closer and closer to me, rolling her hips, all the time holding my gaze with mocking eyes, which told me she knew that I would not dare to respond. I pushed through the Bacchantes and fled.

Maasai women have to do what the elders tell them, but they are skilled in asserting their rights. During the wet season, women may process from village to village, singing and dancing, demanding food and money from the men in return for their blessing. They might beat up elders who have mistreated their wives, and steal some of their cows. Sometimes, if they

63

are anxious about the possibility of becoming barren, these gangs will ambush men in the savannahs and rape them: this is believed to be a cure for infertility. The terrified men keep out of their way.

But when the women were at home and sober they had, as I found, a quiet dignity that sometimes seemed to put the noisy warriors to shame. They worked so smoothly and quietly that I sometimes wondered how water had arrived, a fire been started or food materialized in front of me. Like the women of most nomadic societies, they trudged through the community's unglamorous tasks, while the men fought their enemies, raced across the savannahs with stolen animals, and spent hours confabulating under the thorn trees. They worked with grace, good humour and sometimes even visible pleasure, which had much to say about the way they shared their tasks.

On this second visit I also came to see a little more of the elders. They were perhaps as diverse as any group of men who had grown up together could be. While most survived by keeping animals, among them were several civil servants, a councillor, a policeman, an engineer and even a magistrate, wearing their red cloaks over trousers and city shoes. These urban people had returned to the savannahs for the ceremony; other Maasai townsmen, whose jobs were lowly or who were unemployed, could not afford to come.

They were a proud, volatile, argumentative group of men who, when drunk, appeared to find nothing more satisfying than to pick quarrels and resolve them with dramatic gestures of friendship. But what I found most striking was the way in which they held their tongues and listened when somebody else was speaking, gave his points serious consideration and answered them without belittling his argument.

I spent the night in Toronkei's house, kept awake by smoke, lice and the children who lay on the bed with me, kicking me in their sleep. At dawn I walked out with Toronkei, around the manyatta and over the savannah. In the first, uncertain light, the moran, with cloaks pulled over their heads for warmth, stood like hooded grey ghosts in the smoke billowing from the doors of their huts. As the sun rose, it flared in the fur of the donkeys and cows, reducing them to outlines of gold neon, their substance faded to the same grey as the mist-strewn savannahs beyond them.

We ducked beneath the branches of the thorn trees, talking quietly. Something started up from the bush and hurtled away. Toronkei raised his spear: he said he thought it might have been a hyena. From the manyatta I heard the coughs of the cows and the sleepy laughter of the women coming out to milk them.

'This is the last graduation there will ever be at Enkaroni,' said Toronkei.

'What did you say?'

'There will never be another graduation. No more moran, no more elders.'

I stopped and stared at him. His steady, downcast face showed that he was telling me what he believed to be the truth. Enkaroni, he said, was breaking up. The elders were losing their interest in the community; they wanted to attend to their own affairs.

'But if there are no more moran,' I reasoned, 'then there will be no more Maasai.'

'That's right,' said Toronkei.

The people of Enkaroni had been forced to divide up their territory five years before my visit. Their land had become a group ranch in the 1970s, and a small committee of elders had been appointed by the government to control it. They soon awarded themselves the community's best land and many of its springs and wells. No one else was allowed to use them.

When the other people at Enkaroni complained to the government, they were told that the only option they had was to divide up their group ranch into private farms, which could not be seized by the committee. This seemed, at the time, an appropriate response. Privatization was the only legal means of stopping the committee members. Private landowners, the government reasoned, would have an interest in trying to develop and profit from their land. By trading more of their livestock or converting to agriculture, the Maasai could improve their standard of living. Many of them wanted cars,

brick houses, city clothes and televisions. As traditional nomads they had no hope of affording these things; as private
farmers they would at least have the possibility. In striving to
make money, they might generate some of the foreign
exchange the country so desperately needed to pay off its debt.

But when their land came to be divided, the Maasai of
Enkaroni found that the only people whose decisions the
government recognized were civil servants and the committee
members. Instead of splitting the land equally, these people
awarded themselves the biggest and the best properties. One
committee member bribed the others to let him have four
thousand acres; some ordinary Maasai received as little as ten.
Women were not registered at all, so those who had been
widowed or divorced found themselves with nothing.

In fifteen years the age groups, which had governed every
aspect of life at Enkaroni, had become an anachronism, usurp-
ed by the committee, undermined by the interests of the biggest private landowners. There was no communal land for
manyattas or ceremonies. The current manyatta had been built
on the plot belonging to Samson, Toronkei's father; but none of
the other elders was prepared to have the moran and their
cattle on his own land, and Samson did not want to do it again.
Without a manyatta, without a role for the age groups, there
would be no moran. Without moran and the ideals they
embodied, there would be nothing to distinguish the Maasai
from other people.

To find out how these changes were affecting the people of
Enkaroni, we visited a Maasai researcher living in the nearby
town of Kajiado. Jonathon Kamumon had small holes drilled in
the cartilage of his ears. Two of his lower incisors had been
removed with a steel hook when he was twelve; otherwise, in
jeans and a sweater, there was little to distinguish him from
other urban Kenyans. He came from a community in another
part of Maasailand, but had been working with the Enkaroni
people to see if there were ways out of the mess they were now
getting into. He knew everybody there, and took us over the
savannahs to meet some of his friends.

In a high, wind-stricken patch of thorn scrub, we came to

the home of Tepeney, an old woman whose husband had been given one hundred acres when the group ranch was divided up. She had been sitting on the threshold of her house, making bead necklaces, but when she heard the noise of the Land Rover she leapt up. Both pleased and a little alarmed, she stood peering through the bush until she recognized Jonathon, when she ran to the car window with a smile. They talked rapidly for a few minutes, then Tepeney invited us in to tea. Her house was a square concrete block, one room divided by a curtain, with a corrugated metal roof.

Tepeney's face was a mesh of fine lines which, pulled up into a smile, was like the sun rising out of a bank of clouds; hanging with unhappiness, it was like a streaked window on a rainy day. While talking to Jonathon, the sun gradually disappeared, for a moment her face was clouded, then the long lines began to sink and she soon looked the picture of dismay.

The necklaces she made, she said, were not for herself or her friends, but for tourists. There was no point, she told us, in making more beadwork for yourself, when there was nobody to see it. Before she came here, she had seldom bought or sold anything for cash, but now she was in almost constant need of it. She would take the necklaces down to Kajiado when they were ready and sell them to the curio shop for a fraction more than the cost of the materials.

Before the land had been divided up, Tepeney and her husband had lived with five or six other families, in a group of huts made from earth and dung. They had sometimes depended for their survival upon the other people in the Enkaroni community, who would help them if they got into trouble by lending them a cow or a couple of goats, or sending a spare herdboy to drive their cattle to new pastures. All day long, people had come to the village, to exchange news or advice, to take a cup of tea, to ask for a loan. Today, Tepeney said, nobody came to her home. All those who remained on the lands of Enkaroni had built houses on their own plots and were keeping to themselves. They had their own land to manage, and they were the only ones with an interest in it. Tepeney's plot was not big enough to support her children so they had moved away, leaving just her and her husband, who spent most of his time in Kajiado.

She admitted to being lonely. She had only herself and her cows to talk to. She would sometimes visit her old friends, but the spark had gone out of it now that there were no real reasons to go. And everyone was so busy. In the old days they had plenty of time to talk and have fun.

Before the land had been broken up, Tepeney and her husband had nearly one hundred cows. Every year they had left their houses in the hills, where they grazed their cattle in the dry season, and moved down to the plains, in time to catch the rain. There they would build their camps and graze their animals on the green shoots the rain brought up: the cows would get fat, give birth and produce plenty of milk. Meanwhile, the grass back home would have had a chance to recover and the parasites that waited there to feed on the cattle would die of starvation: when they returned the pastures would be rich and healthy enough to see the cattle through to the next wet season.

Now their cows were down to just a dozen or so. The places where they had grazed in the wet season were owned by other Maasai: there was nowhere for their cattle to feed but on their own patch. Trapped there throughout the year, they gave the vegetation no chance to recover. The parasites, never deprived of their food supply, rose in number, and most of the herd sickened and died. The surviving animals were feeble creatures, grazing on a degraded scrub of thorns and bitter herbs. But Tepeney was more fortunate than most. She cultivated a few acres and sold some of the maize and beans she produced. If necessary she could rent some of her land to other Maasai or people from farming tribes. Occasionally she bought and sold cows.

'In the old days,' she told me, 'we had cows but no money. Now we have money but no cows.'

People who had been given less land than her husband now had neither. Their cows had died and they had been forced to sell their plots, often for a tiny amount of money, and to find some other means of keeping themselves alive.

For most of the Maasai, herding was the only life they knew. So the men who lost their land tried, at first, to find work on the big ranches owned by the committee members. This was humiliating. The Maasai pride themselves on being their own masters. They defer to the wishes of their age group, and must respect the decisions of the age groups above them, but when a man is with his cows he and he alone governs his life. Herding for other people is the job of twelve-year-old boys. So when a grown man had to go to the ranch of another, who may even have been of an age group below his, to beg for work, it was as if he renounced his claim to manhood.

The humiliation was compounded by some of the jobs they were given. Traditionally, the Maasai only tilled a patch of land when they had to, when they could not afford to buy grain for the dry season. They did so with reluctance, for true Maasai, in their view, were people who did not farm. Men coming in from a field with mud on their feet would insist that neither they nor anyone they knew had ever broken the ground. But now that the committee members and the other rich Maasai had cheap labour, they could have a field tilled every year, saving the greater expense of buying maize and beans. The workers could hardly claim not to be farming, as they had no other status. They were despised by their employers for the very task they had been set. In one step they had lost both their manhood and their identity as true Maasai.

But there was herding work or farm work for only a few of the dispossessed Maasai. Others had to find something else to keep themselves alive, and they were woefully unprepared. In Maasailand there are fewer school places than anywhere else in Kenya. Even so, the parents of many of the children who might have attended cannot afford the high fees. So those with neither cattle nor work at home would have to try to make their way in the outside world, illiterate and, in some cases, speaking only Maasai.

To show us how they were coping, Jonathon took us back to Kajiado, a small town inhabited half by Maasai and half by people of other tribes. He introduced us to one or two successful Maasai, people who had used the money from the sale of their land to set themselves up with market stalls or small businesses, buying and selling cattle, cloth or grain. But for every one of these men or women there were ten who had no idea what to do with their money. Some had seldom even handled a banknote before they had sold their land, and had no understanding of modern commerce.

We visited a bar, where men in red cloaks with shining eyes and hoarse voices alternately argued and fell on each other professing undying friendship. As we watched, one man was dragged from his chair by the barman and dumped in the street. Swearing, lashing at imaginary enemies, he collided with a tree and crumpled to the ground, where he lay for the rest of the day, face down in the dust. Another old man, spluttering the same two words again and again, tried to climb into our Land Rover. He fell off the footrest three times, then lurched into the road, where he tottered backwards and forwards among the tyre squeals and the hoots of passing cars. In the past, the elders had only got drunk on special occasions, when they restrained each other's bad behaviour. Men who drank by themselves would be punished by their age group. Now that the traditional sanctions no longer applied, the dissolute men could do as they pleased, until the money from their land ran out.

Nor could the elders now restrain the behaviour of the young Maasai. Unscrupulous government ministers were using the warriors to fight their political battles for them, bringing lorryloads armed with sticks and knives into Nairobi to beat up opposition supporters. Some moran now roamed the small towns at night, mugging people and breaking into shops, activities about as far from their traditional ethics of honourable warfare and daylight raiding as they could stray. But for those Maasai who could not survive by these means in Kajiado, the alternative was still worse: to move to Nairobi, into desperate slums where nearly everyone was under-employed and there were few means of making a living except theft and prostitution.

Jonathon's story was not yet complete. It was, he explained, not only the people but also the land which was

70

suffering from privatization. To show us what Maasailand stood to lose, he took us to a wooded valley a few miles from Kajiado. On the upper slopes the grass was heavy with caterpillars. Shrikes and glossy starlings flew down the valley with full beaks to their nests in the woods below. I noticed, as we pushed through the grass, that I stepped over ten or a dozen species of plants with every stride I took. We disturbed zebra, wildebeest, elands and gazelles. On the far side of the valley a herd of giraffes loped across the sky in slow motion. In the woods a seasonal stream had burst its banks, filling the hollows that surrounded it. Hadada ibises and grey herons stalked their margins for frogs, while a pair of red-billed ducks courted in a flurry of spray.

The land, said Jonathon, had been kept this way by the Maasai. Tilling only small patches, moving their animals whenever they began to exhaust the vegetation, they had stayed within its limits. They tolerated most wild animals: Maasai herds could often be seen grazing side by side with elands, zebra or kudu. But now, on private land, doing what the market and not the environment demanded, the remaining Maasai herders had to choose between the wildlife and their own animals. They were driving the wild animals out, in some places putting up fences to stop them from returning. Their own herds, confined to one place all through the year, were compacting the soil and reducing the diversity of plants. By destroying the respect and understanding with which the Maasai had managed their land, privatization had achieved exactly what it was designed to avoid.

Travelling around Kajiado and Enkaroni with Jonathon, it was not hard to see that most of the committee members, who had added the poor Maasai's property to their own, were doing well. Big red-tiled ranch houses had sprung up in some places; new Landcruisers or Mercedes were parked in front of them. Traditionally, the richest Maasai were obliged to distribute some of their wealth to the poor: gangs of men and women would come to their houses to beg or even demand some of their animals. If they refused they risked losing respect: if they were consistently mean, they would be ostracized. Mean

71

people knew that if the tables were turned and they were ruined by a disaster, no one would help them. But these Mercedes men, the *wabenzi* as they are known in Kenya, felt they owed nothing to anyone. They had enough money not to rely on their communities: if there were a drought or an epidemic, they could pay for cattle feed, tanked water and veterinary medicines. As a result, the rich Maasai were becoming permanently rich and the poor Maasai permanently poor. The men with the money were getting more political power, which in Kenya means the power to grab more and more of the country's wealth for oneself.

Even with their cattle feeds, their tanked water, their consultants, their vets and imported machinery, the Mercedes men were producing fewer cattle on their land than the traditional herders who lived there before them. Their imported techniques were less efficient in the savannahs than the nomadic herding which evolved there. For all the wabenzi's show and sophistication, they contributed less to Kenya's economy than the traditional Maasai, who bartered cattle for grain, iron and cloth.

In Enkaroni the Maasai were being dispossessed by their own people, but in other parts of the Maasai districts they were being pushed off their land by outsiders. Under these circumstances they had even less opportunity for legal redress. As I was soon to discover, they also had less hesitation about taking the law into their own hands.

From the summit of the Ngong Hills, twenty miles from Nairobi, it is sometimes possible to see both Mount Kenya and Mount Kilimanjaro. The intervening land is curiously foreshortened, compressed into a thin dark line, while the mountains float in front of one's eyes, hanging in the foreground haze. It looks as if one could stroll down onto the plain, up either of the mountainsides and onto one of the white peaks before nightfall. Reaching out to those phantoms, leaning into the bolstering wind as if I, like them, could float there without the mooring of reality, I realized that nothing is as it looks in Africa.

When the ghost mountains dissolve and the hundreds of miles of intervening land unscramble, the new prospect is as unreal as the one which it usurps. From a green and undulating land, shot with bright water as the wind hurries the clouds across the sun, comes the shout of a herdboy or the cry of a bateleur eagle. Looking south, only the occasional flash of corrugated iron shows that anything has changed since the first European explorers slapped their walking sticks against their boots in satisfaction, as they exclaimed upon a scene as ancient and as tranquil as the pastoral idyll of the Psalms. Standing on the crest of the Ngong Hills, it is not hard to imagine that the world is at peace with itself.

I found Amos close to the foot of the hills, in the sparse forest of fever trees where we had arranged to meet. Green wood hoopoes churred and swooped from tree to tree. On the distant road the big white cars of district officials rumbled past, but out of the wind, in a hollow between two trunks, Amos felt safe.

When the lands of his community were divided up in 1988, the Maasai there discovered that 2700 of them had been left off the list. Their places had been taken by 200 outsiders, rich businessmen from Nairobi, who had bribed the government-appointed chief. When the Maasai complained to the Lands Ministry they were told they were squatters and had no right to be there. They later discovered that the Minister of Lands had, like the businessmen, helped himself to a few thousand acres of their savannah. They complained to their MP, who refused to help. They waited outside State House and petitioned the President, who told them that all possible measures would be taken to respond to their complaint, meaning that nothing would be done. They pooled all the money they possessed, hired a lawyer and took the case to court. The businessmen gave the judge 1.8 million shillings – about £30,000 – and the case was dropped.

Thus far, the Maasai of Loodariak had been able to stay on their land, because the businessmen were using it as collateral to raise loans and had no interest in farming or ranching there. But some of them were now beginning to sell parts of their ill-gotten properties to settlers. Hearing that the Maasai were hostile to their presence, none had yet dared to arrive, but Amos had heard that a posse of these farmers was planning to move in to take their new land by force. They would not, he told me, find the Maasai amenable.

'Let these people come. Let them come and say "this is our land".' Amos looked over his shoulder and scanned the thin wood. 'We are ready. We have prepared our weapons. We have tried everything to stop this peacefully. The only option left for us is bloodshed. We are going to kill people here. We have to kill them, because if we don't, they will kill us.'

Throughout the lands to the south-west of the hills I met men like Amos, who claimed to be ready to kill anyone who settled there. They said they had laid up supplies of machetes and spears: anyone foolish enough to ignore their threats would be hacked to death. They had, they told me, been left with no alternative.

Travelling around Maasailand, I found that some communities had lost nearly all the land they owned to outsiders. Between the towns of Athi River and Kajiado, the entire savannah had been divided among politicians and their friends. Some of the best land belonged to President Moi; the second best to George Saitoti, the Vice-President, and the inferior places to their colleagues. Some of the new owners had fenced their properties, taken the titles to the bank and raised money on them. Marooned in the midst of the savannahs were three- or four-storey concrete blocks, like the monstrosities Ceauşescu built in the Romanian countryside. They were uninhabited – some were no more than empty shells – but they raised the amount of money the banks would lend against the land. The expelled Maasai, driving their remaining cattle up and down the grass verges of the roads, were bitter and impotent.

Iniquitous and destructive as these land seizures were, none of the effects I had yet seen compared to the catastrophes now visiting the places being put to the plough. Leaving Nairobi on a day stiff with hesitant thunder, I drove to the top of the Limuru Escarpment and looked across the floor of the world's next ocean. From the Red Sea to Lake Malawi, East

Africa is pulling away from the rest of the continent, driven by convection beneath the crust of the earth. Between the rift wall on which I stood and the matching fault line hidden in clouds in the west, the land looked as if it had been stretched flat. Only in a few places had it crumpled, as if it had rucked around some subterranean obstruction. In the middle of the plain, amid a stipple of smaller hills, was the dormant cone of Mount Longonot, where pelicans wheeled on straight wings, gaining height on its exhalations.

This sunken land was, until Independence, almost wholly owned by the Maasai. Now, as we descended the rift wall and crossed the yellow plain, I found that much of it had been handed out to other people: Kikuyu who had been granted land by President Kenyatta; politicians who had bribed or threatened the group ranch committees; big businesses; government ministries. In the unearthly shadow of a satellite tracking station, a Maasai man in a red cloak whistled to his goats. Soon after that, we passed into another country.

The ploughing season in north Narok district had begun a few weeks before. I left the road to watch a tractor towing a disc plough through the grass sward. The savannah flowers, the many hundreds of grass species, rolled over to expose clean slabs of earth. Nothing had been spared. Gallery forests, thorn bush, grasslands, swamps had all been prepared for ploughing then overturned. Even a school football pitch, which had harmlessly occupied a patch of the Maasai's savannah, had been tilled, and the broken goalposts swung forlornly in the wind.

There were no hedges and no windbreaks, simply monotonous miles of churned earth. The only evidence of the Maasai that I saw was a small boy, standing on a path between two vast fields, clutching his herding stick. The thunderstorms of the night before had left puddles on the track, in which his image fluttered, gathering then dispersing, against the grey sky. He had no animals. Beyond him, far away across the furrows, was a house and two lone trees. It was as if the ocean had already filled its trough, and the land and its inhabitants had disappeared beneath its choppy brown waters.

The government chiefs, the committee members, businessmen and politicians had taken nearly all the land the Maasai possessed in this region. Some individuals had seized as much as 30,000 acres. As the rainfall in this part of the valley was sufficient in most years for wheat, they had bought tractors and hired people from farming tribes to replace the savannahs with fields. After the wabenzi had taken their share, and the government and the courts had refused to help, the ordinary Maasai were left with just ten acres each: not enough land to support one cow. The only use to which they could put it was to rent it to the people who had stolen the rest. For this they received £3 an acre, for the three or four years that the land could stand to be ploughed.

The soils here, like many of the savannah soils of East Africa, are shallow and fragile. When they broke down, the farmers would abandon them and invest the money they had made in other businesses. Recovery, if it happened at all, would take forty or fifty years. Standing on the roof of the Land Rover, scanning the bleak wastes around me, I realized that this was probably the first time this land had been uninhabited in three million years. 'Where have all the people gone?' I asked the brown seascape. The answer was to come sooner and louder than I could have imagined.

Driving into Narok town I found the streets strangely deserted. A Kikuyu woman sat beneath a tree, having extensions braided into her hair. A Maasai businessman in a black safari suit, carrying an ebony club, swaggered up the main road, glancing at me from the corner of his eye. A minibus emblazoned with the trade mark 'Nuclear Missile' screeched despondently around the streets looking for targets, sagging at the back on broken suspension. But there was none of the bustle characteristic of Kenyan towns: it looked as if the place had closed down for the day.

Walking along the main road, past the plaster-fronted shops and the mosque, glowing with green lights like an alien spacecraft, I heard the murmur of people, out of sight where the road sank into the valley of the Narok River. When the crowd came into view, it seemed to consist of most of the population of the town. Large women with babies on their backs raised their hands and shook their heads among lanky Maasai men in plastic hats, town boys in jeans and ragged tee-shirts, waiters from the nearby restaurant, men in suits and ties, a gaggle of schoolgirls in faded uniforms. Most were staring across the basin of the river. Others had turned to discuss what they saw. One woman had buried her face in her hands.

It took me a minute or two to get close enough to the edge of the road bridge to see what they were looking at, and still longer to work out what it was. There seemed to have been a spectacular traffic accident in the middle of the river. Two cars were half submerged on their backs in muddy water. A tractor lay upside down on the bank. Twenty feet from the ground, most of a Land Rover was lodged in the branches of an acacia tree, as if it had fallen out of the sky. But looking closer, I saw other things that had nothing to do with traffic. A building site twenty yards from the river-bank had been stripped bare, and the bricks and stone slabs that had been piled there were scattered around the muddy basin, while the pillars of reinforced concrete around which the house was to have been built had been bent to the ground. A little further upriver a tree trunk had plunged straight through a shop, transfixing two walls, as if it had been fired from a gigantic bow. The kiosks around what had been a minibus station were now no more than splintered wood; metal billboards with splayed legs looked like strange twisted beasts perched on the corpse of the centre of the town. A man leaning over the bridge beside me told me there had been an unprecedented flood.

I walked up the river-bank. A mad Maasai elder, wearing a dirty grey mac over his cloak, copper earrings swinging from the long lobes of his ears, paced, bent and swift, up and down along the bank, pointing at the wreckage with his stick and shouting that this was the judgement of God. A minibus, rolled over and over, had been crushed into a cylinder, its wheels bent inwards, its roof crumpled, the glass sprung from its windows. The storm drains were choked with the wreckage of flimsy houses. In the empty market-place crouched a man who had lost all he owned, cooking on a fire of broken boards.

A woman I spoke to told me at least thirty people had been swept away, of whom nineteen had so far been recovered dead. They had found the bodies crushed between cars, swept into the branches of the trees, lodged in the bank of the river like human battering rams. One family had been swept two miles downstream in their car: only the youngest child survived the battering. The abattoir had been demolished and the livestock waiting for slaughter had been whisked past the town.

No one could explain why the flood had happened. The storm on the evening before had been no worse than many that fell on Narok, but fifteen minutes after it broke, the people heard a rumble like an earthquake in the hills, and a wall of filthy water roared into town. Nothing standing in its way had survived. Several people I met suggested that the flood had been sent because the local MP was a necromancer. As I looked into what had been happening in the hills, however, I saw that there was a more prosaic explanation.

The Maasai, pushed out of their pastures by the wheat farmers, had nowhere to go except the land too steep for the tractors to plough. With their herds and accompanied by the displaced wildlife, they crowded into the hilltop forests. As their remaining animals consumed the vegetation and compacted the soil, the rain, which would previously have been absorbed by the forest, had flashed off the indurated ground. It brought to the settled people of Narok a final roar of despair, as the nomads of the region reached the end of their migrations.

CHAPTER FOUR

Leakey's Cattle

If Nairobi is obsessed with the Maasai, it is governed by wildlife. Tourism is Kenya's biggest industry and, even more than the people and the beaches, it is the wildlife which draws its visitors. As a result, walking around the centre of town, you are beset by men falling into your stride and either pushing into your hands a grubby leaflet with a picture of a lion or a buffalo on the cover or whispering 'Safari sir, safari,' as if trying to sell you drugs. Outnumbering the postcards, hoardings, picture books, batiks and carvings of the Maasai are images of the country's famous animals: its elephants, rhinos, buffalo, lions, cheetahs, giraffes and zebras. East Africa is the best place in the world for seeing large mammals, and for many foreigners Kenya is a synonym for wildlife.

To the first Europeans arriving in East Africa the region was everything that their own countries were not. While their land had been crowded, enclosed, ploughed and polluted, the savannahs remained open, sparsely inhabited and unspoilt. Long before palaeontologists showed that human beings arose in Africa, comparisons were made between these regions and the Biblical Eden, where Man had only to pick of the land's abundance to survive. The agricultural sons of Cain, kept out of their grandfather's paradise, set to work to reclaim their birthright in Africa.

The first entitlement they awarded to themselves was hunting. In Europe hunting had long been both the preserve and a defining characteristic of the aristocracy. Here, as the settlers' guns proclaimed, they were all aristocrats: and Africa was their shooting estate. The carnage, in the first few decades

79

of European penetration, was staggering. The hunters eliminated the blaubok and quagga, both of which had survived three million years of contact with Africans. Some men boasted of shooting two hundred elephants on one safari; others included Africans in their bags. Theodore Roosevelt and his son, who called themselves nature lovers, led an expedition which killed five thousand animals of seventy species, including nine of East Africa's few remaining white rhinos. East Africa was, to them and their contemporaries, a paradise, an unspoilt wilderness, a land where every pent-up fantasy, frustrated in their own walled gardens, could now be realized.

The game was also of some economic importance. During the Second World War, hundreds of thousands of wild animals were killed to feed British troops. The authorities established regions which they called game reserves, where the amount of hunting was controlled. They tried to limit the number of animals killed by white hunters elsewhere but, in practice, many of the settlers ignored the regulations and continued to take what they wanted. Eventually, the Europeans came to see that they could not continue to massacre the savannah animals without destroying them for all time. Having regarded the game as little more than nature's providence, set on earth for man to exploit, mzungus began to see it as a phenomenon which they had a moral duty to protect. Among these conservationists were some people of extraordinary courage and resourcefulness, who dedicated their lives to wildlife. But, perhaps understandably, many of these people chose to look elsewhere when ascribing the blame for the wild animals' decline. They conceded that the white man's hunting had been damaging to the game, but most of them maintained that the real threat came from the Africans. Local hunters, conservationists said, were cruel and wasteful. Local nomads over-grazed the land and overwhelmed the wild animals. If East Africa's wildlife were to be saved, it had to be protected from East Africa's people.

The best, the only way to do this, they argued, was to create places in which human residence would be prohibited, places set aside exclusively for the game and the people who paid to watch it. In the words of the most effective champion of such exclusive parks and reserves, the German conservationist Professor Bernhard Grzimek: 'A National Park must remain a primordial wilderness to be effective. No men, not even native ones, should live inside its borders.' Starting in the 1940s, enormous areas of land were swiftly designated as parks and reserves. Among them were places which have since become world famous, such as the Serengeti, the Maasai Mara, Tsavo and Amboseli. The only people who would, eventually, be allowed into them were the wardens, the rangers and paying tourists. Anyone else would be regarded as a trespasser or a poacher.

The only problem was that the places chosen were the homes of thousands of local people. Far from being 'primordial wildernesses' they were, in fact, among the longest-inhabited places on earth. Most of the regions in which the game concentrated were the regions in which the best grazing was found and the best water sources were located: the places, in other words, which were most important to the survival of the local people. When these areas were turned into exclusive parks and reserves, some peoples were deprived of most of their dry season lands. Few tribes lost as much as the Maasai. The British government, having broken its promises to respect their northern lands, had pledged that the entire southern region designated Maasailand would be theirs in perpetuity. But the promises were broken again and, between 1948 and 1988, the Maasai lost all but two of their major dry season pastures and drought reserves.

There were and there remain good reasons for keeping people out of the reserves. Local people throughout East Africa want change. Much of this change, for example, new roads, housing developments and, above all, the cultivation of savannah land, conflicts with the need to protect wild animals and their habitat. As the human population rises – and it is rising fast throughout East Africa – the pressure exerted by communities upon their land and resources will increase. Kenya's economy is dependent on tourism, and anything that threatens the wildlife – commercial poaching, for example – threatens Kenya as a whole. Some scientists have maintained that local people have always been a threat to wildlife: that they hunt the game with destructive methods and over-graze the land. These arguments have been well-rehearsed among conservationists, and are known to many of the tourists visiting Kenya. What I have found striking is that the alternative case has seldom been forcibly argued.

It is now clear that most of the activities of traditional peoples who lived in areas where game abounded did not threaten the wildlife. In the late nineteenth century, hunting tribes such as the Yaaku killed elephants for their ivory, which they sold to Arab traders, and abandoned the carcasses. But most hunting peoples, most of the time, appear to have taken only what they needed to survive. Far from being wasteful, as Europeans suggested, they seldom abandoned a wounded animal, tracking and despatching any beast they hit.

Throughout East Africa the nomads have been accused of over-grazing. The British noticed that while much of the savannah was covered in long grass during certain seasons, at other times it would become a dustbowl, incapable of supporting livestock or wildlife. The observers maintained that this was the result of over-grazing by the nomads. More recent ecological work has shown that during a drought the vegetation of the savannahs disappears, whether or not there are livestock on the land: it simply dies back and regenerates when the rain falls. It is probable that some genuine over-grazing by nomads – compaction of the soil or long-term replacement of edible plant species by inedible ones – did occur in some places. But the work of the early ecologists was so clouded by colonial disdain for the nomads and genuine misunderstandings about savannah biology that it is now hard to tell which were natural and which were manmade phenomena. Many modern ecologists maintain that over-grazing was the exception, not the rule. The resilience of the savannahs was such that they would rapidly bounce back, even after heavy grazing pressure.

What is incontestable is that a fantastic abundance of wild game continued to exist alongside the herds of the Maasai and

1. Matayo

2. The desert around Ngilukumong

3. Herdsman in the Lokwanomoru mountains

4. *Above:* Waiting for the Toposa

5. *Right:* After the rain at Ngilukumong

6. The massacre at Kokuro

7. Fleeing the Pokot

8. *Left:* Maasai herds moving down onto the stubble of the wheat fields

9. *Right:* Amboseli: torn apart by tourists

10. Narok: after the flood

11. *Above:* Tourists
haggling with the Maasai
in the cultural manyatta

12. *Right:* Catching the
white ox

13. Toronkei losing his moranhood

14. *Above:* Canada comes to Tanzania

15. *Right:* Ntalon and the Nkunono outcasts

16. The water that kept the Samburu alive, in the Sarova Shaba hotel

17. Waiting for the rain in Samburu district

18. *Above:* Out of death's valley: fugitives in Nachola

19. *Right:* The civil servant's among those murdered by the army in Wajir

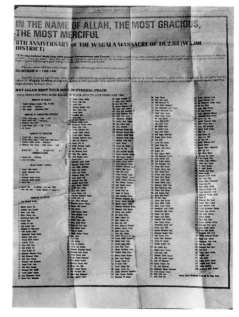

20. Drawing water in Wajir

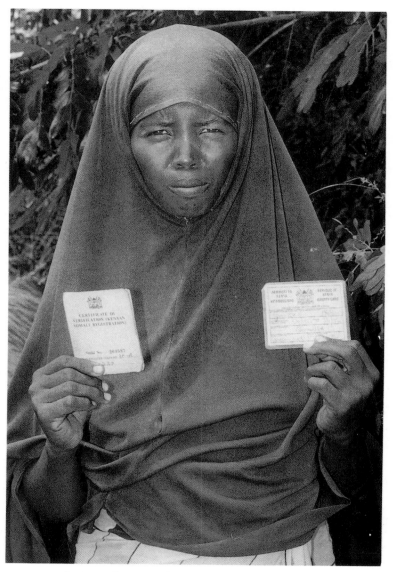

21. Two identity cards: the Somalis are registered twice

22. On the streets in Kitale . . .

23. *Right:* . . . and on the trash heap

24. *Below:* Daudi and Margaret in Kibera

25. Moses leaving the wilderness

other nomads up to and beyond the arrival of the British in East Africa. It was, indeed, because the Maasai had not destroyed the populations of game that the Europeans wanted to conserve their lands.

It is at least as easy to curtail development and, in particular, agriculture within a park as to keep people out of it. In other parts of the world, including Britain, conservation authorities do just this, allowing people to remain inside national parks, but imposing restrictions on what they are allowed to do there. Population growth is a more difficult issue to tackle and if people were to be allowed to continue to use the parks, might demand such authoritarian policies as forbidding permanent settlement there, ensuring that they were used only for seasonal grazing. But these, surely, would not be as unacceptable as the policy which has been adopted: depriving all the Maasai within these conservation areas of their traditional livelihood.

Perhaps most significantly as far as conservation is concerned, there is evidence to suggest that the negative effects of exclusion from the parks and reserves outweigh the positive ones. Excluding the Maasai from their best grazing lands means confining them to places too small to support their herds. The result is just what conservationists are trying to prevent: over-grazing. Many of the parks and reserves are now becoming islands of bio-diversity in a sea of degradation. Unable to support themselves on their diminished lands by herding alone, more and more of the Maasai are now turning to agriculture. Moreover, keeping the Maasai out of the parks excludes some of the practices that are now known to be of benefit to wildlife: the burning of coarse grass, for example. There are many ecologists who now believe that much of the landscape so valued by conservation is partly the product of human management.

Many of those who were expelled from the reserves feel bitter about conservation. As a result of both this and their declining standards of living they have, in some places, taken to poaching. In the past, commercial poaching was organized and executed by outsiders. Today some of the Maasai feel few qualms about joining in. Conservationists are doing their best to win them back to wildlife, but much of the damage has already been done. Conservation may have also encouraged population growth. Traditionally, a Maasai woman would not allow herself to conceive until her previous child could carry a bowl of soup to his father. Large numbers of infants were a hindrance to people trying to migrate. But once the Maasai have lost their traditional livelihood, the sanctions limiting population growth are abandoned. They need as many children as they can produce, for children are the only form of security that people without land or money in East Africa possess. Taking all of these points into consideration, it strikes me as astonishing that, in the 1990s, conservationists in East Africa are still trying to take land away from its inhabitants.

It was after the first national parks had been established that the ivory trade, which had been encouraged and largely supplied by the British at the beginning of the century, became a serious threat to the survival of the elephant. Poachers, many of them equipped or employed by foreign businessmen, slaughtered elephants in and out of the reserves. Corrupt ministers in the Independent Kenyan government became involved, both organizing poaching and hampering attempts to prevent it. Only when the East African elephant looked as if it might go the same way as the quagga and the blaubok, taking with it much of Kenya's appeal to tourists, did the government make serious attempts to stop the poaching. They began, in 1989, with the appointment of a man whose name has already featured in this book, the famous and charismatic palaeontologist, Dr Richard Leakey.

Dr Leakey's task was monumental. He had to safeguard Kenya's most important industry by stamping out practices supported by some of its most powerful people. He had to protect some of the world's greatest natural assets, and at the same time encourage more people from overseas to come to take advantage of them. He had to persuade the ordinary people of Kenya that conservation was good for the nation and good for them. Against him was ranked one hundred years of

history, during which effective means of destroying wil
had been established in Kenya and many local people had been
turned against conservation. On his side was enormous international enthusiasm for protecting wildlife, and the widely
held perception that the government's premise was sound: that
tourism, unlike many other forms of exploitation, was compatible with and even supportive of conservation.

Before he became director of the new Kenya Wildlife Service, Dr Leakey had not had any professional conservation
experience. He was a brilliant manager, a clever and persuasive
speaker and a workaholic of unflagging determination. But his
views about conservation were the views of three generations
of expatriates in Kenya: that the wildlife was threatened by
local people and better protection meant better exclusion of the
one from the other. To keep animals away from people and
people away from animals, he proposed at first to build fences
around the Maasai Mara Reserve and the Tsavo National Park:
a plan he withdrew when horrified conservationists pointed
out that this would stop the wild animals from migrating. But
he went ahead with the plan to allow his rangers to shoot to kill
trespassers suspected of poaching in the parks.

His anti-poaching policies were extremely successful. His
wardens were trained like soldiers and equipped with helicopters and automatic weapons. Hundreds of poachers were
caught and tons of ivory and rhino horn were confiscated. Both
to encourage them to support the anti-poaching operations and
to persuade them to continue to tolerate the wildlife living on
their lands, Dr Leakey designed a plan to share some of the
money made by the parks and reserves with local people. They
would also be helped to set up tourist camps and safaris on
their own land. In return they would be expected not to sub-
divide or plough their land; not to kill wildlife; and to report the
movements of suspected poachers.

At the same time, he was considering setting up some new
reserves and extensions of the existing ones, from which, it
seemed, the local people would be excluded. With the rest of
his conservation proposals, these plans earned the Kenya
Wildlife Service a promised $290 million from foreign donors,

led by the World Bank. The Kenya Wildlife Service soon established a reputation as one of the most principled agencies in Africa. To find out how the wildlife programme was affecting the Maasai, what the results of their exclusion from the parks and reserves had been, and whether Dr Leakey's attempts to involve them in conservation were welcomed we set off for southern Maasailand.

Even before we reached the gates of the Maasai Mara reserve, it was clear that we were about to visit one of Africa's most famous attractions. On each side of the road was an almost constant stream of white Combi vans carrying tourists. When we reached the reserve, on a normal weekday, out of season, we had to wait for twenty minutes in a queue of other vehicles. The visitors were each charged the equivalent of $9 for every day they stayed. Their hotel bills, fees charged by the safari companies, money spent on souvenirs, taxis and tips, made the Maasai Mara one of Kenya's most valuable resources.

So what draws tourists from all over the world (I saw and heard Europeans of every description, Americans, Canadians, Japanese, Australians, South East Asians, Mexicans and South Africans) to this corner of Kenya? It did not take us long to find out. Before we had travelled two miles into the reserve we saw a clump of Combi vans gathered around some bushes, with tourists crammed into the ceiling hatches, leaning forward with long lenses and video cameras to photograph something hidden in the shade. Driving closer I spotted what appeared to be a ginger snake raising its head, hovering in the air for a moment then flicking back into the grass. Coming closer still, I saw that it was attached to a large ginger sack, which soon resolved itself into a lioness, stretched out, apparently asleep in the shade. A drowsy, half-grown cub batted at the flicking tail; another lioness raised her head and yawned a nightmare of yellow fangs. The cameras crackled like applause.

There was no mystery about the source of the second commotion I saw, for the objects towered over the subjects like rock stacks surrounded by white breakers. The elephants were standing beside the reserve's airstrip, tearing up clumps of grass with their noses and gently cramming them into their mouths, their small rheumy eyes swivelling to watch their visitors. A baby elephant, still covered with black down, flicked mud from the airstrip onto its back. It seemed as if, for that moment, a peace treaty had been struck between nature's monsters and man's rapacity, for neither party appeared to give a moment's thought to the idea that the other could do it harm.

In a pool of a sluggish creek an industrial boiler rolled and made the waters surge. When it heard us, the hippopotamus staggered to its feet, crashed out of the stream and through the papyrus beds, plodding away on huge flat feet, sleeves of loose skin rolled up above its elbows, an enormous belly swinging from side to side. Hidden in the long grass not far away were the arch black horns of a herd of impala.

In Keekorok Lodge, a hotel in the middle of the reserve, large white tourists, cameras perched on their bellies, wandered on wooden walkways over swamps that bubbled with frogs and air-breathing fish. A lily-trotter scuttled around the margins and egrets stalked along the trails of mud and flattened grass left by grazing hippos. On the verandah we met the person we had arranged to talk to, a man involved in negotiations with the Maasai whom, to protect his position, I shall call Peter. Employed by a conservation group, he was becoming concerned that conservation, in the form it was now taking, was doing neither the people nor the wildlife any good.

Keekorok, Peter explained to me, is Maasai for black trees. The lodge had been built around a clump of acacias both culturally and spiritually important to the western Maasai. The warriors of the area had held their meat feasts in the shade of these trees. As a result they were said to provide the shelter in which the age groups grew strong. The Maasai would point to them as one of the coordinates which mapped the progress of their lives.

Now the only Maasai to come near them were the men employed as waiters in the hotel or as rangers by the Narok County Council. In place of the feasting moran were tourists, circling a vast buffet in the restaurant. To them the lodge and its trees seemed to represent something quite different, a backdrop to their photographs of luxury in the midst of wilderness.

The swamp over which they strolled had been a crucial watering-hole for the Maasai herds, reputed never to dry up even in the most severe droughts. None of the sources the Maasai visited outside the reserve was as reliable as the ones they were now denied within. Until the second half of the twentieth century, the Maasai Mara had been infested with tsetse fly, so its pastures were not in permanent use; but its marshes and scrub brakes were a critical refuge from the worst droughts. Together with their drought reserves and their waterholes they had lost places which were spiritually important to them: the places in which their parents were buried or around which they had woven their traditional myths and tales. The only way in which the Maasai could legally enter their old territory was to turn up at one of the gates in a vehicle and pay the entrance fee.

The reserve had taken one of the Maasai's most important refuges in the south of Narok district, Peter told me, but the effects of conservation did not end at its borders. To show us what the Maasai were now losing, he took us out of the Maasai Mara and into the surrounding savannahs. The places he showed us belonged to the Koyiaki Group Ranch. They were drier but almost as spectacular as the parts of the reserve I had seen. There were woods bearded with lichen and lit with flowers; there were grass savannahs in which jackals slunk away, as low and as smooth as snakes; there were secret valleys where spoonbills and little bitterns trembled in the rushes. I saw a mongoose, a bull elephant, giraffes, warthogs, zebras, wildebeest and topi. This land, said Peter, had as much potential for tourists as the reserve itself. Conservationists had been urging the local people to take advantage of this and charge visitors to camp or tour there. The men who controlled the group ranch needed little encouragement.

As soon as they saw how lucrative conservation could be, the committee members unilaterally declared that the Koyiaki Group Ranch had been sub-divided. The lands immediately to the north of the reserve were annexed by the committee and their colleagues in the Narok County Council. This handful of men claimed exclusive rights to take money from the tourists there. Now, in the adjoining group ranches, county councillors had started collecting tourists' money on behalf of the community. Rather than spending these funds, as promised, on projects of benefit to the Maasai, the councillors bought themselves new cars and country villas. Most scandalously, some of them were buying up land close to the reserve to plant barley and wheat. Conservation was being used to finance devastation.

Throughout Maasailand we heard similar stories, of people expelled from their most critical lands, watching their herds decline, faced with the possibility of losing even more of their territory. Some of the conservationists we met, like Peter, were alarmed by what was happening to the Maasai and were trying to find ways of alleviating their problems. The Maasai were grateful for the help they were getting from them. There had been schools and health clinics built, wells dug and cattle dips installed, all of which were helping them to survive the loss of their land. But their fundamental difficulties had not been addressed: everywhere we went people told us that conservation had made them poorer and less secure. Of the many complaints I heard from the nomads I met, the most arresting were the allegations made by people living outside the Tsavo National Park.

We had arrived in Loitokitok the day after the long rains began. Though the town lay in the skirts of Kilimanjaro, there was no sign of the mountain, just a ragged fringe of cloud hanging above the houses. 150 miles away, the peak was almost close enough to touch. Here in the foothills it might never have existed.

The streets of the little town looked as if they had suffered from several months of trench warfare. Lorries were buried to their axles in mud; minibuses were trapped in chasms stripped from the edges of the roads by the rain. People skidded from one building to another with newspapers over their heads, their trousers and skirts splattered with orange gore. Rain fell throughout the day, and in the night all the heavenly artillery was unleashed upon Loitokitok. At three in the morning the town dogs started howling, then the earth shuddered as if shaking off the water: there had been an avalanche on Kilimanjaro.

Soon after dawn I stepped into air so fresh and clear it was as if the rain had washed all but the oxygen out of it. Thrushes sang in the pine trees, and in the townspeoples' rejuvenated gardens sunbirds fluttered around *Leonotis* flowers. I looked up and there, as vast and other-worldly as the moon rising from just behind the earth, was the smooth white dome of Kilimanjaro.

In Loitokitok we visited a Maasai man who was helping the other people of his tribe to defend their lands. Daniel Somoire was an incisive, diplomatic man, with a big head, a wide mouth and gaps between his teeth that made him look like one of the early dinosaurs. His work was confined to informing the Maasai of their rights, and how they might legally try to uphold them, but he had been rewarded for his pains by midnight visits from the police, constant monitoring and one prolonged and vicious interrogation. He agreed to take us to meet some of the local Maasai. Before we left Loitokitok we were joined by Paul Ntiati, who worked for the African Wildlife Foundation, a charity closely linked to the Kenya Wildlife Service. Like some of the other conservationists I met, he was trying to help the Maasai with new projects, to encourage them to welcome conservation.

Trapped on the road to the Tsavo Park were half a dozen white Combi vans, back wheels in the ditches, front wheels slewing and spurting through the mud. Tourists in white trousers and new safari boots had left their vehicles to push, and were beginning to look as if they had been tarred and feathered. At one point we skidded off the road and into a trench: we only got out when a truck carrying members of the Christian Brotherhood Society fortuitously came our way. Having driven sideways for about forty kilometres, we came to a sign beside the road welcoming tourists to The Olgirra Cultural Boma. We drove in. When they heard the sound of the car, scores of people ran from their huts with incredulous smiles. Children leapt into the air, shouting 'mzungu, mzungu'. Hands were thrust through the windows to seize ours and shake them as if we had just won the Paris–Dakar rally. I have never received such a welcome anywhere in Africa.

The land on which the 'cultural boma' had been built belonged to a group ranch which had not yet been privatized. The entire ranch was composed of wet season pastures. All the dry season land had been enclosed within the Tsavo Park. In a normal dry season the herders could keep their animals on the ranch without too many ill effects. But if the dry season lasted longer than usual they started getting into trouble. They could either stay on their land and watch their animals lose weight and die off; trek the many miles to the waterless Chyulu Hills; or try to sneak back into their old grazing grounds in the Tsavo Park. 1991 and 1992 had been bad years, with poor rains and long dry seasons.

They petitioned the Kenya Wildlife Service to let them back into the park. KWS said this was impossible, because if tourists saw them there they would complain. They kept trying until, at length, KWS relented, and allowed them to graze in a small section of the park for a limited time. Before their animals had recovered they were told to leave the park. KWS said that they could make up for the losses they suffered by encouraging tourists to come to their land.

But the Rombo Group Ranch is flat and unattractive. To tourists it is simply a place to pass through on the way to Tsavo; there is nothing worth stopping for. Although the Maasai tried hard to get them to stay in campsites or pay a fee to shoot birds on their land, the entire group ranch earned a total of £83 in the first year, or just over four pence a head. Exasperated, some of the Maasai decided that if there were no attractions on their ranch, they would have to create one, so they had built this village, or *boma*, beside the road, to draw in tourists who would pay for the privilege of visiting them and seeing their traditional dances.

The village had been established eight months ago, and ours was the first foreigner's car to have entered. No one had told the Maasai there that they needed to bribe the drivers of the Combi vans if they were to get them to bring their passengers in. Though they stood on the road in traditional dress, holding up bunches of beads and grinning widely, they had watched the vehicles stream past. The men and women I spoke to were bitter. They said they felt that all the government cared about was the wild animals.

'We are getting nothing from all this conservation,' one old man told me. 'They say it's good for Kenya, but it's only the government and the businesses that benefit. The only thing Leakey's cattle do for us is to destroy our crops.'

'Leakey's cattle?'

'The wild animals.'

As they could not afford to buy grain, the Maasai here had planted small fields of maize. These had been trampled by elephants and eaten by zebras. Both cows and people had been attacked by lions. One old man came forward to show me the stump of his leg, which had been bitten off by a lion two years before. The people said that they were now thinking of moving away from this village, but there was nowhere better to go. They were worried about the possibility of starvation.

I told them it seemed to me that anything was better than starvation: why did they not try to sneak into the park and graze their hungry animals there? The Maasai laughed and looked away. I pressed the point, and one of the old men stepped up to Daniel and whispered, 'Who is this man? Is he from the Kenya Wildlife Service?'

Daniel told him that I was a journalist. The old man looked around in hesitation then sat down beside me. I felt a wave of nervousness pass through the watching Maasai.

'I took my animals into the park after they stopped us grazing there in the last dry season. There was nowhere else to go. I was caught by the rangers.' He coughed, spat on the ground and rubbed it out with his foot. He looked up sharply. 'They took my stick and beat me with it.'

'What happened to you?' I asked.

'I fell to the ground. They kicked me and dragged me around. They carried on beating me, taking turns. I was hit again and again. Then they arrested me. They took me to court and I was fined. I spent a week in hospital.'

'Who were these rangers?'

'They were from Kenya Wildlife Service.'

I questioned one man after another. In the last two years nearly everyone there had been caught grazing his animals inside the park. All the culprits had been beaten up. I was shown scars where their sticks or the butts of the rangers' guns had broken their skin, and hospital bills detailing treatment for bruising or concussion. They told me that if the rangers chased the men and failed to catch them, they would go to their homes and arrest the women and children, holding them illegally until their husbands gave themselves up. On several occasions the women had also been beaten. When the rangers came to a village they would 'confiscate' anything they deemed to be an offensive weapon, including cooking utensils and cow syringes, as well as spears and knives. Sometimes they gave the men they caught a choice between being taken to court and paying a bribe: if they could afford it the Maasai paid up. Cattle had been chased away by the rangers when the herders were dragged off: some men had lost every animal they possessed. I asked whether they had complained to the Kenya Wildlife Service. They told me they were too frightened to complain; they thought they would be beaten up again.

Paul Ntiati, who, as the African Wildlife Foundation representative, had earlier been trying to explain why conservation was good for the Maasai, was listening to these accounts with a weary, grave expression. I asked him if what he was hearing were true.

'Yes, it is all true.'

'Why is KWS doing this?'

'The rangers are not well-educated perhaps. They need to be educated and that will take a long time.'

I found what these people told me astonishing. Kenya Wildlife Service claimed to have trained all its wardens and rangers in community relations. The rangers were supposed to be the best disciplined force in Kenya, and Dr Leakey had convinced foreign donors to KWS that his staff were both accountable and untouchable. Yet these serious and well-attested allegations told of torture, false imprisonment, theft and corruption, and implied that the sainted rangers here were no better than a bunch of ill-disciplined thugs.

From the lower slopes of Mount Kilimanjaro it is possible, on a clear day, to see all of eastern Maasailand. The verdure of the mountain makes the savannah below look hard and inhospitable, a mustard-coloured, dull-burning plain in a frame of soft blue shade. The deep, feathery *Grevillea* trees, the small fields of potatoes and maize, the thatched huts of the Kikuyu farmers whisper that they are the sanctuary of comfort and civilization, while the lowlands are a chaos of turbulent heat and bright futility.

But even from the seductive slopes I could see that eastern Maasailand was not consistently arid. There were patches of land which to the naked eye looked greyer than the rest, like the shadows of low clouds. Through binoculars they appeared the dull green of fading bruises. Close to Kilimanjaro three of these blemishes caught the eye. The broadest I could see was in the east, the shallow valley of the Tsavo River, entirely enclosed within the Tsavo National Park. In the west was a swampy grey depression, tinged now with red, which I knew to be the empty lake bed of the Amboseli Basin, also a national park. Directly ahead of me, and most prominent, was the saw-toothed range of the Chyulu Hills.

These are, or were, three of the four major dry season grazing lands used by the eastern Maasai. I stood on the fourth, the greenest of all, the slopes of Kilimanjaro itself. Over the last forty-five years, the Maasai had been excluded from three of these territories. Tsavo and Amboseli, as national parks, had been closed to them. The slopes of Kilimanjaro had been privatized by President Kenyatta immediately after Independence. The Maasai swiftly lost most of this land to the Kikuyu – people of the President's own tribe – who had settled in the region. In a bad season there was now only one place left to graze: the thorny and forbidding slopes of the Chyulu Hills.

To the Maasai the Chyulu Hills were the place to move to only when there were no options. In their tangled seasonal forests the cows walked with difficulty, found little grass, were plagued by lions and weakened by thirst. There were no water sources in the hills themselves: the nearest were three days' walk away. But, in bad years, they had kept the cows and the people from starvation. The hills had been a national park for several years, but the conservationists had recognized that stopping the Maasai from grazing there was equivalent to condemning some of them to death. They imposed some restrictions on the herders, but accepted that they did no significant harm to the ecosystem. In 1992 settlers from the Kamba tribe were caught clearing some of the bush for farmland on the northern side of the hills. They were immediately expelled by the Kenya Wildlife Service.

The Kamba people, as the conservationists knew, had nothing to do with the Maasai. They were farmers who came from a different district. Like the conservationists, the Maasai were glad when the Kamba departed. Settlement and farming on the hills were as detrimental to them as they were to the wildlife. But KWS panicked. Its foreign backers would be concerned and tourists would be upset if they discovered that a national park had been damaged. To show that it was not treating the matter lightly, KWS announced that it was considering plans to keep everyone but tourists out of the Chyulu Hills.

The Maasai, Dr Leakey argued, no longer needed to rely on herding to survive. Instead, the nomads could take advantage of the new opportunities opening up in Maasailand, provided by conservation and tourism. To see what he was talking about, I travelled with Daniel Somoire to the Amboseli National Park, where the Kenya Wildlife Service had been testing its ideas about sharing some of the money it collected.

No one was sure what was wrong with Amboseli, but the Basin which had once displayed one of the world's most spectacular concentrations of wildlife was now, in places, as bleak and dreary as an empty playing-field. The long grass, the scrub and the acacia woods in some parts of the park had died: all that remained was mud with a dusting of green shoots. In the mirrored wilderness of grey land and grey sky even the elephants were dwarfed.

The most popular theory was that the lake which had once occupied the Amboseli basin was refilling. This might have been because either atmospheric warming or local pollution was causing the snows of Kilimanjaro to melt more swiftly, swelling the underground rivers that ran to the basin. As the salty waters of the old lake rose through the soil, they were poisoning the roots of the tree and shrubs. The decline of the vegetation and the dreariness of the scene had been exacerbated by the shredding of the basin floor by visitors' vehicles. Finding the roads too swampy to negotiate and the wildlife too far away for tourists to photograph, the drivers had left the official routes and carved tracks of their own across the dying savannah. Parts of the Basin had been so badly damaged that in early 1993 Amboseli had to be closed to allow its wounds to heal.

Though studies had shown that they were causing no significant harm to the wildlife, in 1977 the Maasai were persuaded by conservationists to leave their dry season lands in Amboseli, in return for money and new water sources. Both these inducements had dried up within a few years. As the Maasai's cattle began to die through want of good grazing and lack of water, the herders became so alarmed by their declining fortunes that they began to talk of dividing up their group ranches and renting the land to farmers. As conservationists soon realized, this would be disastrous for Kenya's wildlife.

The animals that had made Amboseli famous spread out in the wet season over the lands of the Maasai. Many of them migrated north to another great tourist attraction, the Nairobi National Park. If the Maasai divided up and fenced or ploughed their land, both parks would be completely cut off. Neither could sustain more than a certain number of resident animals, so their value to tourists and hence to Kenya would decline.

When the Kenya Wildlife Service was founded, one of the first things it did was to look for ways of preventing the Maasai from breaking up these lands. It decided that the most effective means was to offer them some of the benefits of conservation. In return for keeping their lands intact, the thousands of Maasai living around Amboseli would be given a total of about £70,000 a year, which KWS had collected from tourists. If this worked, similar deals would be struck with local people living around some of the other parks and reserves.

To find out what the Maasai thought of this scheme, we travelled with Daniel to the Olgulului Group Ranch, just to the east of Amboseli, to meet some of the recipients. I found that they were pleased to be getting some money at last, after a long series of broken promises from conservationists. They were using it to help finance projects such as schools, cattle dips and bore holes, that would be useful to the whole community. As intended, money was helping to persuade them not to divide up their lands. Everybody agreed that this was beneficial. But at the same time the Maasai I spoke to felt that the revenues could not in any way compensate for the land they had lost. Standing by the small field he had planted, fenced with help from the Kenya Wildlife Service, a middle-aged man waved to Daniel. Then he rolled up the trousers under his red cloak and came wading across the storm-flooded ground to meet us.

'Kenya Wildlife Service said it would give us money and it has given us money, so in that sense it has treated us fairly. We are grateful for the projects we have been able to afford,' Metoe ole Lombaa told me, when I asked him how he felt about the deal. He paused and stabbed the wet mud with his stick.

'But how could any money compare to what they have taken from us, to the grazing we have lost, to the human lives we have lost by being kept out of Amboseli? We did no harm to the park. If anything we did it good. Our cattle manured the ground and made the vegetation grow. Poachers kept away because they were frightened of us. Since we were thrown out, the park has been destroyed. The animals have followed us to the group ranch.'

Now Dr Leakey was suggesting that the Maasai around Amboseli could supplement the money they received from KWS by attracting tourists to their own lands. They would then be less dependent on cattle-herding to keep themselves alive. I asked Metoe what he thought of these proposals. He hesitated a moment, then slowly drew his stick across the mud, scoring a frown.

'We know there is money to be made from tourism. We already have tourists staying on our land in tented camps. And yes, they bring us an income. We don't need KWS to tell us that. But you can tell Dr Leakey this. We don't want to be dependent on these tourists. We are Maasai and we want to herd cattle. If we stopped keeping cattle and depended on tourists, we would be ruined when the tourists stopped coming.'

It was around Amboseli that the Maasai had most notoriously turned against the wild animals when they felt they had been given a raw deal by the conservationists. Before the Kenya Wildlife Service had started sharing some of its money, the Maasai had speared rhinos to death and poisoned some of the park's watering-holes, killing the lions. Several tourist buses had also been attacked. But, as I was beginning to discover, this was not the only place in which conservation appeared to have set the nomads against the wildlife. To find out more, I crossed the border into Tanzania, and drove towards the remote savannahs of the Maasai Steppe.

Drought had emptied much of the Steppe of both its people and its wildlife. They had crowded into the river valleys on the edges on the plateau, leaving behind a void of yellow scrub and grey dust over which, for mile after mile, not a living being moved. There were brakes of forest in which parrots clattered away through dry branches, a dikdik skidded across the track, or a goshawk as grey as the sky peeled away from a stump and drifted off across the trees on limp wings, like a shred of windblown paper. But I would soon emerge once more onto the open plains, where the only signs of life were an empty tortoise shell or the cracked white skull of a buffalo.

Nowhere in the world have I felt further from help or human habitation. Had the Land Rover broken down or had I taken the wrong track and run out of fuel somewhere in the midst of the grey plains, I might have walked for a week without coming to a house. My anxiety mounted when I saw lightning shudder against the sky a few miles ahead of me and I realized that, for the first time in nine months, the rains had broken on the Simanjiro Plain.

The track took me down to a gully between two low hills, in which a stream jostled around the rocks. I took off my boots and trousers and waded across to test its depth. Finding it shallow enough to ford, I returned to the Land Rover. I was about to pull on my trousers when the ambience of the little valley seemed subtly to change. I turned round and stared incredulously at the little river. The water, which ten seconds before had swirled harmlessly round the rocks, now foamed and snapped at the banks, piling up in waves against the boulders in its way. As I watched, a branch swept down the torrent and hit one of the boulders with a crack. A gravel bank rustled into the water. The rain had reached the hills.

Throwing my boots and trousers into the Land Rover, I leapt into the driver's seat, crunched the ignition and charged at the rising waters. If I failed to cross now I would not get over for days. The river surged around the door sills, the back end slewed in the current, but before I had a chance to breathe I felt the wheels dig into the gravel of the far bank. I looked back at the stream with a mixture of relief and dread: having crossed it I could not turn back.

I ran into the rain after just a few miles. It rattled against the windscreen so fiercely that at times I was blinded, and pitched into the potholes and furrows hidden by the barrage. Afraid of missing my turning, I leant forwards over the wheel, my nose almost touching the windscreen, only to be jolted back into my seat when I hit another hole. I could not stop and wait since I had been warned that too much rain could make the tracks ahead impassable, whereupon I would have been trapped between the rising waters and the impenetrable mud. Driving as fast as I dared, I cracked an engine mounting and fractured the exhaust, but I reached the southern side of the Steppe before the roads dissolved.

There, as I discovered as soon as I hit it, the soil changed suddenly from grey clay to black mud. I slid straight off the road and into the bush. The next thirty kilometres took two hours to cross. The first rains had arrived here ten days before, and in places the road was little better than a river of slurry. When the camp of the man I was visiting came into view I was so relieved that I laughed. Delighted to be there, astonished to have found my way through the dreadful labyrinth of trails, I grinned, waved and stepped out of the car to shake hands with the people who came to greet me. Apparently sharing my elation, they shouted and laughed. I felt like a hero. Only when I returned to the Land Rover to get my bag did I realize that I was wearing no trousers.

Jock Conyngham had built his camp around the roots of a giant fig tree, which overhung the seasonal stream where the Maasai watered their animals. The roots had flowed over the rocks of the bank like lava, and in their crevices glittered ferns and the webs of tiny spiders. The tree was in fruit and when the wind shook the branches figs spattered the clear water. At dusk vervet monkeys, green pigeons and go-away birds squabbled in the canopy; at dawn robin chats sang from the lower branches.

The soft rocks downstream had been scoured by the hooves and tusks of wild animals. The soil on this part of the Steppe was so poor in nutrients that the animals ate anything that could supplement the little they got from the plants: as well as consuming the rocks, zebras had been seen feeding on ant hills; warthogs chewed the bones of dead cattle. In a tangle of roots, overhanging a pool where antelopes came to drink, lived a rock python. Its track was said to be as wide as a tractor tyre. Lions, buffaloes and elephants passed at times within a few yards of the camp: Jock himself had twice been driven up a tree by a lioness and had once had to flee from a wounded buffalo. In the glades of green trees along the river's valley were the huts of the Kisongo Maasai.

Jock Conyngham was a laconic, self-contained man. His contentment, in his tent beneath the trees, made me feel that, in spite of all my grand ideas and rushing around, I had still not got the point of life. By day he walked from one Maasai village to another, collecting data on the size of the people's herds, how they looked after them and where they took them to graze. At night he sat outside his tent with his computer, writing up his results for his PhD, or talked with his Maasai friends about their animals, the weather or the wildlife. He had been brought up on an American dairy farm, and his interest in cattle was as inexhaustible as the Maasai's.

Assuming that Jock would welcome a change from meat and maize meal, I had filled the back of the car with water melons, pineapples, lettuces, carrots, spring onions, courgettes and aubergines from the market in Arusha. The Maasai watched me unload them with astonishment. One man sidled up to Jock and whispered,

'What are those things?'

'They're vegetables,' said Jock.

'You mean,' the elder asked, 'they are that man's food?'

'I think they probably are.'

The elder beckoned to his friends, pointed at the vegetables, pointed at me and whispered something. They shook their heads in consternation. Later I cooked up some spaghetti with vegetable sauce and offered a plate to one of the Maasai. He stared at it for a minute, then prodded the spaghetti with his finger. He started back as if it had moved. It struck me that vegetables were at least as repulsive to the Maasai as meat is to vegetarians.

I was soon to become the region's richest source of scandal. On my left wrist I wore a bracelet of monkey teeth which I had been given by the Tukano Indians of north-western Brazil. I was proud of this decoration, as I had been presented with it on the day when they had proclaimed me an honorary *tuxuau*, or respected elder. But to the Maasai it meant something quite different. They believed that the killing and eating of monkeys was an act of the most atrocious barbarity, scarcely distinct from cannibalism. When the warriors around Jock's camp first noticed the teeth, they clustered round, touched them and turned them over as if it were daring to do so, whistled and shook their heads. Later, when a party of elders visited Jock and started pointing at me and whispering questions, I could see from their faces that they were discussing the teeth. Confidentially, Jock leant over and told them something. They nodded, never taking their eyes off me. When they had gone, I asked Jock what he had said.

'I said that they weren't monkey teeth after all.'

'Good.'

'I told them they were the teeth of little children.'

For the next two days, Maasai boys came down to the camp, sneaked up to the bole of the tree, stared with horror-filled eyes at the vegetarian cannibal who exposed himself in public, gasped when I looked up and ran off screaming. I could see that I was not coming across very well.

Jock took me to meet his best friend, a big, gentle man with a reputation for generosity and plain dealing. Olurie had recently been castrated as treatment for elephantiasis of the testicles, and walked with a shuffle, but this defalcation did not appear to have damaged his self-esteem. He was witty and shrewd and, according to his friends, the best herder in the community. I had told Jock that I wanted to know more about what the Maasai thought of the wild animals on their land, and whether their attitudes were changing. Jock steered Olurie off the subject of bulls and asked him whether he thought wild animals were good or bad for the Maasai.

'There are different groups of wildlife,' Olurie replied. 'The wildebeest and zebra, they can certainly be a problem. At the moment there are far too many of them. They eat too much of the cattle's grass and they spread diseases. When the wildebeest calve and their afterbirth gets in the water supply, the cattle catch malignant catarrh and die.

'Buffalo compete a bit, but they're not really a problem. The antelope eat some of the goats' food; but it's not as bad as the impact of the wildebeest and zebra on the cattle. But rhinos and elephants: it's a real shame there aren't more of them. The rhinos keep back the thorn bush by browsing it, and the elephants pull down some of the trees, opening up more grazing. They dig wallows as well, which we can use as watering-holes. No, rhinos and elephants are a good thing. We just need more of them right now.'

It struck me that this was exactly what some savannah

ecologists had been saying: that the number of wildebeest and zebra had climbed too high, and that the rhinos and elephants, whose populations were reduced by poaching, should be encouraged. This was not, I knew, the only way in which the interests of the Maasai and new ecological thinking appeared to concur.

After nearly a century of reviling the Maasai for keeping too many cattle and over-grazing the savannahs, ecologists were now coming round to the view that they had, after all, been doing the right thing. Not only had the way they kept cattle remained within the limits of the environment, but in some respects they had helped to make the savannahs more productive for wildlife. In the Ngorongoro Highlands of Tanzania, for example, the Maasai used to burn parts of the grassland. This stopped the coarse grasses from growing, while encouraging the growth of fresh green shoots. Conservationists, associating burning with destruction, banned the practice, and the result is that the coarse grasses have overwhelmed the edible ones: the unburnt areas are less attractive to wild animals. Burning and selective grazing have helped to create the mixture of grass and scrub so important to wildlife in Maasailand.

There are also ways in which the Maasai are harmful to wild animals. In some places they put up temporary thorn fences around waterholes to prevent the game finishing the water. While for the most part it is the cattle which suffer from wildlife diseases, some cattle diseases can be passed on to the game. Maasai who have lost their herds may turn to hunting for a living, though this is considered to be such an ignoble means of survival that they should no longer be allowed to call themselves Maasai. On the whole, their impact on the game was neither lasting nor profound. It was, I had begun to see, largely the changes imposed by outsiders which had turned the Maasai into a serious threat to wildlife. Olurie picked up the story.

The lands of his people, he told me, had until 1970 included the area now known as the Tarangire National Park, which began just to the west of Jock's camp. Like the Maasai of Tsavo and the Maasai Mara, his community had been thrown out by conservationists.

'The swamps and all the best dry season grazing are inside the Park, but we're not allowed to use them any more. In the wet season the wild animals come out of the Park and eat our grass. Fair enough. But in the dry season they all return to the Park and our cattle can't follow them in to eat their grass. So the wild animals are increasing while the cattle are declining. The balance between us and the wildlife has been upset.

'I said to the government when the Park was created: "Let us in. We'll act as guards for you and we'll promise not to do anything to harm the wildlife." But they didn't listen to me. All they did was to grab people who tried to graze their animals there and throw them in jail.'

Since the Maasai had been expelled from the Tarangire Park, Olurie said, lions had become a serious problem. Before the Park was created, the Maasai herds had some protection from lions because they were accompanied by large numbers of wild animals wherever they went. The lions normally chose to hunt the wild game rather than cattle and goats. But now, when the wildlife retreated into the Park, it seemed that some of the lions were staying behind to feed exclusively on the Maasai's livestock. They were cunning and audacious, dragging their prey over a family's corral before anyone woke up. They were becoming a serious pest.

Traditionally the Maasai had the greatest respect for lions. The warriors hunted them largely for sport, by what they considered the most honourable means. They chased them until they were cornered, then speared them to death. Most lions escaped. When the warriors did manage to surround one, they had to spear it before it pounced. Often they were too late, and the lion was killed as it was mauling one of them to death. They chose on the whole to hunt the adult males, the least important part of a breeding population. To the Maasai it was sinful to cause the death of the young or unborn of any species, so they did not hunt lionesses which were in cub or suckling.

But now that the lions were taking such a toll on the herds, killing them had become less a matter of sport than of survival. The Maasai had given up chasing them with spears and had started to lay down poisoned carcasses instead. In one dry season they had killed twenty-three lions. As they could not select their victims, lionesses and cubs were killed as well as adult males. Over the next few weeks I began to discover that this was just one of several ways in which conservationists had turned the Maasai against wildlife.

That night Jock and I sat under the canopy of the fig tree, drinking from tin mugs, covering them with our hands to stop beetles drawn by the paraffin lamp falling in. From time to time the drowsy rhythm of the frogs was broken by a piercing yelp from the bush: the warriors of the region had learnt the trick of crushing their windpipes between finger and thumb and forcing air through them. The sound carried for several miles and was said to frighten lions away.

When Jock sat back in his chair, most of his body disappeared beyond the ring of light. All I could see were his high forehead, gleaming as if it were waxed, the glints of light trapped in his beard, and his hands, cradling his tin mug.

'I'm at the last waterpoint in a big area here. It's a seasonal river, but there's about a kilometre of it that continues throughout most dry seasons. And so wildlife and cattle from a huge area focus here during the dry seasons and during the droughts. And it amazes me how eight or nine hundred cattle can water right there—'

One of his hands left the tin mug and, flaring in the ring of light, pointed to the pool just beneath the tree.

'— in a given day and that evening, an hour-and-a-half later, lions are moving through there. And bushbuck are feeding there, watering there and feeding all along this river bed. And oh, there's so many impala, so many giraffe round here, there's one group of two elephants and another group of ten that come down and water about half a kilometre from here every night. There's both a tremendous concentration of wildlife and a tremendous concentration of domestic livestock and people round here. The conflicts are really minimal.'

There was no doubt, Jock said, that the two groups of animals competed with each other, but neither excluded the other from the land. On the whole they used the savannahs as they used this stretch of river: one group would move out and the other would move in. Now, for the first time, the Maasai were becoming a serious threat to the environment. In many parts of Kenya and Tanzania, both privatization and conservation had prevented the Maasai from migrating. Confined to one place throughout the year, their cattle were grazing out the edible plants, making way for poisonous shrubs. In some places the ground was compacting, becoming too hard for the roots of plants to penetrate. Genuine over-grazing was taking place, and it was, in part, the result of conservation.

Travelling around Tanzania, I saw that there were several ways in which conservation was damaging the Maasai's relationship with wildlife. After the Maasai had been thrown out of the Serengeti National Park, the conservationists had broken their promises and expelled them from the Olduvai Gorge. They had been told that in the Ngorongoro Conservation Area, where much of their best remaining grazing lay, their interests would take precedence over wildlife. But now the conservationists were restricting their movements so severely that it was becoming almost impossible for them to keep themselves alive. They found it hard to see what they had been doing wrong. Olduvai, they were told, had to be protected from them in case they disturbed its famous palaeontological deposits; yet the tourists who crawled up and down the rock faces, taking away stones as souvenirs, were encouraged. The Maasai were banned by the conservationists from the Ngorongoro Crater 'to make it look as natural as possible'. At the same time, several tourist camps and a network of new roads were established on the crater floor and the Tanzanian President gave permission for hotels to be built on the crater rim. They saw new safari lodges being built over waterholes, forests being cut by rangers to provide firewood for tented camps, roads being carved through some of the most beautiful landscapes in Africa. Yet they were told that it was they who were spoiling the view.

With the help of a British conservation group the Maasai were expelled from the Mkomazi Game Reserve because the tourists did not like to see them there, and they were dumped in the surrounding farmland. There they were promptly arrested for criminal trespass and fined. They tried to return to their old grazing lands, but when they got there they were once more arrested for criminal trespass and fined again. Their cattle died of starvation.

Like the charges of over-grazing, the accusations of damaging wildlife and destroying the savannah that the conservationists levelled against the Maasai soon became self-fulfilling. Impoverished by the decline of their herds, some of them began to farm, destroying their own pastures. Others started to poach. At first they took only the odd wildebeest and zebra for the pot, but if they were caught they were treated like professional poachers, and imprisoned for many years. Like everyone in northern Tanzania, they knew that it was the rangers themselves, in the wildlife department's trucks, with the wildlife department's guns, who were doing the real poaching. Seeing that they might as well be hanged for a sheep as for a lamb, some of the Maasai were now borrowing automatic rifles from Somali middlemen and shooting the elephants and rhinos on their land. They were paid the equivalent of thirty pence for a kilo of ivory. Conservation had helped to turn the Maasai into farmers and poachers. It had turned the friends of nature into its enemies.

In both Kenya and Tanzania the parks and reserves are, as a result, becoming pockets of intact savannah surrounded by degraded land. Because conservation has failed to regard human beings as part of the ecosystem, because it has alienated the people with whom it should have been working, most of the land once used by wild animals is becoming hostile to them: in some regions their migrations in and out of the parks have been severely restricted. Some of these places are likely to become little better than free-range zoos. Conservation has done as much as anything else to destroy the East African environment.

In the hills close to Kenya's border with Tanzania, in the south-east of Narok district, is a forest called Naimina Enkiyioo. The name means 'Where the Little Girl was Lost'. There is a story, as old as the Maasai's occupation of the hills, of a little girl whose father had put her in charge of his calves. She took them to graze in the shadow of the trees. As they wandered around the pasture she peered into the forest which grown men feared to enter, where the trees, many of which were sacred to the Maasai, were said to have wills of their own.

She rounded up the calves and drove them into the bushes at the forest's edge. It seemed so dark and still and mysterious that she felt that somewhere, in the green gloom beneath the trees, there must be hidden an extraordinary secret. Though the calves were frightened, she drove them on. The forest echoed with the calls of hidden birds. From the ground came the stupefying odours of fungi and the sickly smells of forest flowers. A black and white monkey, high in the forest canopy, bounded away in silence on elastic limbs. She went on, further and further into the forest.

At nightfall her brothers left their houses to look for her. With trepidation, gripping their spears, they stalked into the forest. They shouted and their calls echoed among the trees and were lost. In the darkness the forest appeared to be creeping into life. They searched and searched, but the little girl and her calves, drawn into the never-ending trees, were gone.

The Maasai of these hills are the only people of Kenyan Maasailand to have prevented the government from turning their land into group ranches or private farms. They are proud of the fact that their territory has remained a common, and many of them are determined to keep their savannahs and their forest in the hands of the whole community. But the Narok County Council has other plans. While I was travelling in Kenya, it proposed a project to turn the forest into a national reserve. The Maasai responded by setting up a trust and producing a conservation plan of their own: the forest could become a reserve, they said, but this one would remain in their hands. They gained the support of the Kenyan forestry department and it seemed, for a while, that they would set an example of local conservation which nomads throughout Kenya could follow.

I first met Ntoros ole Baari on the bleak campus of Reading University, where he was completing a dissertation on tourism in Maasailand. In his tiny concrete room, he had made Kenyan tea for me and spoken excitedly about the salvation of his people. Now, standing on the grassy slope overlooking his father's corral, he was subdued. The sun had just risen, and the clouds that had settled in the lap of the valley were streaked yellow and blue. Cows stood at the gate of the corral, breathing mist onto the air, their hides warmed red by the sun. As Ntoros's sisters, with shaven heads and bead necklaces, led them out into the pastures, they left dark hoof prints in the dew. At my feet, encrusted with dewdrops, flowers began to uncurl into the light. Two crowned cranes skimmed down the valley, folded their wings and dropped through the cloud. On the far hill the sun touched the crown of the Naimina Enkiyioo forest.

The forest, Ntoros said, was the holiest place in western Maasailand. In its midst was a cathedral of seven trees, to which the prophets of the tribe would bring offerings of grass for the Maasai God, Nkai. There was another tree under which every age group's spiritual leader would spend a night guarding a sacred fire and trying to overcome his fear of the forest. There was a river rising from the hills in which Maasai boys were washed before they were circumcised. The forest was indispensable not only to the spiritual life of the Maasai but also to their material survival. In the dry season the local people grazed their cattle on its undergrowth. They used its dead wood for fuel and its live wood for building houses. Among the trees they found their medicinal plants and the honey they used for brewing mead. The forest protected the watershed from which all the local rivers flowed. It was also the home of elephants, lions, leopards and buffaloes. Though it had been managed only by the Maasai, the forestry department admitted that it was the most pristine forest in Kenya.

Narok County Council made most of its money by administering the Maasai Mara Reserve. It collected not only the gate fees the tourists paid but also much of the money they spent elsewhere in the district, on the surrounding group ranches, in hotels, lodges and tented camps. The money had made the councillors fabulously wealthy. Having discovered what a good thing conservation could be, they had been casting around for another reserve. The Naimina Enkiyioo forest possessed all the necessary elements.

The forest regions administered by the County Council elsewhere in Narok had been devastated by illegal logging and encroachment by settlers. This was because the Council had no vested interest in their long-term survival, and the people it employed to guard them were demoralized and greedy. Naimina Enkiyioo had been protected because the people who lived there knew that their livelihood depended on its survival. They kept illegal loggers and settlers away, and the elders prevented each other from over-exploiting the trees.

Because the land on which the forest grows had never been divided up into registered properties, the councillors argued that it did not belong to the local Maasai but to the Council. The Maasai had to be expelled from it, they said, to protect it 'for posterity'. The tourists who came would generate revenue, which would be of benefit to the district as a whole, and provide employment for the Maasai. As if to confirm their environmental credentials, leaks revealed that the councillors had also made plans for the surrounding grasslands. They would throw out the Maasai and plough the land for barley and potatoes.

To the Maasai the scheme was the most momentous disaster. They would lose everything they possessed. Their expulsion would leave the forest to the tender mercies of the hotels and the safari companies. They threatened to do to it as tourism had done to the Ngorongoro forests in Tanzania: tear it apart to meet the enormous demands for fuel wood and building materials made by tourist lodges and camp sites. The holy places would be defiled and the water catchments would be broken. The Maasai of this region, Ntoros told me, did not need employment. They were self-sufficient because the forest and the surrounding grasslands answered all their needs. They would welcome a little, closely regulated, tourism in their land, but only if they were in control. If the County Council took charge, none of the revenue would get back to the community. The Council wanted to turn the forest into a reserve not in order to conserve it but in order to exploit it.

In September 1993, a few months after I left Naimina Enkiyioo, the County Council decided to go ahead with its plan to take over the forest and throw out the Maasai. Contacts had already been established with foreign businessmen who were keen to build safari lodges. The Maasai prepared to take the Council to court. In the labyrinthine law courts of Nairobi they would, like the little girl in the forest, be drawn ever further into the darkness.

111

CHAPTER FIVE

People with Eyes

The Maasai believe that to certain people the bodies of everyone else are transparent. These men and women, whom the Maasai describe as 'having eyes', cannot prevent themselves from seeing through their neighbours. Whether they want to or not, instead of clothes and skin they see bones and blood and guts. If they harbour any resentment towards the person they gaze upon, his vital organs will suffer from this exposure: adults can fall ill and little children can be struck dead. There are, of course, striking similarities to the pan-European belief in the evil eye.

In order to neutralize any evil effects they might be perpetrating, those considered by the other Maasai to have eyes are required to spit whenever they see someone. Spitting, invoking the falling of rain, is, by contrast to its significance in Europe, considered to confer a blessing. While people with eyes within the community are scrupulous about fulfilling this obligation, the Maasai do not trust strangers to be so considerate. This is why, when newcomers enter a village, the little children will run off and hide behind their mothers' skirts: being seen by an ill-disposed stranger with eyes who does not spit can be fatal. It takes time to discover whether someone has eyes, so all visitors are initially treated with a measure of suspicion.

Soon after X-ray machines arrived in Kenya, the Maasai heard that there was a device used by the mzungus to see people's bones and guts. They heard that long exposure to its rays could make people ill or even kill them. It did not take a great leap of the imagination to make the connection between X-rays and having eyes. When mzungus then arrived in their villages and stared at them through their cameras, the Maasai equated these one-eyed machines with the ones they had heard about. They concluded that the tourists had deliberately endowed themselves with eyes. Seeing that they never spat when they took a photograph, some of the Maasai assumed that the mzungus were intentionally doing them harm. They did not dare to attack them for fear of the consequences from the government, but they became, and have been ever since, resentful of tourists and photography. This is just one of the hazards of introducing tourism to the Maasai that may not be immediately obvious.

Beside the road to the Maasai Mara Reserve are scores of what the Maasai call 'cultural *manyattas*'. Although almost identical to the true manyattas where the warriors graduate, these are false villages. They are not fully inhabited by the Maasai, but were built, like the 'cultural boma' I saw outside the Tsavo Park, to attract tourists. The van drivers have been sufficiently bribed, some of the safari companies have even included a visit on their itinerary, and the Maasai who commute to these fake homesteads to dance for the tourists are doing quite well. It is their one remaining option for survival.

The Maasai in the cultural manyattas are people who have lost most of their land and most of their animals as a result of both privatization and conservation. With neither a full education nor experience in business, many of them do not have the skills required to get a government job or to set themselves up as traders. They have one remaining commercial asset: their culture. The Kenya Wildlife Service, the African Wildlife Foundation and many of the other powerful conservation groups have been encouraging them to make the most of it.

Ntoros ole Baari, my friend from the Naimina Enkiyioo forest, took me into one of these manyattas just before a pair of tour buses drove in, carrying Swedish and American tourists. When the Maasai heard the sound of vehicles, they left their huts. They looked like something out of a 1950s movie where the hero comes across a band of inarticulate savages in the jungle and becomes their master. The warriors' bodies were

113

hideously splattered and streaked with dye. On closer inspec-
tion I found that it was not the traditional red ochre mixed with
sheep's fat, but, because it was cheaper, orange emulsion paint
(red ochre, mined far away, fetches exorbitant prices in
Maasailand). When I saw that instead of dreadlocks they were
using the sort of nylon hair extensions I had seen women
wearing in Nairobi, raddled, like their bodies, with orange
paint, I began to suspect that these were not warriors at all.

Instead of gathering in a circle, with the moran on the
inside and the women on the outside, as was traditional in
Maasai dances, the men and women assembled in front of the
tourists in two straight lines. The tourists scrambled for their
cameras and video recorders. I had the feeling that they
believed they had caught the Maasai starting a rare and secret
ceremony. One of the painted warriors shouted something and
all the men started leaping up and down while the women rose
and fell on their toes. It reminded me of an aerobics class.
Staring straight at the tourists or, rather, at the line of lenses
pointing their way, they muttered a few words over and over
again.

They carried on leaping up and down for a few minutes,
with set expressions, then suddenly they stopped. Some of the
women wandered into the huts and brought out cow hides
which they spread on the ground, and bunches of jewellery,
wooden masks and miniature spears which they laid out on the
hides. The men stood around, mumbling and scratching. One
of them ostentatiously picked his nose.

The tourists, keeping their distance from the Maasai,
spread out over the manyatta, filming everything they came
across. Several clustered around a pile of cow-dung and
zoomed in and out on the flies. Other people thrust their heads
into the huts.

'My God, do you think they really live in there?' one
woman asked.

'Sure they live in there,' said the man beside her.

'The whole place smells of shit.'

The tourists were obsessed with excrement. When the
guides told them that the huts were plastered with cow-dung,

they cooed and whistled with astonished delight. The lack of toilets was a theme they kept returning to, with evident satisfaction.

'Do you think they just go wherever they happen to be?' somebody asked.

I stopped some of the tourists and asked them what they thought of the people they were visiting. Everyone I spoke to enthused about these 'simple people' – one man called them 'original man' – who had no electricity or toilets and who 'have not changed for thousands of years'. Three people told me it was just like *Out of Africa*. When I asked them if they knew that the village had been built specially for tourists, none of them believed me. A Swedish man replied:

'So, it is just like those other villages I saw by the road. So, it is evidentally a traditional village.'

As they were all on their way to the reserve, I asked whether they thought the Maasai should or should not be allowed to graze there. Most did not know that the Maasai were prohibited, but some were indignant about the destructiveness of people who, in the words of one woman, 'don't know any better'. They must be kept out of the reserve, I was informed, or they would kill all the wildlife. I asked how they knew that, and was told it was in the guidebook or on TV. Others disagreed. They were shocked when I told them that the Maasai had been expelled from the Maasai Mara. An American teacher said: 'I figure that tourists need to adjust themselves to the country that they're visiting, and if that is how the people choose to live we should adjust our needs to meet their needs. It reminds me of what we did to the Navajo, who were put in the least desirable areas.'

When they had shot all they wanted, some of the tourists asked their guides to help them bargain for the beadwork and carvings on the ground. They haggled with furious relish, beating the nomads down to the last shilling. Some offered old plastic biros in part payment, which did not endear them to the Maasai. After half an hour everyone got back into the buses, the tour guides paid the dancers and they drove away to the main attraction, the reserve. The Maasai drifted off to their real homes, the morning's charade at an end.

When the tourists had gone I realized to my astonishment that none of them had spoken to the Maasai, except to bargain, though their guides spoke Swahili and some of the dancers spoke good English. I tried to work out why this was. Doubtless the shyness and formality from which many Westerners suffer had contributed to their reserve, but it struck me that something else was at work. The tourists seemed to have found all they came for, without having to exchange a word with the Maasai. Thinking about the way in which the Maasai and the visitors skirted each other, as if deliberately avoiding contact, it struck me that both groups were conspiring to preserve the otherness of the nomads. If the tourists left the manyatta with less understanding and more mystification than they had arrived with, this might not have been entirely accidental.

It was as if the Maasai were models, not only for paint and beads, but also for the foreigners' concepts of who they were. They flaunted the outside world's impression of their primitivism, and they became what the travel agents had told the visitors they would be. Neither party wanted to disturb this lucrative impression by trying to cross the barrier between the savage and the civilized. None of the mzungus appeared to have the faintest notion that they had been visiting a people whose society was as complex as their own; whose intellectual life was, if anything, more active; and whose circumstances were changing perhaps as swiftly as those of any people on earth. The tourists took away their fantasy – the noble savage inhabiting the primordial wilderness – intact.

I stopped one of the painted dancers as he was leaving, and asked him how successful the cultural manyatta had been. He was a young man named Johnson Pesi, curt and rather aloof. Half-turning, as if impatient to be gone, he told me that it was doing quite well. I asked if he had any other ways of making money.

'No, none. My cattle are all dead. Without this we would starve.'

Ntoros came along, and Johnson began to relax: I was not,

as he had suspected, another tourist getting a free showing of the manyatta on the tail of the Combi vans. I asked him if he felt he was damaging his culture in any way by displaying it to the tourists. He said he was not, because what they were showing the tourists was not real; the dances were different, and the songs they sang were made up for the occasion. I asked him what the words were, but he smiled, shook his head and said nothing. Ntoros said something rapidly in Maasai, and they both laughed. Johnson looked around bashfully. 'We sing: "Come on you tourists, buy our beadwork, and give us all your money".'

Ntoros disagreed with Johnson about what tourism might be doing to the Maasai's culture. He said that because the Maasai here were tailoring their culture to suit the tourists, they were losing their self-respect. In some parts of Maasailand the government had been trying to destroy the Maasai's identity: moran had been caught by the police and had their heads shaved, manyattas had been pulled down. At the same time this distorted version of Maasai life was being used to sell Kenya to foreign tourists. As the charade gradually replaced the reality, the Maasai would soon cease to be what they were. They would instead become what they appeared to be. As the original meaning of their ceremonies disappeared, they would lose the sense of self that maintained them as a people.

I asked Johnson what he thought of the tourists. He said they were not badly behaved, but he did not understand them. He could not see why they had to take so many pictures. What would they do with them when they got home? Were they trading them? Were they using them as pornography? He felt uncomfortable about being photographed. I asked him if this had anything to do with the belief in people 'with eyes'. He said it did not: he did not believe that cameras were harmful, though some of the other people in the community did. He simply felt that photography was rude. But, as that was what the tourists wanted, he and the other Maasai had to go through with it. As we were talking, a man walked past us who was dressed as a moran, but carried the club of a senior elder. I asked Johnson how old the man was, and he said he must have been forty or fifty. He confirmed that he was not a moran.

'Are you one?'

'No. No one here is a moran.'

'So why are you all dressed as moran?'

'The real ones are away at a meat-eating camp, so we have to pretend to be moran until they get back. It's what the tourists want to see.'

Johnson, I found, should have been at school, but six years before his father had been mauled by a lion. His ribs and left arm had been crushed and blood had got into his lungs. He had not been able to leave his bed since. The government, as part of its effort to persuade people that wildlife was good for them, had promised to compensate anyone injured or killed by a wild animal on their own land. Johnson had spent six years trying to collect the money due to his father. He had travelled all over Narok district, getting a doctor's letter, visiting the local chief, the Kenya Wildlife Service, the district commissioner and the district wildlife committee, but had come away with nothing but promises. The same had happened, he said, to nearly everyone who had tried to get compensation. People had waited ten years and received nothing; those who had been paid said it was hardly worth the effort: in southern Narok a human life was valued at £150. Johnson had had to leave school to support his family.

'If a Maasai kills a lion,' Ntoros said, 'the helicopters are hovering before the body is cold. He gets an enormous fine and up to seven years in prison. If a lion kills a Maasai, his family waits for years and gets promises.'

Ntoros felt that he and the other Maasai were being mocked. In the hotels many of the people performing Maasai warrior dances for tourists were not only not warriors, but not Maasai at all. Habits essential to Maasai survival were to the tourists a source of sick fascination. In many places the Maasai were asked to bleed their animals and drink the blood, while the tourists writhed in horror. Playing at being primitives, the Maasai were becoming ashamed of what they had once been proud: of their knowledge, their abilities, their identity as savannah nomads.

Tourism, Ntoros suggested, might be less damaging if it were organized by the Maasai themselves, rather than by hotels and safari companies run by outsiders. This was beginning to happen, but they did not have the capital or the marketing skills to compete with the big companies. In some places the Kenya Wildlife Service and other conservation groups claimed to be helping them, but this could not protect them against the failure of the industry. Tourism was the world's most volatile trade. For big businessmen to dabble in it, with the risk of losing some capital if the tourists stopped coming was one thing, for the Maasai to stake their lives on it was quite another. While nomadic herding had proved it could persist for hundreds of years on the savannahs, tourism carried no such guarantees of survival.

Travelling around the parks and reserves, I had begun to suspect that much of what was being done in the name of conservation was actually being done for the sake of tourism. Several times I was told by conservation officials that the Maasai had to be kept out because the tourists did not want to see them there. Whether or not they caused any harm to the environment was of secondary importance. The idea that tourists might do more damage than the nomads was seldom addressed. When I asked Grace Lusiola, head of Kenya Wildlife Service's Community Conservation Department, what her priorities were, she told me, with admirable if astonishing frankness, 'At the moment the tourist is top priority. But this doesn't mean that KWS will completely close its eyes to conservation.'

Tourists have become the new aristocrats of East Africa, around whose wishes the lives of local people and the use of the land have to be shaped. The Maasai are kept out of lands that have been theirs for centuries; the tourists are welcomed in. It appears that the nomads are treated as a problem to be dealt with, and the tourists as a people whose beliefs and culture must be protected.

With the exception of Antarctica, there is no such thing as wilderness. Every region of the world has long been inhabited by humans and altered by their presence. Yet wilderness is

119

what tourists want and travel agents sell. So the job of East African conservationists is to make the myth a reality, by continuing to empty the land of its inhabitants, inventing more wilderness to satisfy the growing demand. In doing so they are beginning to destroy the very system they are trying to conserve.

By throwing out the nomads, the conservationists are getting rid of the people who helped to shape the landscape, who are partly responsible for the complex pattern of forest, scrub, grass and swamp that is so important to the wildlife. Tourists pay to see what the TV programmes show them: huge numbers of large wild animals roaming across the plains. If they are to keep the tourists happy, the conservationists cannot allow the natural boom-and-bust cycle of the savannahs to take place: they cannot allow the massive decline of game that occurs naturally in certain years.

To this end, water troughs are being built for the wildlife; veterinary medicine and dried food for wild animals have been contemplated in some places. The continued expulsion of the Maasai from their dry season grazing lands is partly motivated by the need to stop them from competing with the wild animals during the toughest years. One result, coupled with the control of rinderpest, has been a six-fold increase in the population of wildebeest moving between the Serengeti and the Maasai Mara. This is said by conservationists to be a great success. Yet it is an unnatural phenomenon: the conditions created by the conservationists have allowed the herds to get bigger than they have ever been before. If their numbers do not fall, they will change the composition of the savannahs. Far from protecting the existing system, the conservationists are creating a new one. The savannahs are in danger of becoming uniform both in space and in time. The wildlife is becoming a monoculture.

I returned to Nairobi and, on a warm calm day when the traffic fumes hanging over the city smelt like dread, I drove across town to the headquarters of the Kenya Wildlife Service, to keep my appointment with Richard Leakey. I had been worrying about this meeting for the last two months. As I sat in the waiting room, listening to the clatter of his secretaries, the tapping of keys, a printer, a fax coming in, I found myself unbuttoning my collar, wiping the back of my neck and buttoning it up again. I felt overawed by the thought of the man whose name had accompanied me wherever I went, a man as well-known for his shortness with people he felt were wasting his time as for his ruthlessly efficient administration. I felt as if I were waiting outside the headmaster's study for a caning.

The door to Dr Leakey's office swung open, someone was ushered out and a tall, heavy man filled the doorway and stared at me with raised eyebrows. I untangled my limbs and stepped forward to meet him.

'Good morning. I can give you ten minutes,' he told me.

Dr Leakey never took his eyes from my face. They were sharp and determined, and seemed to see right through me. I noticed little tufts of hair beneath his eyes, bushy eyebrows which met in the middle, a sharp nose, large brown cheeks and an enormous gold watch. (This was before the plane crash that deprived him of parts of both legs.) He was precise and authoritative, and answered my questions without a second's hesitation. I put it to him that the land set aside for conservation was the property of local people.

'We're dealing,' he told me, 'with a modern nation state . . . The setting aside of land for the purpose of wildlife conservation, to support the tourist industry, is a strategic issue. The morality of evicting people from land, whether it's to establish a wheat scheme, a barley scheme, hydroelectric scheme or a wildlife tourist scheme is the same. Basically nation states have got to function.'

There were also, he said, sound conservation reasons for excluding people from parks and reserves. 'People today want to have modern homes, they want to have pipes and running water, they want to have vehicles and roads and schools, and the infrastructure of modern society is entirely incompatible with conservation. You can allow people to graze like they used to one hundred years ago, but they're not grazing like they did one hundred years ago, because they've introduced veterinary medicine that doubles the size of the herd, we've introduced modern medicine that doubles the size of the population, and those areas can't take the pressure.'

Taking the Maasai Mara region as an example, I said that the papers I had read suggested that herd numbers were not rising. The way that people grazed their animals had changed partly as a result of their exclusion from the parks: it was this, not the size of their herds, that was causing degradation.

He told me, 'I think the question of whether the Maasai Mara herds have increased and the country degraded because people have been excluded is a fair comment; but tourism is very critical to this country, and tourism is not compatible with lots and lots of cattle in national parks. People don't pay a lot of money to see cattle.'

When I suggested that conservation policies were helping to destroy the nomads' economy, he replied, 'I think that the semi-arid pastoral economy is doomed to fail anyway, because the cash requirements of the people who are herding cattle in a traditional way are growing and the value of bush cattle isn't growing. There is absolutely no way that the Maasai living around Amboseli can educate their kids and put 'em through university and deal with the modern needs in the way they were doing it twenty years ago.'

We moved on to the subject of the beatings of people entering the Tsavo National Park. Dr Leakey said he did not believe it. He said that occasionally a ranger might get annoyed and lash out, but that regular physical mistreatment was certainly not taking place. If it were, why had the Maasai not told KWS? I told him they were too frightened to complain.

'I think that's absolute arrant nonsense. I'm a very straight-forward person, I built my reputation on integrity and I simply don't believe that.'

He agreed, however, that the payment of compensation to people attacked by wild animals was not working well, but said that this was the responsibility of another government department. KWS's priority had been to stop poaching and attacks on tourists. Now that it had done so it was beginning to work on the problems between wildlife and people. He was aware that the survival of the wildlife required the goodwill of local people. The best way to obtain it, he argued, was to share some of KWS's money. But where there was a conflict of interests, the strategic needs of the country had to come first. It was effectively impossible, he told me, to control the movements of nomads and the size of their herds, so there was no question of allowing them back into national parks. You could not put the clock back. 'If you allow excessive numbers of stock, or any stock, which will become excessive by definition, [into the parks,] you will destroy the wildlife potential very quickly.'

When I left Dr Leakey's office, I wandered around the animal orphanage at the gates of the Nairobi National Park, turning over in my mind what he had said. Dr Leakey's arguments were logical and persuasive when seen from the perspective of traditional conservation, but were, in the light of what I had seen and heard, both counter-productive and unjust. It is true, as Dr Leakey pointed out, that Kenya has to attract foreign exchange, not least because of its growing debt. But it seemed to me unfair that the nomads have to bear the cost of it. Other parts of the economy have failed partly because government ministers and their colleagues have stolen the money. Yet, while few serious attempts are being made to solve this problem, the Maasai and their lands are being squeezed for every penny they can produce, to fill the hole made by Kenya's leaders.

Tourism is, of course, essential to Kenya's survival, and it would be madness to suggest that it should be stopped. But at the moment its net effect is to take wealth away from the impoverished nomads and to give it to the country's richest people: the men and women who run some of the hotels and safari companies. As Dr Leakey said, the morality of evicting people for a wheat scheme, a barley scheme, a hydroelectric scheme or a wildlife tourist scheme in Kenya is the same. In every case local people are being thrown off their lands so that a handful of businessmen and politicians can make enormous amounts of money.

I have already argued to the effect that the problems of

123

development, population growth and agriculture can all be restricted within parks and reserves without expelling their inhabitants. I have shown how poaching may be exacerbated rather than suppressed by keeping people out of the parks. Allowing them to stay inside, on the other hand, could contribute to its suppression. The Maasai, being so widespread, so mobile, so disdainful of hunting and so ready to use force against their enemies, could, if won back to conservation, become the best guards against commercial poaching that conservationists could wish for.

Dr Leakey is correct in suggesting that the Maasai are in trouble, but incorrect in his assumption that their traditional economy is doomed. It will only collapse if agencies like the Kenya Wildlife Service continue to push. Their cash needs are growing; but taking away their only reliable means of making a living is going to exacerbate, not solve, this problem. Nearly all Kenyans have difficulty paying for such things as education, but none more so than those who have lost their lands.

Yet conservation and tourism could work far more effectively than they do today without stamping out the most vulnerable people in Kenya. If the lands of the Maasai were returned to them they would have an active interest in ensuring that the parks and their surroundings were not degraded or poached. If they, rather than the big businessmen, controlled tourism, its benefits would penetrate much further into Kenyan society, without destroying the very attractions that bring tourists to the country. Far from putting the clock back, returning the parks and reserves to the Maasai is the only sure means of securing the future of both the people and the land.

A few weeks after my meeting with Dr Leakey, I received a letter from Toronkei, telling me that the next part of the graduation process was to begin at Enkaroni on the following weekend. We were welcome to come, and to stay in his house if we wanted. We left Nairobi at six o'clock on the Friday evening, as a pale moon rose over the savannahs. By the time we passed Kajiado, darkness had fallen and the moon, now tinged with yellow, was roving through the clouds. We drove into swarms of flying termites, induced by the recent rains to leave their colonies and flock away to start hills of their own. They whirled into the headlights and piled up on the windscreen like snow. On the dirt track to Enkaroni were scores of Maasai men and women, their cloaks flaring in the headlights. Several people flagged us down. Like us, they were moving in to sleep at Enkaroni, to be ready, the next day, for the biggest ceremony of all. I immediately caught their excitement.

In the manyatta I found Toronkei. He took me by the arm and led me to the edge of the houses. As if divulging a state secret, glancing around as he spoke, he whispered that the ceremony the following day would determine the future of the moran. If it went well, their lives would be prosperous. If it went badly, they would all be blighted. He led me to the centre of the manyatta where the warriors' animals were gathered, the donkeys sleeping on their feet, the cows beginning to sink to the ground with grunts and belches. In their midst was a white ox, almost a head taller than the other animals. It was pacing around, tossing its head and flaring its nostrils.

'Tomorrow,' whispered Toronkei, 'we will suffocate that ox to death, then every one of us will drink its blood.'

Watching the animal jogging and huffing around the manyatta, I fancied that it knew what was to come. Close to the sleeping livestock, the moran and some of their girlfriends had huddled together to dance, to a rhythm softer than those I had heard before at Enkaroni. They swayed up and down, singing what sounded like a lament. As I watched, a young man strode up to the edge of the group carrying the long, loosely spiralling horn of a greater kudu antelope. He put his mouth to a hole in the horn and blew four loud blasts, so deep that I felt them vibrating through my body. Screaming and howling, the dancers scattered, knocking me over. Four or five warriors collapsed and lay on the ground, quivering and groaning. People tried to pull them to their feet, but they seemed to be unconscious. They growled, drooled and vibrated their lips. Their heels drummed on the ground like the last spasms of the dead. After a few minutes, as the screaming moran around

125

them began to calm down, all but one recovered. The last lay limp on the ground, his eyelids flickering and his limbs twitching. He was carried to his house, and a little later the dancing resumed.

The sound of the kudu horn, Toronkei later told me, signalled the approaching end of graduation, and hence of the period of being moran. It filled the warriors with grief and anger. Some of them had deflected these feelings by means of what anthropologists call 'ritual shivering': falling into bodily spasms that lead to an ecstatic trance. It was not uncommon for moran in this state to pass out, and they could take days to recover from the shock. On some occasions people had even died of anger.

That night the ox had to be given a flask of beer, in order, the Maasai said, to pacify it for the sacrifice the next day. As this operation could be almost as dangerous as a lion hunt, the moran had been building themselves up to it all night. At about ten o'clock they surrounded the herd. The ox buried itself among the other cattle, its eyes rolling. Several warriors ran through the animals and caught it by the horns and tail. The other beasts scattered. The ox bucked and danced. It broke loose and the moran swirled away in panic. It turned towards me. I found myself pressed against the thorn fence. But it turned again and ran at a moran. Someone caught it by the tail; others leapt on its head and haunches. It ploughed across the manyatta, bellowing and dragging the warriors. More and more of them piled on, until they brought it to a halt. They held up its head and a gourd full of beer was poured down its throat. With a shout they released it and leapt back. The ox ran about wildly for a few seconds, then dived back into the herd.

There was no room in any of the houses, as several hundred people had come for the ceremony, so we pitched our tent beside Toronkei's hut. News of this device soon spread around the manyatta, and the flap was repeatedly unzipped and zipped up as warriors and children peered inside and asked us if we had fallen asleep. Half an hour before dawn, when I had slept for just four hours, I was woken by the braying of donkeys. I crawled out of the tent. The manyatta was already awake, and even before I knew what they were saying, I could hear the Maasai's excitement.

The ox seemed to be displaying what I could only imagine were the bovine manifestations of a hangover. It trotted up and down, groaning loudly and pawing the ground. It stopped from time to time to urinate. Failing to notice that everyone else was pressed against the doors of their houses, I wandered into the middle of the manyatta. Toronkei ran up and grabbed my arm.

'Keep away from the ox,' he told me.

When the sun had risen and bloomed in the hides of the cattle and the cloaks of the Maasai, the moran formed a semi-circle on either side of the manyatta. Slowly, with nervous smiles, they started to close in. The ox, sensing their fear, jostled through the other cattle, its head twisted back, breathing noisily. A moran seized a leather thong from the hands of an elder, ran forward and caught the creature round a back leg. It charged through the herd, dragging him with it. Another youth ran in and caught it round the other leg. Someone tried to seize it by the horns, but it ran straight over him, ploughing him under the hooves of the panicked herd. When the cattle had passed, he staggered to his feet, dazed but apparently unharmed. Warriors swarmed in on the ox, grabbing the straps attached to its legs, but it towed them swiftly towards the huts. Only when twenty or more people had caught it, clinging to its horns and haunches, could it be turned round and pushed back into the middle of the manyatta. A gourd of milk was emptied onto its back, then it was wrestled to the ground.

One of the elders took the leather mantle off his shoulders and pressed it to the muzzle of the ox. It paddled furiously, and the people holding it used all their strength to stop it breaking loose. The mantle was bound round its snout with a strap. The leather rose and fell over its nostrils, ever swifter and shorter, until, after a minute or two, it began to fall slack. A few feeble puffs of air lifted the mantle and then it lay still: the ox was dead.

Bunches of papyrus were stacked around the corpse, and the elders cut the skin of the throat and dewlap and flayed it from the flesh without piercing any vessels. They hooked their fingers into the holes cut in the edge of the flayed skin, and lifted it to form a wide basin around the throat. The jugular vein was punctured and blood frothed into the basin, filling it almost to the brim. Women poured gourds of milk and beer into the blood, and the moran queued up behind the elders.

In turn the warriors stepped forward, knelt down and drank from the basin of skin. They were, I was later told, taking the gift of life from God, who had brought the ox and their other cattle into being with rain. It had to be suffocated so that the gift did not spill from its veins, but remained in the beast for the moran to consume.

A shout went up when all had drunk, and the warriors began to sing. The elders finished the ceremonial beer. Then some of them, arguing noisily, turned the dead ox onto its back and started to skin it. They kindled a fire by rubbing two sticks together and laid the butchered meat over the flames on a rack of green wood. The mothers of the moran built a circle of stakes and cow hides around the fire.

When the meat was cooked, the moran and their girlfriends paraded around the central enclosure, dancing and chanting. After circling it several times, the moran marched in, leaving the girls outside. They took their places on a ring of hides strewn with papyrus. Two of them vomited with nerves. The old men spat mead onto the cooked meat. The heart and lungs of the ox were taken from the grill and carried to the first moran. They were smeared over his nose and forehead, then held in front of his face. Using only his teeth, he tore a chunk out of each of them. They were passed around the circle, followed by a strip of fat from the breast of the ox and a strip of lean meat, similarly smeared over the warriors' faces and then torn by their teeth.

To the Maasai the hard fist of the heart represents reality. By eating its meat a moran ensures that reason governs his life. But the Maasai say that if a man were to live by reason alone he would become a brute. His character must be moderated by the soft, accommodating lungs, which represent compassion and tolerance. The fat eaten by each moran is success, the lean meat is failure: by consuming them together the age group learns that it must share both its conquests and its defeats.

When the moran had finished eating they stood up and started pacing around the inside of the enclosure, their sticks raised in the air. The elders fell on the rest of the meat, shovelling it into their mouths and sawing through the bones with their knives to get at the marrow. A kite wheeled round the enclosure, trimming the hot air with the fingers of its wings, turning and swooping above the elders' heads. The remaining bones and gristle of the ox were burnt, to ward off the possibility of sorcery.

It was not easy to get much sense out of the elders that afternoon, as they had been drinking mead and maize beer since the killing of the ox. But on the following day I sat down with some of the survivors, who crouched in the shade with their cloaks over their heads, trying not to move. I asked them if this were truly the last graduation at Enkaroni. Most agreed that it was. For several years they had tried hard to survive in both worlds, adapting their culture to the demands of Kenyan society. They told me they had cut down the period of moranhood from twelve years to just eighteen months. This allowed those boys whose parents could afford it to go to school, and it cost the community less.

The ceremonial lives of the moran had been skilfully compressed. Traditionally moran would live for several years in a manyatta built soon after they were initiated, then they would move to a new one for the graduation ceremonies. This time there had been just one manyatta – the graduation village – and they had stayed in their parents' houses until they moved into it. Traditionally there would have been many sacrifices of oxen. Now the sacrifice I had seen the day before had acquired new significance as a unique and critical event. But even these fundamental changes were not enough to keep Maasai culture alive. The moran, who produced little and consumed a lot, were becoming too expensive for the impoverished Maasai to support.

Yet the Maasai knew they would be diminished without moran. Throughout the ceremonies, despite their dislike of cameras, they had pressed Adrian to photograph everything that took place. These events brought hundreds of years of history to an end, and no one wanted them to be lost from memory. Oleiti, the spokesman of the warriors, told me, 'The government has always blamed the moran for the problems here. It may be right. Moranhood has discouraged people from going to school. We eat a lot of meat; it's not very economical. But we also see that there's something very important in moranhood. It keeps us together and makes us who we are.'

Without age groups, the Enkaroni Maasai would lose the sense of identity which made their lives meaningful. They would become like the other dispossessed of the earth, like people everywhere who have lost the attachment to a place and a culture which tells them who they are and what they stand for. They would join a society whose social relations could be measured in figures, whose loyalties extended to nothing more meaningful than a football team or a political party.

While they were being forced to abandon their traditional life, nothing – no training, no education, no opportunities – was being put in its place. For most of them, the only foreseeable future was as atoms in the human sea of Nairobi's stinking slums. As I spoke with the elders and watched the last of the moran feinting and tussling in the manyatta, I was overwhelmed with a sense of futility and waste. The Maasai had so much to offer, so much energy and innovation, and none of it would be put to use. Forced by their environment to experiment, to take risks, to keep learning throughout their lives, the Maasai were swift to grasp new languages and principles. Had development been organized for their benefit, rather than just that of the businessmen and politicians, the Enkaroni Maasai could have both kept their identity as herders and become involved on their own terms in the affairs of the rest of the world. For most of them it was now too late. For the Maasai of other communities there is still a little time. To prevent them from sliding into the slums, the government and its foreign funders will have utterly to change their attitudes to the Maasai.

Three weeks after the sacrifice we returned to Enkaroni to watch the final moments of the moran's transition to elderhood.

When we arrived at the manyatta, the kudu horn was blaring, and several of the warriors were being carried away unconscious, moaning and twitching. The remainder of the moran were dancing, slowly and sadly, with a gentle murmur like the wind in the trees.

When my eyes had become accustomed to the darkness inside Toronkei's house, I noticed an unfamiliar face, a dark woman with a bashful smile, who turned away from me and said nothing when I introduced myself. I turned to Toronkei in some puzzlement and saw that he was laughing.

'This,' he told me, 'is my wife.'

Three days before, he had been visiting a friend about thirty miles from Enkaroni. He caught sight of this woman near the friend's home and fell in love. He spent the day with her and at nightfall persuaded her to elope. They waited until everyone was asleep, then slipped out of the compound and ran. The dogs woke up and her brothers set off in pursuit. The two lovers darted through the scrub, zigzagging along the narrow goat trails to try to lose their pursuers, but soon after midnight the brothers surrounded them. Toronkei's lover refused to return home. She told her brothers that if they wanted to talk to her they would have to come to Enkaroni. She had made up her mind and would not be dissuaded. The brothers went home and she and Toronkei reached the manyatta before dawn. Her father was furious, but there was little he could do. Toronkei had opened negotiations and the father had demanded five cows and ten thousand shillings as his bride price. This was considered excessive, and Toronkei and his parents had been trying to talk him down. His wife came from a rich family, and the bargain was going to be a tough one. To the other moran, Toronkei had become a hero.

Once again there was no sleeping space in the houses, so we put up the tent. After another fitful night, I was woken by a commotion at dawn, and staggered out to see the moran stalking in from the bush with long straight sticks, which they sharpened as substitute spears. On this day all real weapons were forbidden and the blood of neither humans nor beasts could be spilt.

The moran stabbed their sticks into the ground, then rubbed fat and red ochre into their hair. They each took a stool from their houses and sat by the entrances. Their mothers came out with tiny gourds full of milk and emptied them over their sons' heads. With razor blades they shaved off the moran's long hair. When all the warriors had been shaved, they clustered together in the centre of the manyatta, trembling a little, saying nothing. The moran, and the Maasai of Enkaroni, had come to an end.

CHAPTER SIX

The Scattering
of the Dead

To the Barabaig people of Tanzania, home is where the dead lie. When a man dies, a mound is built for his spirit to inhabit. A holy tree is planted beside it, under which his descendants pray for his blessing and protection. The mounds, which the Barabaig call *bung'eding*, are, to these nomads, the fixed points around which their migrations range, the spiritual focus of their lives. The spirits of the ancestors keep the land fertile and the cattle in good health. Anything that drove away the dead would make the land uninhabitable for the living. A land without spirits is a no man's land.

Tanzanians, like many of the people of Africa, are short of food. Their country has abundant farmland, but much of it is far from the centres of population. Disintegrating roads, mismanagement and official corruption ensure that harvested grain rots before it is collected. Some of the land farmed closer to the towns is used for growing not food but crops such as coffee and cotton for export to other countries. Tanzania has long been forced to import much of the food its townspeople consume.

In 1970 Tanzania came as close to bankruptcy as any country could get. It had no reserves of foreign money and it was exporting next to nothing, yet it needed to buy food from abroad. The only sensible solution was to increase the amount of food produced and sold in Tanzania. The government asked for help and Canada came to the rescue, with a dramatic plan for producing food on an enormous scale.

At the time, agricultural science had been advancing at a

tremendous rate. New seed varieties had been developed which allowed certain grains to be grown in places hitherto considered hostile. New machines and new chemicals meant that, according to the scientists' predictions, previously unproductive land could be persuaded to yield fantastic quantities of food. The problem of how to feed the world is an enormous one. The gigantic fields, hybrid seeds, fertilizers and new expertise of what came to be called the Green Revolution provided an enormous solution. Tanzania, the Canadian government argued, could feed its urban people without having to spend its precious foreign money: by ploughing some tens of thousands of acres for wheat.

While there is no doubt that Canadian scientists genuinely believed that this was the answer to Tanzania's problems, there was also, of course, an element of self-interest in the proposal. If Tanzania adopted the techniques of prairie farming it would need the equipment and chemicals of prairie farmers, and the companies that made those were Canadian. By helping to finance a wheat project in Tanzania, Canada would support its own businesses. There is nothing unusual in this: few large-scale aid projects are approved which are not designed to be at least as beneficial to the giver as they are to the receiver.

Even at the time it might have been possible to see that the plan had certain flaws. The scheme was, and would remain, extremely expensive. Bread is not an important staple food in Tanzania: most people there subsist mainly on maize and beans. Wheat is a temperate, not a tropical plant and scientists, while hopeful, had not proved that it could continue to produce good yields without destroying the soil. But at the time nearly all the countries involved were wildly optimistic about what the Green Revolution could do for their people: neither Tanzania nor Canada should be singled out for blame in this respect.

A huge farming scheme needs a huge amount of land. As it would rely not on manual labour but on the use of enormous machines, it was clearly not something in which Tanzania's peasant farmers could engage. So new land had to be found, land the authorities considered under-used. They turned, unsurprisingly, to the territory of the nomads. It has long been the conceit of governments in East Africa that nomads contribute nothing to their countries. In Tanzania they are classified by the government as people with 'no productive employment'. The problem is three-fold. Nomads tend to live in the driest regions, where the environment is so sparse that they can seldom produce more than a small surplus. The livestock and hides they sell have tended, historically, to be bartered, not exchanged for cash. In the remote regions they inhabit, nomads can generally avoid paying tax, so their contribution to the economy, while real, is often invisible. In truth they tend to extract as much as they can from their land without destroying it. They trade their stock, when they can afford to, for grain, clothes, metal and beads. Most importantly they keep themselves alive, without relying on the efforts of other people for food. There is, in fact, almost certainly no use of the savannahs which could sustain more people's livelihoods.

But, because their contribution is often invisible and may, even when it surfaces, be small, nomads can be written off by governments as of no economic value to the country. When this interpretation is compounded by the traditional attitudes of the civilized towards the hordes – nomads everywhere are considered backward, destructive, dirty and ungovernable – it is easy to see how a government's dislike of nomads can be translated into a determined effort to get rid of them.

I am not suggesting that this was what prompted the Tanzanians and the Canadians to choose the land they did, but it does seem clear that the fate of the nomads they were displacing was the last of their considerations. The area they selected was fertile, well-watered and wide and flat enough for Canadian prairie tractors to be used. The fact that it was also critical to the survival of 40,000 nomads was of limited significance.

The Barabaig are an isolated and little-studied people of the Tatog group of tribes. Like many of the nomads of Kenya and Tanzania, they were driven into the lands they occupy today by the Maasai, before the British arrived in East Africa. Their wars were bloody and prolonged. Though they sometimes trade with the Maasai today, their mutual mistrust survives:

both the Maasai word for Barabaig and the Barabaig word for Maasai translate as 'enemy'.

When, a little more than a century ago, the Barabaig migrated into what is now Hanang district, they found that they could prosper by moving their animals between eight different ecological regions. This allowed them to respond to subtle changes in rainfall and vegetation so successfully that their cattle soon became famous in Tanzania. They built small dams and wells to supply their animals with water throughout the year. They made their land habitable by peopling it with the spirits of their ancestors: building the bung'eding in which the souls of their dead fathers could live and watch over them.

Of the eight regions used by the Barabaig, the most important were the lowlands to which they would move just after the rains began. Here their cattle recovered from the dry season and started producing calves and milk again. Being the most fertile and productive part of Hanang, the plains were indispensable to their survival. They were, for the same reason, the place chosen for the Tanzania Canada Wheat Programme.

The Basotu Plains, described by the government as 'idle', were declared state property and handed over to the National Agriculture and Food Corporation, or NAFCO. NAFCO used Canada's money to buy Canadian tractors, seed and pesticides, and started ploughing the savannahs. As the Barabaig, following their rotation, tried to return to their pastures with their animals, they were told they were trespassing and were forcibly evicted. When they tried again, they were beaten up, fined and imprisoned. Homes were burnt down, dams were destroyed, and the mounds of the ancestor spirits were dragged under the plough. The government had given NAFCO 70,000 acres of the Basotu Plains, but even this was not enough. Without permission, it soon began to expand its farms beyond these limits: by 1991, when I first visited the Basotu Plains, 102,000 acres had been swallowed up. The Barabaig, who had kept themselves alive by using the parts of the plains which had not been ploughed, were now threatened with extinction.

In July 1991, in the course of recording a radio programme

for the BBC, I drove with a Barabaig man I shall call Jotham across a scrub of dark acacias and yellow grass, beneath the serrated blue dome of Mount Hanang. The sky, thinned by the five months of the long dry season, was now dirty with the cobwebs of yellow savannah dust. As we passed I saw beneath the trees tall men and women in tasselled brown cloaks. Around their necks, wrists and ankles they wore jewellery of beaten brass. I saw flat-roofed huts surrounded by thorn corrals.

The scrubland ended abruptly at the foot of an escarpment. My eyes, bleached by the yellow grass, accommodated as we climbed to a rubble of black rocks. When we reached the crest I was almost blinded by an explosion of silver light. Screwing up my eyes against the glare, I stared across what at first seemed to be an enormous lake, filling the twenty miles or so between the escarpment on which we stood and a mist of pale hills in the distance. As my eyes adjusted once more, the wash of silver faded a little to a lucent pale yellow, divided into squares. Across one or two of these crawled what must have been enormous machines, which from the ridge looked as tiny as ladybirds. In climbing the escarpment I had crossed the division between two continents: I had left the savannahs of Tanzania for the prairies of Canada.

Only when we descended into the plains did I realize just how vast were the fields of the wheat project. Counting the miles, I worked out that the largest farms of southern England could have fitted into any one of them several times. The combine harvesters were the size of houses. There were no hedges, no trees, nothing but stubble and the last few squares of standing wheat. Whenever the road took us close to one of the machines, Jotham covered his face and sank beneath the windowsill: he told me that if he were seen and recognized as a Barabaig he would be hauled away and imprisoned, and I might get into trouble for bringing him there. Otherwise, as a mzungu, I would not be challenged: the farm workers would assume I was Canadian and leave me alone.

Wherever the land dipped, the road descended into a gully, ten or fifteen feet deep and about twenty feet in width. The rain, Jotham told me, had ripped through the soil when ploughing had left the land bare. The earth was too soft and the rain was too hard. With every ploughing, more and more stones appeared in the furrow. The fertile soil was gradually giving way to a stiff grey clay. We followed the mesh of gullies across the plain to a lake, surrounded by marshy ground, trapped in a ring of forested hills. This, Jotham told me, was Lake Basotu, the most sacred of the Barabaig's holy places. On the wooded shores the most revered of his people's ancestors were buried. He pointed to a small hill in the midst of the marsh where the Son of God was said to live. But the lake was disappearing.

Until the mid-1980s the hill in the marshes had been an island: Lake Basotu had filled the whole depression. There had been flocks of flamingoes in the shallows, pelicans, fish eagles, crocodiles and hippos. Giraffes, elephants and lions had come down to the water to drink. The fish had been so abundant that, when wooden rowing boats came to Tanzania, thirty or forty of the Barabaig had given up herding and become fishermen.

The soil stripped from the land and flushed down the gullies had come to rest in Lake Basotu. Already it had shrunk to half its former size. The hippos and crocodiles had died or moved away. The birds and some of the fish they fed on had been poisoned by the pesticides which ran down with the earth. The rowing boats lay cracking in the shade beneath the trees, and the fishing settlement was largely deserted. The wild animals no longer came down here to drink, as there was nothing to eat along the way.

Lake Basotu was still critical to the Barabaig's survival. Together with the ponds and troughs they had built on the plains it was one of the few water sources on which the herders could rely all round the year: if their animals were to survive, they had to bring them here to drink. The Tanzanian government had recognized this, and instructed NAFCO to leave cattle tracks across the wheat fields. The tracks, the government said, must be forty metres wide, because cattle travelling long distances like to move in a broad front.

Over the last twenty years, as NAFCO had sought to increase the size of its fields, the tractors had gradually encroached upon these tracks until many of them were now no more than two metres wide. Even the most skilful herders found it impossible to confine their cattle to such paths, and it was inevitable that some of the animals would step on to the margins of the fields. The NAFCO workers were vigilant. As soon as a cow strayed from the track they would move in to arrest the herders for criminal trespass. The Barabaig were taken to the district court where they were invariably convicted and fined. Those who could not pay were imprisoned for between one and five years.

Jotham took me to a village in the midst of the scrub on the other side of the escarpment, a circle of low houses built of mud, cow-dung, sticks and corrugated iron, to meet eleven old men who herded their cattle together. Beneath their brown robes, they were as thin as xylophones. One man brought tea in chipped enamel mugs, put out a pair of rickety chairs for us, then sat down on the ground, his knees pulled up to his chest. Two weeks before, he told us, three of their cows had been caught walking on the margins of a field. They had not strayed into standing wheat, but onto the stubble of fields that had already been harvested. He and his friends had tried to head them off and push them back onto the track, but they were too late: NAFCO workers had seen them. Driving over the stubble they were supposed to be defending, they rounded them up in Landcruisers and took them to the police station. Within a week the old men appeared in the district court. Each was ordered to pay NAFCO the equivalent of £90 by way of compensation, even though the court accepted that no damage had been done. The only way they could pay this fine – enormous by Tanzanian standards – was to sell some of their cattle: he himself had lost all that remained of his herd.

'What is left for me now?' he asked. 'Without cows, I don't know what I can do. I think I shall just die. Why are they doing this to us? Are they trying to finish us off? I think they want to be rid of the Barabaig, so that we stop causing them trouble.'

Several other people had been convicted of criminal

trespass in the month before my visit. A man and his wife had taken three guests to see their cattle. They were driving them down to a pond in the middle of the farms when they were caught by NAFCO workers, who claimed that the cattle had strayed one metre into a field. The herders denied this, but they were allowed neither a lawyer nor witnesses in their defence. The husband and wife were sentenced to three years each and the guests one year, although they had nothing to do with the cattle. A nine-year-old boy who let his cows stray onto the stubble had been remanded in prison: I later discovered that he was kept there for four months before being sentenced to twelve strokes of the cane. A ninety-year-old woman had been fined and imprisoned for a year. Two younger women had allegedly been raped by NAFCO workers before being taken to court. Their cattle were 'confiscated' by the farm as a supplementary fine.

There were, in fact, no legal grounds for arrest or conviction for criminal trespass, as the ownership of the land was still in dispute. But NAFCO is the biggest power in Hanang district, and the authorities seem prepared to do whatever it wants. There are well-documented cases of the police and courts fabricating or suppressing evidence, and the Barabaig were seldom given an opportunity to defend themselves.

With help from human rights lawyers, the Barabaig have been petitioning the High Court in Arusha to recognize their rights to the extra land NAFCO had seized. They won the first case they brought in 1984, but NAFCO took it to appeal and had the decision reversed on a technicality. To celebrate their victory, the corporation's employees hospitalized several of the plaintiffs. In 1990, when the Barabaig appeared to be on the verge of winning two critically important cases, Tanzania's Prime Minister stepped in. Violating the country's constitution on two counts, he decreed that all Barabaig rights to the land were extinguished, and he backdated the announcement to 1987. Thousands of Barabaig, despairing of ever regaining the land they needed for their survival, terrified by the beatings, rapes, fines and imprisonments, had fled to the towns. For the first time in their known history, many of the remaining herders were now suffering from malnutrition. Jotham told me that if there were a bad drought the Barabaig would start dying of starvation. If the old man's assertion – that NAFCO was trying to get rid of them – were true, then it was clear that the corporation was enjoying some success.

Officially, Canada was soon to stop funding the project, but in 1991 it could still determine how it was run. Employees of the Canadian International Development Agency occupied a complex of offices in Arusha, from which they oversaw the management of the farms. When I phoned the offices they refused, at first, to talk to me. I tried again, asking them if there was something they wanted to hide. The research director gave me a five-minute appointment, on condition that I did not bring a tape recorder.

When I entered his office he stood up briskly and clumsily, shook my hand and, without a word, gestured that I should sit down. He was a Canadian of around fifty-five, with a thick neck and cheeks of an unhealthy purplish-yellow colour. I noticed that he was nervous. Clinging to the edge of his desk, he squeaked his revolving chair from side to side. He stopped every few seconds to push his glasses back up his nose. The string of letters after the name on his business card showed that he had enjoyed the best education any man could hope for.

I asked him first about the way the land was farmed. He listed the types of machinery used, the style of ploughing, the quantities of chemicals, the yields of wheat. When I suggested that these techniques seemed to be responsible for a good deal of soil erosion, he told me that studies had shown the erosion rates were well within the expected range, and were not a cause of concern. I asked him what he felt the change in land use was doing to the Barabaig people. His chair squealed to a halt. He stared at me.

'The Barabaig people?' he said at last.

'Yes. Surely you must have heard of them?'

'The Barabaig people—' he paused. 'The Barabaig people don't live on that land.'

It was my understanding, I said, that they did, or they had

done until the project dispossessed them. Now they were trying to survive around the margins of the wheat farms. Did he not think that their rights had been violated? The chair started squeaking again.

'The project has been a success. I don't think we could have expected it to have been any more successful than it has been.'

'But the rights of the Barabaig people?'

'I don't know anything about them. My job is to make sure the project is a technical success, and as far as I am concerned it has been.'

'But it has deprived forty thousand people of their best grazing lands. Is that a success?'

The chair started squeaking furiously. 'The Barabaig are nomadic. They can go to another place.'

As I left he advised me not to return to the Basotu Plains. 'If they catch you, they'll probably shoot you.' His Tanzanian assistant, Anna Shilcombe, had been listening to our conversation through an open door. Bristling with indignation, she strode up to me as I stepped into the corridor. The Barabaig, she told me, were under-developed people who were impeding the progress of Tanzania. I told her that it seemed to me that the project was impeding the progress of the Barabaig, as they were now in danger of starvation. She drew herself up.

'I won't shed a tear for anybody,' she announced, 'if it means development.'

While I appeared to have caught the staff in Arusha off guard, when I telephoned Dar-es-Salaam to speak to the over-all project director I found him well-briefed and, in his own words, 'pleased to have the chance' to speak to me.

'There are strong views, and I think we have the same feelings,' Dr Lorne Heuckroth told me, 'that there have been downsides to the project. . . . If this project were brought to us today we would certainly want to see a project that has more immediate and direct benefits to the target group: the poorest in this country.'

More direct benefits? I asked. He told me that, yes, the effects on the Barabaig had not been entirely beneficial, but it would be wrong to say they had not been beneficial at all. I pressed him on this point and he told me that the wheat farms had created employment. I said I had heard that the farms only employed two hundred and fifty people, of whom ten were Barabaig. He told me that was correct, and hoped that this might be improved. But now Canada was due to start paying for some development projects for the Barabaig, which would help to make up for the benefits they might have missed.

Dr Heuckroth seemed to have accepted that the project had not been the one that Tanzania needed. It was, indeed, providing the townspeople with food, but it was now clear to nearly everyone that there were more efficient and less destructive means of achieving the same end. Tanzania has a lot of human labour and very little money, so a project that requires a lot of money and very little human labour is clearly not using the country's resources effectively. A great deal more food could have been brought to the towns simply by means of repairing the roads: in many places this is, at last, being done. At least as much grain as NAFCO produces – and grain of a variety that Tanzanians wanted to eat, rather than the wheat that Canadians wanted to grow – could have been produced by helping peasant farmers on existing farmland. There are, and have always been, ways in which this can be done, without destroying the environment. Helping small farmers rather than big business does not require the expulsion of local people from their lands.

I asked Dr Heuckroth about the complaints of rapes, beatings and false charges of criminal trespass. He said that these were being investigated, and such things would never be allowed to happen again. NAFCO would also be made to stop expanding its farms. He was very glad I had shown an interest in the project, and would be happy to accompany me if ever I returned to the Basotu Plains.

I did try to take advantage of Dr Heuckroth's kind offer, but received no reply to my letters and telephone calls. So, in December 1992, seventeen months later, I set off for the wheat fields once more with Jotham, the man who had accompanied me on the previous journey. Even before we reached the

Basotu Plains I could see that not all of Dr Heuckroth's promises had been kept.

From the midst of the savannahs on the nearside of the escarpment rose a pillar of yellow smoke. I drove across to see what was happening, then left the Land Rover to walk towards the fire. At first I could see only the shimmering heat haze, a smear of grey, black and orange, like reflections on the surface of a river. I could hear the crackling of the fire and a steady dull roar. When the wind turned I smelt the smoke, a rousing, dangerous smell. For a minute I hung back. But I soon realized that the flames were not travelling: the heat haze hung over a fixed line on the savannah. As I approached I saw that the fire was consuming a row of uprooted trees, which must have been bulldozed off the land and pushed together into a sort of tideline. Standing around the edges was a flock of storks, waiting for any small animals that might bolt from the flames. When they saw me they left the ground, and were swept up like smuts in the thermals.

As I came closer, I picked out beneath the roar and crackle of the fire a deeper sound. Beyond the burning trees, grinding up the savannah towards me, was a gigantic red tractor. As it came closer I saw that it was towing something, and that the ground behind it was turning from yellow to brown. Only then did I realize that the land had been cleared of its trees to prepare it for ploughing. As the tractor came up to me I raised my hand and, to my surprise, it stopped. The driver left his cab and stumbled across the grass towards me, grinning widely. As he approached, he saw that I was not the man he had expected and his face changed a little, but he kept smiling. He shook my hand and asked me if I were from CIDA (the Canadian International Development Agency). I told him I was and he said he was very glad to meet me. He confirmed that he was working for NAFCO and told me the work was going well. I asked him what he was doing.

'I am making fields.'

'You're expanding the farms?'

'Surely.'

For miles along the road to the escarpment, the land had

been cleared and was now being ploughed: the Canadian tractors beetled up and down the sward, leaving, as they closed in on each other, not a tuft of savannah grass. In the middle of the overturned ground stood the village, now empty, where I had met the eleven old men.

Jotham told me that the last wet season grasslands of the Basotu Plains, on the other side of the escarpment, were also being ploughed. The inhabitants were being evicted: if they tried to stay, their houses were burnt down. Women had been brought back to the farm compounds by NAFCO workers and raped. Everywhere I went I met Barabaig who, since my last visit, had been dispossessed.

Jotham took me to a market close to the town of Basotu. On a patch of trampled grass, merchants from Arusha were selling shirts, trousers, knives, mirrors, lung tonic, blackcurrant cordial, sandals, tobacco and washing powder. Barabaig men and women crowded around the stalls. The women's faces were tattooed. Chains of raised scars fell from their shoulders to their breastbones like necklaces. The tassels on their cloaks jingled with brass beads.

We met a friend of Jotham's called Gidamwaghwela, a short, muscular man in a fawn cloak, with deep, melancholy lines around the edges of his mouth. He told us that the place in which his life was rooted, the bung'eda inhabited by his father's spirit, was about to be ploughed up. NAFCO's new fields now came within a few hundred yards of the mound and the season's ploughing had not yet finished. Hundreds of bung'eding had already been destroyed.

'When the mound is ploughed,' Gidamwaghwela told me, 'the dead man's spirit is lost. You don't know any more where your father has gone. My children won't know where their grandfather is. We can no longer belong to this land.

'We didn't know about these farms until they started ploughing. The same has happened with the extension of the farms. They never tell us anything. They just arrive with their tractors and plough up the land. They've taken our best lands and yet still they want more.'

Gidamwaghwela told me there was no wet season grazing

that could substitute for the land they were losing. The only places they could go to were the lands of the Gogo and Nyaturu people, many miles away. Until now those tribes had been friendly, but they were becoming intolerant of their Barabaig visitors and would soon forbid them to return.

Gidamwaghwela's problems were not confined to the continuing expansion of NAFCO's farms. A few days before I met him, he and five others had been heavily fined for letting their cattle step onto the margins of a bare field. He was one of scores who had been charged since I had last visited Hanang. Dr Heuckroth's assurance that the arrests for criminal trespass would stop was as empty as his promise that NAFCO would cease to expand its farms.

Travelling around Hanang district, I heard a series of horrendous accounts, some of which have since been independently recorded by the International Institute for Environment and Development. In July 1992, four women and five men whose cattle had died of starvation went gleaning in NAFCO's harvested fields. Gleaning – picking up the grains left on the ground when the crop has been removed – has been the right of the poor for thousands of years: even during the most repressive periods of European history serfs were allowed to collect the spilt grain. Though NAFCO was happy to leave the gleanings to the birds, when these Barabaig started gathering them they were rounded up. In the district court all nine were sentenced to three years in prison for stealing wheat. The women had young children, whom they would not see again until they were released from jail.

A month later another party of men and women, pursuing their last chance of avoiding starvation, were found gleaning. Most managed to escape. But a middle-aged woman named Udaghowed, her teenage son Ginada and two other women were caught by the farm workers. Ginada was ordered to have sex with his mother. When he refused, the women were told to beat him. When they failed to beat him hard enough, they were beaten themselves, and one of the women was raped with a stick. Ginada was told to lie on the ground and bare his buttocks. The women were forced to flog him so violently that when they had finished he could not get up. Jotham showed me a photograph of what had been done to him. The sticks had shredded his buttocks.

Returning to Jotham's house from one of our excursions, we found a man waiting for us, crouched in a dark corner. He stood up, breathing heavily. At first I could only see his body, a strange, hunched form in a long cloak. His face was in shadow. When he stepped forward into the light I caught my breath. The top half of his face was a tumult of scabs and fresh scar tissue. The wounds ran through his eyebrows and up into his hairline. The skin over his cheekbones was split. Holding on to the back of a chair with one hand, he tried to raise the other, but it fell back limply to his side. His shoulders were bunched around his neck and his arms were trembling.

Emmanuel had enclosed a patch of land as his own and tilled it. In Tanzania land classified as 'productive' – under crops in other words, rather than used for grazing – could be registered in the name of the person who cultivated it. Though the Barabaig knew that farming would reduce their grazing lands still further, they also knew that this was the only claim to their land the courts would recognize: they found that if they surrounded their homes with small fields they could prevent them from being burnt down. NAFCO saw this as a threat to the expansion of its farms.

Two weeks before I met him, Emmanuel was returning to his home, which had been completely surrounded by the wheat fields of one of the seven NAFCO farms. To get to his house he had to cross the farm compound: if he took any other path through the fields he would be arrested for criminal trespass. As he was passing the buildings, the farm's storeman, Mr Mgoma, came out and called him over. He told Emmanuel that he wanted to buy his fields. Emmanuel said he did not want to sell. Mr Mgoma asked him to come into his house to discuss the matter. He stepped through the door. Mr Mgoma head-butted him and he fell to the ground. The farm's driver, Mr Mrema, who was hidden behind the door, joined in.

Mr Mgoma started beating Emmanuel over the head with a piece of timber, while Mr Mrema kicked him repeatedly in the ribs and kidneys. He curled into a ball on the ground and, when he was asked again, still refused to sell his land. Mr Mrema held him while Mr Mgoma left the room. He returned with a length of electric flex. Emmanuel struggled to his feet. Mr Mgoma poked one end of the flex into the wall socket and lunged at him with the other. Shielding his head, Emmanuel received five shocks to his arms. Each one threw him to the ground. The men let him get to his feet before Mr Mgoma electrocuted him again.

Mr Mgoma left the room to find something else with which to torture him. Seizing his chance, Emmanuel picked up an empty charcoal stove and threw it at Mr Mrema, who dodged, leaving the way to the door clear. Emmanuel fled. Later that day, a friend took him to report the incident to the police. They refused to charge the two men, and suggested instead that Emmanuel ask them for compensation, to help pay his hospital bills. Emmanuel told me he was too weak to work. A journey that had once taken him an hour now took the best part of a day. He said he felt his insides had been burnt.

I drove out to the farm where Emmanuel was attacked and found the most senior man present: Mr Lupondo, the production manager. He claimed to know nothing about the Barabaig, as he had only been working there for two years. He said he did not know whether or not his farm was being expanded. Canada, he told me, was no longer supposed to be funding the project: it had completed its twenty-one years of official payments to NAFCO in 1991. But the field director, he admitted, was a Canadian and was paid by the Canadian International Development Agency. NAFCO, he said, was still asking Canada for money, as it was still obliged to buy Canadian machinery, and was currently in financial difficulty. Pests were getting out of control and the corporation needed to use more and more chemicals to suppress them. He was certain that Canada would provide the money, as the Canadian ambassador was a regular visitor to the farms.

I asked Mr Lupondo if he had heard about the incident involving Mr Mgoma and Mr Mrema. He told me that he had and I asked him what he thought of what they had done to

Emmanuel. He said it was 'maybe not a good thing'. I asked him if he were going to do anything about it.

'I do not think so.'

'Why not?'

He looked around, at his desk, at the calendar, at the open door, as if somewhere among the papers and the woodwork there was an answer to my question. 'I do not know. Maybe it is a personal matter.'

Despite the continued beatings, rapes and imprisonments, the Barabaig had not given up the struggle for their lands. They were now fighting both NAFCO and the Prime Minister's order in court. The authorities had tried to delay or frustrate these cases: the court files had been officially 'lost', only to be found a year later in the Prime Minister's office. But, at the time of my visit, there seemed to be a real chance that the Barabaig would get back some of their land, as a report commissioned by the government concluded that the traditional land rights of local people should be recognized. For a while the government seemed prepared to act on this. Soon after I left Tanzania, without warning or consultation, it suddenly decided to take the opposite course. An act was pushed through Parliament extinguishing all customary land rights and terminating all court cases. It seems that the government came under pressure both from new landowners and from foreign banks who were trying to persuade it to privatize Tanzania's land.

The Barabaig, with the help of their lawyers and supporters in other countries, are still fighting for the recognition of their rights. They see that there is simply no other means to survive. Canada has tacitly acknowledged that its project has destroyed the lives of the Barabaig, by setting aside money to spend on schemes for their rehabilitation. Unfortunately these, too, appear to be grossly misconceived and are likely, if they go ahead, to do the people more harm than good. If the Barabaig are to survive Canada must do more than simply throw money at the problem. It must insist that NAFCO returns the extra land seized and compensates the Barabaig for their losses. It must force the Tanzanian government to release the people falsely imprisoned and stop the arrests, the thefts, the torture and the rapes. Only then can it make good its claim to be a morally enlightened nation. Only then will NAFCO's ploughs be prevented from scattering the living as they have already scattered the dead.

CHAPTER SEVEN

The Astromancer

I had heard of Ol Doinyo Nyiro, the holy mountain, long before we travelled to Samburu district. It was here, among the arid lands south and east of the Turkana's territory, that God, or Nkai, was said to live, in a cave on its wooded flanks. But I had not heard, until we reached the decrepit little town of Baragoi, that Ledumen, the great Samburu prophet, also lived on its slopes. I was told by one of the townspeople that he had greater powers than any other soothsayer in Kenya. Intrigued, we decided on the spur of the moment to visit him. With two Samburu friends we had made in the town, Peter and Julius, we set off across the shrivelled pastures of one of the most spectacular peoples in Africa.

The land was as dry and creased as a paper bag. In places it looked pink, as all that covered the ginger soil was a furze of knee-high bush, bleached as grey as driftwood. In the empty cusps of exhausted volcanoes grew the remnants of a fishbone forest. There had been no rain in this region for four years. We climbed into the mountains, the white sun glittering on andesite and obsidian, shards of heat-shattered rock scraping the undersides of the Land Rover. Only in the narrow valleys were there flashes of green: coral gardens of candelabra cacti or banana trees watered by a missionary. Baboons loitered beside the road, listless as youths on a derelict estate.

But as we passed the mission settlement of South Horr and climbed towards Ol Doinyo Nyiro, the flanks of the hills turned lichen green. The further we travelled the denser the scrub became, until the road was hedged by woods of cactus and thorn trees. I looked up and saw the mountain, capped with a bluff of orange rock in the shape of a recumbent lion. A small track took us to the base of one of its foothills. We left the Land Rover and climbed through the scrub to four or five small houses where Ledumen and his family lived.

I was surprised to find a crowd of twenty or thirty men standing around the huts, staring hard at us as we came into view. They half-raised their hands as we approached and I heard them whispering something. As we stepped among the huts they moved in a little, but no one came forward to greet us. The elders among them watched us with quick red eyes, chewing the dregs of their tobacco. I looked around the ring and asked if Ledumen was there. No one replied. I asked Peter and Julius what all these people were doing. Peter addressed them, but the men just shuffled their feet and looked around. I began to feel uncomfortable.

The elders, like the elders of all the nomad tribes in Kenya, were a ragged bunch of men in dirty jackets and broken hats; but the warriors who stood beside them were more splendid even than the moran of the Maasai. They wore triangular headscarves, chokers and necklaces, cuffs of beads around the stretched lobes of their ears, rings and bracelets. On their eyelids and high on their cheeks, delicate patterns of red ochre had been painted in filigree. They carried maces with metal heads and javelins with orange pennants fluttering from the shanks. At first I assumed that these were the special flags distinguishing their age group, but later I discovered that they were household dusters, bought in bulk from a merchant in Baragoi.

An old woman crawled out of one of the huts and straightened up in front of us. She was tall, thin and shaven-headed. A blue cloak covered one shoulder and one breast. She did not seem remotely surprised to see us. I introduced myself and asked her if she knew where Ledumen was. She tilted her head towards the valley and the pendants hanging from the lobes of her ears swung away from her skull. Then she stepped into the goat corral, lifted her skirts and, behind the fence, still standing, still watching us, she urinated. In Samburu district it is the men who squat.

While we waited, Peter and Julius told me about the

prophet. His father, Leseven, had been the greatest diviner the Samburu had ever known, whose predictions of rain and raiders invariably came true. On his death there had been a prolonged debate among the elders as to which of his two sons should succeed him. Normally the elder son would take his place, but in this case the younger one, Ledumen, had shown more promise. To his brother's disgust, Ledumen was chosen, and swiftly justified the elders' faith in him by some astonishing feats of prophecy. He had foretold the drought and a recent enemy raid. He could predict, they told me, exactly what visitors to the district would do – whether enemies or friends – and where they would go.

We sat down in the middle of the village and waited. The crowd of men sat down as well. They spoke, if at all, in whispers, scratched the ground with their sticks, and seldom took their eyes off us. I felt as if they were expecting me to do or say something. Twice I almost resolved to get to my feet and make a speech, but decided it would be better to wait and see what was happening. I had been sitting on the ground for half an hour when there was a sudden stir among the men, and several of them got to their feet.

'The prophet is coming,' said Peter.

I saw two elders striding up the hill towards us. The man on the left was small and grey, but the man on the right was tall and sharp-faced, with penetrating eyes. He carried a club, beautifully decorated with beads, and stared around him as he walked, as determined and dignified as a hawk. Behind them came an unadorned young man wearing a red cloak and a digital watch, whom I took to be the prophet's disciple. I stared as the tall elder strode into the centre of the village, raised his hand with stately gravity and disappeared into one of the huts. Peter tapped me on the arm.

'This is Ledumen,' he said.

I turned round. Standing beside me was the young man with the digital watch. He had a smooth, innocent face and a soft moustache. He smiled, shook my hand, said 'Yes,' when I introduced myself and followed the elder into the hut. After a few minutes he came out again, smiled his brief, businesslike smile and asked if we had brought any gifts for the crowd of men. Perplexed, I told him we had not: we had had no idea that so many people would be here. Ledumen turned to the crowd and, rapidly, authoritatively, passed on what I had said. I saw them deflate a little and, grumbling, casting occasional stares at us over their shoulders, they walked off down the hill. Totally confused, I turned back to Ledumen, but he had disappeared into one of the huts. A glance at Peter and Julius showed that they were as confounded as I.

The prophet kept to his hut until evening. I sat among the houses, scant frames of sticks partly covered in hides and tarpaulins, which nestled like blown litter between the boulders of the mountainside. A warm wind blew up the hill. I lay back and let it run over my face and through my hair. From the valley below I could hear the clunk of wooden cowbells, bleats, shouts, the crying of a goshawk. The cicadas started strumming in the trees. I opened my eyes. Leaning back on the roof of a low hut, her young breasts rising naked from layers of beads, was a girl with the smooth, curved features of a Benin bronze. When our eyes met she smiled and we both looked away.

As the sun went down, Ledumen came out of his hut. I stood up to speak to him, but he turned from me. He climbed onto one of the rocks and sat watching the sky above the mountain, his hands folded in his lap, quite still. The beautiful girl – his sister – stood up, stretched and wandered away to milk the goats. Ledumen, as still as the mountain, was silhouetted against the darkening sky, his head thrown back as he watched the stars creeping behind the bluff. As night fell the wind quickened, and the fires inside the flimsy huts roared and sputtered. They looked like Chinese lanterns tumbled amid the rocks. The prophet, the wind tugging his robes, did not move for two hours. A large white planet teetered on the rim of the mountain then slipped away, and Ledumen jumped down from the rock and wandered over to where I sat. He apologized for not having greeted us before.

I asked him what he had been looking for in the sky. Until the children of the village were asleep, he said, he could not tell me much: people who heard his predictions before they were prepared could suffer misfortune. But all his attention had been focused on Venus: he sat out at night in time to see its emergence, stayed there until it disappeared behind the mountain, then woke early to watch it coming over the eastern horizon. His prophecies were based, he told us, on the colour of the planet and the length and direction of its rays. I protested that Venus was white and rayless. He agreed that it was. His gift was to see what other men could not.

Ledumen looked around. The children in the huts had fallen silent. He leant forward and spoke in a whisper. All he could predict, he told me, was rainfall, the movements of people and certain national events, like the outcome of the forthcoming elections. Yesterday, he confided, he had seen that there would be a migration of people from the eastern plains to the slopes of this mountain; today he had seen that rain would fall in a few days' time, not here, but in the south, in places that had received none for four years.

No one had taught him these skills. His second sight, he told me, was the gift of God. It was on God's mountain that he, like his father and his grandfather, had made his home, and God would withdraw his gifts if the prophet displeased Him. Only through solitude and contemplation could he see what he needed to: he kept to himself as much as he could. Unlike Loktelej, the Turkana rainmaker I had met, he claimed no powers to change the future, all he could do was to see it. He fell silent. I could hear the fires roaring inside the huts, the old woman shifting, hawking and spitting. What, I asked him, were all those people doing when we arrived? He smiled.

'They were waiting for you,' he said. 'I told them you were coming three months ago.'

I felt a prickle of alarm run up my spine and through the hair on the back of my neck. I shook my head. I told him I had decided to come only yesterday. I had told no one but Peter and Julius, and they had never left my side. No one else knew. Ledumen simply nodded.

On the following day I found some of the men who had been waiting in the village when we arrived. It was true, they said, that Ledumen had told them of our visit three months ago, and they had eagerly looked forward to the day in the hope that we might bring some presents for the people of the area. They were disappointed when we turned up with nothing. Ledumen had spent the morning of the previous day, before we had even heard of him, trying to find a goat to slaughter for our arrival; but no one had one to spare. Perhaps, I asked them, foreigners came here all the time? They insisted that we were the first mzungus to visit Ledumen for nearly a year. But in just over a month, the prophet had told them, a white woman and her daughter would arrive, so everyone would return to see if those visitors would be more generous.

On my third day in Ledumen's village I set out to climb the holy mountain. While Nkai, like the Turkana's Akuj, is both inscrutable and omnipresent, there are places, like our churches, in which His presence is said to be felt. The cave on Ol Doinyo Nyiro's slopes was one of these, and it was to try to find it that I pushed through the trailing thorn bushes and candelabra cacti – *Euphorbia* – of the lower slopes, looking for a route to the top. The word Nkai means both God and rain. Rain is both God's gift and His substance, just as communion wine is the blood and the bequest of Christ. As one of the wettest parts of Samburu district, the mountain is intrinsically holy. Its waters bring cattle and humans to life: they are the spittle of God, without which the land and its people would be but dry bones. Just as God is both the rain and of the rain, He is in the mountain and the mountain is simultaneously a part of Him. To nomads, God, land and sky are inseparable. A nomad in the city is a man apart from God.

From the bottom of the mountain the ascent looked easy, for the ground sloped evenly up to the bluff, which had been conveniently shattered by the weather into a complex of twisted steps. I was confident of getting to the top and back again before nightfall. But as I walked the bush became thicker and thornier. The only trails were tiny passages made by goats or duikers, and the enthusiasm with which, at first, I followed them on hands and knees evaporated when I startled a green mamba. Trying to find a route up the mountain, I wandered further and further to the south, passing through forests of frilled cacti and plants with stems like upright marrows, swollen with water. Vervet monkeys bounded away through the bush and geckoes edged into crevices in the rocks. I tried innumerable routes, but the door to the house of God was closed to the infidel.

Scrambling down a cleft in the side of the mountain, I came to a thread of water, running along the course of what must have been a torrent when rain fell. I peered into a pool trapped behind a boulder and started back: the bed was shifting and jostling. I looked more closely and saw that it was composed of gigantic tadpoles and freshwater crabs, packed together as the waters had diminished. I sat on a rock and looked out across the land. I confirmed what I had seen on the way from Baragoi: Ol Doinyo Nyiro was the only green point in the landscape. On its lower slopes the white specks of sheep and goats drifted in and out of the trees. Beyond them the land was grey. Though I scanned it with binoculars, I could see no living thing.

Drought had struck Samburu district four years before and, in the lands I overlooked, no rain had fallen since. While in the past the Samburu had survived even longer periods of aridity, this one had brought them to their knees. They had lost the resilience and good fortune that had kept them alive and now, in November 1992, they were faced with the possibility of death through starvation. Change in the lands of the Maasai and the Barabaig had led to dispossession and poverty. In Samburu district, coupled with this terrible drought, it killed.

Before the British arrived in East Africa, the Samburu were no more and no less a distinct tribe than any of the other peoples who called themselves 'Maasai'. Being Maasai was simply a matter of conforming to certain codes of behaviour, living almost exclusively from one's herds and speaking the Maa language. It did not mean working as one group for the defence of Maasai territory and the conquest of the non-Maasai tribes. In fact the people who called themselves Maasai were people of many different tribes, who fought each other with bitter rivalry, like Protestants and Catholics, or the rival Moslem tribes who claim direct descent from the Prophet

Mohammed. Some vowed to wipe each other out, some succeeded: in the 1880s, for example, the Purko tribe effectively
eliminated the Laikipia tribe, driving the last of their moran
into the abyss of the Menengai Crater, close to Lake Nakuru.

The British, seeing people who dressed similarly, spoke the
same language and were equally impossible to govern or
reason with, assumed that they all belonged to the same tribe.
When they seized the northern Maasai territories, and pushed
the Maasai into the south, they forced these different peoples
to live together in what they called 'Maasailand'. Over the
decades the barriers between the tribes there began to break
down. Today the situation is confused, but it may not be
inaccurate to say that, though there are still some conflicts,
most of the Maasai have been turned into what the colonists
thought they were: one tribe, united by their circumstances.

But the British left the Samburu behind. Less warlike, living
in drier lands than the other Maasai, the Samburu were considered neither a threat nor an obstacle to British plans. They
were left where the British found them, in the region now
designated Samburu district. This was just one of several
historical accidents which allowed the Samburu people to sustain their traditional nomadism, for most of the nineteenth and
twentieth centuries.

In the early nineteenth century the Turkana to the north
and west had begun to encroach upon the Samburu's lands.
These desert raiders were, at the time, the Black Huns of East
Africa, daring and ruthless in war, with little respect for peace
treaties or honourable conventions, a terror to both settled
society and other nomads. The Samburu retreated before them.
By the turn of the century it looked as if they would be overrun.
But in 1900 the Purko Maasai, having obliterated the Laikipia,
moved into the fertile lands of the Leroghi Plateau, on the
borders of both the Samburu and Turkana territories. The Turkana made the mistake of raiding the Purko, and received in
return an attack so devastating that they were stopped in their
tracks and have never come further. In their place, the Purko
began threatening the Samburu, but within a few years they
were pushed out by the British.

In 1933 the Kenya Land Commission ruled that white farmers had no right to annex the Samburu's best lands. The settlers were furious, but at the time they or their compatriots had committed so many well-publicized atrocities that Kenya was becoming an international embarrassment, and the British government felt obliged to put them in their place. At the same time the authorities imposed strict controls on the Samburu moran, trying to close down some age groups altogether. In response, many of the warriors, to retrieve the pride demolished with their manyattas, joined the army and helped the British to defeat the Italians during the Second World War. They became the government's most valued troops: even today there are thousands of Samburu in the army and the police force.

This helped soften the British government's attitudes towards them, and the moran, though controlled, were allowed to keep going. Still convinced that nomads were irresponsible and destructive, the authorities went ahead with their plans to reduce the numbers of Samburu cattle and control the way they grazed. Had the scheme worked it could have destroyed the Samburu, as their environment is so dry and unpredictable. But they refused to do as the British demanded. In 1961, some of the chiefs appointed by the government started trying to enforce the grazing plans. The elders came together and issued a collective curse on them and their families. A few days later one of the chiefs told his sons to take his cattle to the Ndoto Mountains. The moment they reached the foothills, an avalanche engulfed them, obliterating both the herders and their beasts. The grazing plans immediately came to an end. So, largely through good fortune, the Samburu had survived until Independence and beyond remarkably unscathed. But, as I sat on the slopes of the holy mountain, I knew that the forces of change in East Africa were now more potent than they had ever been before.

From Ol Doinyo Nyiro we travelled south, towards the black Ndoto Mountains, where the chief cursed for collaboration lost his cattle and his sons. The Land Rover bumped along a red track over monotonous miles of saltbush. A black-backed jackal crossed the track ahead of us and turned to watch us pass. Otherwise I saw no sign of life.

After twenty miles we came to a group of windblown huts, right in the middle of this desolate land. We pulled up alongside and got out. At first I thought it was deserted. The only sound was the creak of the wind in the dry fabric of the houses. The corral, where cattle had once been kept, was littered with grey bones. But a hurried scraping noise made me turn round, and I saw a thin, dirty child crawling out of one of the huts. He straightened up and ran, dodging away through the grey scrub.

I waited for several minutes, wandering around the wretched encampment. I found a couple of hearths, a few chips of metal and several faded cows' skulls, their crania split open by men or hyenas. The inhabitants must have been desperately poor, for their houses were open to the wind: the other camps we had passed in Samburu district, even if they had no cattle to provide hides or dung for plaster, could get hold of plastic sheets or pieces of beaten tin. The clouds that now filled the sky promised, to my eyes, no rain; they served only to make the scene more desolate, as if the people who lived there were trapped between the hard grey clouds and the rough steel sheet of their defeated land. I heard a voice and looked around: the child had returned with a grim-faced, bony woman. She walked slowly across the camp to meet me.

Ntalon was, she explained, one of the Nkunono, the abominated blacksmith clan of the Samburu. Among many of the nomads of Kenya, indeed among tribes of herders or farmers throughout Africa, blacksmiths are said to be polluted. They have supernatural powers, which are normally considered malevolent. As a result they are isolated from the other people of their tribe. The Nkunono, for example, are only allowed to marry within their own clan, reinforcing their ritual pollution: such marriages, the Samburu say, are incestuous. Their curse is potent and ineluctable. They can cause a wound inflicted with iron to fester, or bring about the death of a child circumcised with an iron razor. Anyone of another clan who steps over an Nkunono's forge will break his legs.

160

Fascinatingly, archaeological evidence suggests that black-smiths in Europe may also have been isolated, both physically and culturally, from the remainder of their tribes. Throughout European mythology, blacksmiths are portrayed as malevolent forces. Hephaestus, the lame smith-god of the Greeks, is repre-sented in northern Europe by Wayland, the divine but evil smith tutored by the trolls and maimed and imprisoned by a legendary king. Throughout the continent his unquiet wight is said to haunt his 'smithies', which are typically Neolithic burial mounds. In the fens of eastern England he re-emerges as the ghastly Will-o'-the-Wisp, the vengeful blacksmith spirit embodied in the flickering blue flame of burning marsh gas. There are stories of smiths entering into a pact with the Devil to get fire and the means of forging metal; indeed it is arguable that the medieval vision of Hell represents the smith in his forge. The anti-Christian associations persisted into the nine-teenth century, when British couples who could not get the Church to bless their marriage would leap over a blacksmith's forge together, symbolically passing through the transforming flames. In some parts of Britain, the introduction of iron tools was resisted for centuries, as farmers believed that the evil they contained would poison the soil.

It is conceivable that blacksmiths, throughout Africa and Europe, tried to preserve the exclusivity of their skills by claiming supernatural powers. These could easily have been translated by outsiders into evil powers. As the skills of the smiths gave them the key to both military and material pro-gress – weapons and iron implements – other members of their tribes would have been at pains to prevent their becoming dominant. Ostracism, justified by their association with evil powers, may have been the most effective means. Where people failed to contain their metal workers, the results are clear. In some of the pre-European kingdoms around Lake Victoria, the symbol of monarchy was the anvil: the smiths had become kings.

But here among the Samburu, the power of the blacksmiths had been effectively limited, and their only means of survival was to trade the iron weapons, implements and jewellery they made with other people of their tribe. As a result, Ntalon and her clan could be seen as a barometer of the fortunes of the Samburu, as their prosperity depended not on the vagaries of weather and luck that affected an individual herder, but on the well-being of the tribe as a whole.

I asked Ntalon to make me a metal bracelet, so she wandered off to find a friend to help her. She returned with a woman as tall and shrivelled as herself, and the two of them set to work. The friend blew up a fire on one of the hearths with a pair of bellows made from goat hides, while Ntalon cut strips from a battered aluminium saucepan and melted them over the glowing charcoal in a tin can. She poured out the metal, let it harden, then hammered it flat on a piece of railway track. She cross-hatched one side of it with a flattened nail, then beat it into a circle to fit my wrist.

As she worked, Ntalon explained that the women of the clan concentrated on making jewellery, while the men forged iron knives and spears. Her husband would exchange a spear for a sheep or a calf. He had built up a good herd before the drought, but now nobody came. Almost all the cows in Baragoi division (the western part of Samburu district) had died or been stolen. There were not enough sheep or goats for trading. The Samburu were now selling their weapons to tourists – in an effort to make a little money to buy grain – and buying no replacements. Ntalon's own cattle had died of starvation: the bones in the corral were all that was left of them.

People had survived, she told me, by digging tubers from the ground, eating the pods of acacia trees, finishing their stores of meat and dried milk, taking turns to slaughter their goats and share the meat. Food relief had arrived just in time: without it, she said, she and everyone she knew would have starved to death. Without help she could not see how the Samburu would ever pick themselves up from this disaster and rebuild their herds: there were simply no animals left from which to breed. None of the previous droughts in Samburu district had had such devastating consequences, for both here in Baragoi division and further to the east the Samburu had been kept out of the best grazing lands. While the nomads' story of the loss of their land and the decline of their herds was becoming horribly familiar to me, here in Samburu district it was peculiarly unpleasant.

Archer's Post is a dull, windy town in the middle of a barren plain. It consists of a dozen tiny shops and perhaps one hundred shacks of tin and cement, planted wherever local officials could be bribed to give away a plot. No one here appears to be at ease. The owners of the shops and bars are people of settled tribes – Kikuyu, Kamba, Luo – who have become migrants, taking their commercial skills to wherever they can most profitably be used. They would spend a year or two in Archer's Post then move on to the next commercial frontier. The rest of the population is composed of nomads who have become sedentary, yet who have few means of keeping themselves alive in the town. As no tribe is at home here, no tribe makes its mark: traditional culture has been abandoned and despised, yet the sophistication of larger cities is far out of reach. To many of the people of Archer's Post, the height of elegance is getting drunk in a tin shack.

Not everyone in Archer's Post had abandoned himself to dissipation. In a long low house close to the mission hospital, I found my friend Alois, a tall, fine-boned, very dark Samburu man, with a neat, round head and a wide mouth, from which the lower incisors had been ritually removed. Working in a college in Dublin, he had confounded the farmers of County Wicklow by turning up on their doorsteps and announcing that he had come to study them. While this work had been of limited application in Samburu district, his travels among his own people had afforded him an unparalleled knowledge of Samburu herding patterns. He told me that if we wanted to see what was happening to the nomads, we should visit the village of Nakwamor, a few miles from Archer's Post, and speak to the elders there.

Though Archer's Post was dull and Ntalon's community desolate, Nakwamor came as close as any place could to making them look prosperous and entertaining. Subdued by starvation, the people there were neither welcoming nor hostile. They simply ignored us. Old men sat on stools outside their tattered houses, staring at the horizon or scratching the dust with their sticks, without speaking. I tried several times to start a conversation, but received no more acknowledgement than a shifting of the stare from the horizon to myself, a brief nod, then reversion to the horizon. Even the moran were listless. The only attention I received was from three little girls, who surrounded the hearth at which I sat and said, '*Jambo, jambo, jambo*', like a dripping tap. After an hour I felt oppressed and irritable. I wandered around the village. There was nothing to watch but two pygmy falcons, fighting to the death beneath a tree. Having lost most of their animals, all the inhabitants could do was to sit and wait for the drought to lift.

Only when one of the women of the village had cooked the maize and beans we had brought, and everyone there had eaten, were people inclined to talk. Nakwamor, they told me, had been hit so hard by the drought because the dry and stony land they occupied was surrounded on all sides by mortal danger. If they left it to graze their animals, either they or their herds could be killed. To the east and north-east, Somali raiders were encroaching on their lands. They were well-armed and hungry, and the Samburu had little chance of defending their herds if they drove them there. To the north and west the army was using their lands for artillery and bombing practice and tactical exercises: several Samburu herdboys had been killed by unexploded bombs. To the south were the forbidden lands of the Shaba National Reserve where a herder had been shot dead by rangers four years before. They had been left with the least fertile of their lands, where no grass grew even during the wet season. To see what they had lost, I travelled first to the reserve, and the Sarova Shaba Hotel in its centre, which could just be seen from Nakwamor.

Like many of the safari lodges in Kenya, the Sarova Shaba Hotel is built of raw rock and is heavily thatched. It seemed to me that the whole foreign experience of Africa had been compressed into one building, and rendered exotic enough to be exciting to tourists, while familiar enough not to be frightening. Reed mats and wooden gods hung from pillars of knotted wood. A spring of pure water bubbled up outside the lobby, sank beneath its floor of broken rock and emerged on the other side in a series of little waterfalls and pools, in which cichlids fanned their fins beneath the pads of waterlilies. The bedrooms surrounded a vast swimming pool, with a covered bridge and rocky promontories. Beside it a sunken bar sold cocktails called 'Wild Elephant' and 'Born Free'.

I was reminded that it was in this reserve that Joy Adamson was murdered, after she had set up a tented camp to carry out what she called a 'conservation project', but which was actually the rehabilitation of her pet leopard. She angered and alienated local people, whom she described as 'squatters'; renamed most of the features of the land after her pet; treated her servants with a racist brutality which would have raised eyebrows even in South Africa; and made herself unpopular with so many people that the murder enquiry was delayed for months by a surfeit of suspects. Yet, thanks to her own unblushing accounts of her work, she remains, in the imagination of thousands of people, a heroine, struggling in isolation against the forces of darkness, single-handedly protecting Kenya's wildlife from its people.

I walked up to the restaurant, where large Europeans sat at tables set with white cloths and silver, eating steaks and slabs of fish, drinking European wine. From the restaurant balcony, through the jacaranda trees, I could see the broken houses of Nakwamor, and a starving elder standing, still as a pole, in the dust beneath a tree. The spring on which the hotel had been built, now used to fill the swimming pool and the ponds in which the cichlids swam, had been the local Samburu's watering-hole. Not only had they lost the good grazing lands of the Shaba reserve, but they and their herds now had to drink from the Ewaso Ngiro River. Coming down from the young rocks of the Kenyan Highlands, this river is at times little more than liquid mud. It is turbid in the wet season and diseased in the dry. Now, as the upper reaches were being diverted for irrigation, there was a real danger that it would dry up altogether. The spring provided the region's only pure water.

When we left the Shaba reserve we travelled north, to the savannahs being used for military training and live firing. The people of Nakwamor had told me that the first Samburu children to be killed there had picked up unexploded shells or thrown stones at them. Now they had been taught to keep away; but they could still be blown to pieces if one of their animals stumbled against one. The danger was such that the remaining herders seldom took their cattle there, even though these were their best remaining grazing grounds.

I had discovered that two armies were training in Samburu district: the Kenyans and the British. British regiments visited the area three times a year, set up camp for six or seven weeks and fired live ammunition at cardboard men and vehicles. A few days before my arrival the Coldstream Guards had moved in, so we drove out to meet them, to ask whether or not they were responsible for the munitions the Samburu claimed had been left scattered around the pastures. Beside the track through the savannahs tramped rectangular, self-assured white men with jug ears and crew cuts, dressed in desert camouflage and carrying rifles and radios. They waved and raised their thumbs as we passed. When we stopped to talk to one of the patrols, the soldiers complained of the heat, the food and the camp, but morosely admitted they were having a good time.

As we approached the compound, a helicopter skimmed over our Land Rover and landed ahead of us, raising a tornado of noise and dust. From the activity inside the camp one might have guessed that the Russians were coming. Field ambulances, troop transporters and water lorries trundled in and out; men ran around with messages; the radio buzzed and crackled in the control tent. I had been apprehensive about how we might be received, and had imagined some furious sergeant-major with waxed moustaches barking us out of his camp. But the commanding officer was a slim, refined man in spectacles, brisk but courteous. He was happy to show us around the compound and introduce us to some of the men.

They stood in vests around vast pots of bubbling mince or beans; adjusted the guy ropes of some of the hundreds of green tents; stacked up the scowling cardboard soldiers they would later shoot down; cleaned their weapons or unloaded boxes of fireworks from the lorries. They were well fed, friendly, humorous men, who threw themselves wholeheartedly into their tasks. As I wandered around, it struck me that they believed utterly in what they were doing. The cardboard soldiers lying on top of each other in boxes would, the next day, become real enemies flipping up from the scrub to ambush them; the fireworks would become, in the field, the machine-gun fire they simulated. I found myself briefly envious of their security.

The captain explained that his 550 men came here because it was the world's best available training area for the firing of live ammunition. It was open enough for large-scale movements, but scrubby enough to keep the enemy hidden and the troops on their toes. He claimed to have made a deal with the local people: they had agreed to keep out of the region for six or seven weeks and in return the Royal Engineers training with his men would build dams for them. He said he was scrupulous in accounting for every live shell his men fired: the debris was picked up and unexploded ammunition was sapped.

By contrast, he said, what he had seen of the Kenyan operations suggested that their soldiers manoeuvred with little regard to their own safety or anyone else's. On two occasions his troops had almost been forced to engage, as trigger-happy Kenyan tank commanders had pursued them, firing shells. Live Kenyan ammunition littered the countryside and was a hazard to his men as well as to local people. He resented having to send out his sappers to dispose of other people's shells.

In Archer's Post I checked his story with some of the Samburu people I knew. They told me that they had, indeed, agreed to keep out of the land used by the British during their operations. They were not altogether happy with this, but saw that there was little choice, and the dams the Engineers built were welcome. While they did not know whose bombs and shells were killing their herders, the fact that the Kenyan army had neither consulted them nor compensated them for the use of their land led them to suspect that it might be similarly negligent about cleaning up. The Kenyan army had also taken over land in the south of Samburu district, both for training and for dumping old munitions. Some were detonated, others were left unexploded in the pastures.

I was told that if I tried to reach the Kenyan army training grounds I would be arrested as a spy and thrown out of the country. The army, always resentful of criticism, was now especially jumpy, with the elections just a few weeks away. So I waited until I was back in Britain, several months later, before I sent a request for information to the Kenyan High Commissioner. He sent me the following reply:

> During and after live firing, the troops make every effort to search for misfired munitions and when found are destroyed or taken away. Local residents are pre-warned of the dangers of fiddling with any objects resembling munitions and that they should make a report to local authorities whenever a sighting is made. The Armed Forces who are very mindful of the safety of local residents would swiftly take appropriate measures. Regrettably in the past there has been a case or two when local residents have not reported a sighting of misfired munition and have assigned themselves the responsibility of disposing of such ordnance thus resulting in serious accidents.

The results of the Samburu's exclusion from much of their land, by bandits, conservation and the army, were plain to see. Along the road between Archer's Post and Isiolo, we came across what seemed to be a line of old sacks or discarded clothes. Stepping out of the Land Rover, I was almost overwhelmed by the rich smell of carrion and the ammoniacal odour of maggots. The old sacks were dead cattle, dumped by the road when they had starved to death. They were little more than skin stretched over a casket of bone. I thought this might have been partly the result of emaciation after death; but soon afterwards I saw animals still tottering around which had scarcely more substance. Everyone's cattle were dying of starvation, and all the people could hope for was food relief. But even here their representatives had let them down.

There was a famine relief store in Archer's Post, a square

shed with a corrugated iron roof and padlock on the door. When, after months of denials and delays, the government had finally allowed 5000 sacks of donated grain to arrive at Archer's Post, the civil servants there received a mysterious instruction not to distribute it. The local MP then told the people of Archer's Post that the authorities, despite his best efforts, were refusing to distribute the grain. As their MP, he said, he would do everything he could to get the store opened and the food handed out to them, and he hoped they would remember his efforts during the approaching elections. Several weeks after the grain arrived, he invited the press to Archer's Post. When the television cameras were rolling, he ordered the officials to break open the lock and hand out the food to the victims of bureaucracy. When the doors swung open, the Samburu saw that of the 5000 sacks only 200 were left; the civil servants had taken the opportunity to steal the rest.

All over Samburu district, the people's lands and resources were being snatched by anyone who had political power, big money or good contacts. Much of the Leroghi Plateau, the most fertile part of their territory, had been ploughed by an Italian company for wheat. Government chiefs, councillors and army commanders were helping themselves to the Samburu's drought reserves: the river valleys and the oases which had remained green despite four years without rain. But, in the west of the district, the most immediate cause of famine was not the loss of land but the loss of cattle. For the first time in their recent history, the Samburu had suffered from what had been afflicting the Turkana for several years: raiding by the people of the Pokot tribe.

Travelling around the savannahs on my return to Baragoi division, it struck me that I had not seen a single cow there. I set off in search of one, and the quest took an entire day. There were a few sheep and goats and one or two camels, but, with the exception of a herd of five or six I came across in the evening, all I saw of the cattle was bones and hoof prints. Outside the tiny villages and empty corrals sat bored and sullen herders, dull-eyed and speechless, scarcely bothering to flick away the flies. They reminded me of snails which, when the weather is too hot and dry, withdraw into themselves, sealing up the entrance to their shells.

But in Baragoi I met an old man named Loglai, who hobbled round to the back of my hotel to meet me, and sat down with a sigh which sounded like the air leaving a punctured tyre. He looked, indeed, as if he had deflated, for deep folds of sagging skin hung from his face and arms. He spoke with a soft, thin voice and abstraction in his eyes: watching him, it seemed that he was talking about another place and another age.

Until eleven o'clock on the night of 15 August 1992, Loglai was the owner of 305 cattle, and considered himself a prosperous man. He was woken by gunfire, and stumbled out into his compound to see unfamiliar men in shorts and dirty tee-shirts rushing round his house with AK-47s. He ran indoors and grabbed his spear, but when he came out again the raiders and his cattle had gone. Everything that had made his life meaningful disappeared with the Pokot.

They had come, on that dark night, not just to Loglai's house but to nearly all the compounds in the west of the district. There were hundreds, possibly thousands of them, and all of them had automatic weapons. They had taken the Samburu entirely by surprise since, for several years, the people of the west had had no tribal enemies. The Somalis and Boran were too far away to bother them. Any Turkana who might have been hostile had been driven away from their borders by the Pokot. The Pokot themselves had buried a spear with them several years before as a token of peace. The Samburu, needing no military defence, were content to arm themselves only with spears.

But the Pokot had exhausted what the Turkana had to offer them. They had driven the Turkana herders so far north that it was no longer worthwhile to raid them: most of their cattle had died when they reached the drought zones. Now the government ministers who were reputedly paying the Pokot to raid were getting frustrated: their supplies of cattle and hence of money from the Kenya Meat Commission were drying up. In August, when a government chief in a Pokot district gave (by his own admission) his customary blessing to what he thought would be another raid of the Turkana, the bandits turned east instead, to the richer hunting grounds of Samburu.

The Samburu of the west had possessed 100,000 cattle before the drought. Four years without rain had reduced this number to 25,000. Systematically working around the region over the course of two days and one night, the raiders swept up all but the last 10,000. As they drove away the 15,000 head of booty, the bandits were overflown by two army helicopters. Whether these served to monitor or to assist them, the Samburu did not know. They certainly did nothing to intervene. Nor did the thousands of soldiers in the district – who had so enthusiastically been shooting shells at each other for the strategic good of the country – do anything to hinder the Pokot for the strategic good of the Samburu.

The Samburu complained to the government and the government, characteristically, told them it would do everything it could. It claimed to have instructed the Pokot to give back the cattle within ten days; but when the ten days had passed and no cattle were forthcoming (hardly surprisingly, as they had already visited the KMC's abattoirs), nothing happened. In four years the Samburu had been brought to their knees. In two days they had been crushed flat.

'When the cattle were taken away,' Loglai told me, 'my life went with them. I am not a man any more. I can't return to my home. How can I face my children when I have nothing to give them?

'I've been wandering around here, looking for my cattle. I know they're not here. But what else is there to do? I'll go to Pokot. If I find just one of my cows then my life will mean something. If I don't, I don't know what I will do. The only option is to wander around, looking for my cattle.'

'How will your family survive without them?'

'They're dependent on famine relief. If it doesn't come they will go to bed without food.'

In the village of Marti, to the south of Baragoi, we watched several hundred Samburu men and women squatting on the rocks outside a padlocked shed, holding babies and empty sacks. A Landcruiser arrived and three Samburu men jumped out and unlocked the shed. It was filled with sacks of grain, labelled 'USA Wheat. Not to be sold or exchanged'. The men carried out some of the sacks, opened them, checked a figure with a calculator and called out a name. A woman left the rocks, wandered over and opened her empty bag; the men in charge filled it with the prescribed amount, gave her three packets of cooking oil and called the next name. For more than an hour the Samburu came forward one by one, were given 6.5 kilos of grain and half-a-litre of oil for every family member, and walked away. It was quiet, orderly and fast, and about as far as I could have conceived from the desperate scenes I had seen on television, when people clamoured and fought around the back of a food relief truck. Designed in a hurry, run entirely by local people, Oxfam's system in Baragoi division was being studied by other charities and foreign governments, as it was probably the most efficient food distribution in Africa.

If a famine relief programme loses thirty per cent of its food it is considered efficient. Many lose eighty per cent, some lose everything they are given. But the Samburu distributors had lost only two per cent of the grain they received, probably as a result of spillage and the odd sack being snatched from the back of a lorry by a quick-witted thief. Despite the complete collapse of their economy, not a single Samburu was known to have died of starvation in Baragoi division. The contrast to the government's efforts in Archer's Post could hardly have been greater.

Rosemary Benzina, the Samburu woman in charge of the distribution, said that she and the Oxfam staff there had been reluctant to get involved in famine relief. They were development, not relief, workers and had no training for this sort of emergency. For them, food relief was not a solution but a desperate measure, which should only be applied when there was no other means of helping people to keep themselves alive. They had trained local people in new veterinary techniques and set up a network of food stores selling maize at reasonable prices. They had tried to get a better deal for Samburu women, helping them, in particular, to resist exploitation by middlemen and to get fair prices for their milk and hides. Under normal circumstances, development of this sort would have helped the Samburu to survive, despite all the disastrous changes that had been introduced to the savannahs. But as the cattle started to die, as food disappeared from the shops through exhaustion or hoarding by merchants, and the prices of maize exploded, they saw that none of these strategies could hold back the impending famine. When the Pokot came, the crisis turned into a catastrophe.

The Oxfam workers set up a relief committee to work out what needed to be done. They lobbied the government to ask the World Food Programme for grain, pushing and pushing until the Office of the President at last conceded there was a problem. The government would not accept their estimates of the numbers affected, so they were forced to register the whole population of the division, something officials had not done for years. They found there were far more people than either the government or they themselves had estimated, but still the government refused to accept that nearly everyone needed help.

The register was the key to Oxfam's success. They could use the list to make sure that everyone received his or her due and that no one came twice. The workers built distribution points all over Baragoi division, so that the handouts would not draw people away from their homes. Because of a mix-up between the World Food Programme, private charities and the Kenyan government, and because food relief which should have gone to the starving instead went to prosperous people in President Moi's home region, no fat or protein arrived in the division. So Oxfam spent £100,000 of its own money on cooking oil for the Samburu, as grain alone could not keep them alive.

Despite the ferocious efficiency with which Rosemary and the other staff worked, it was, she told me, not Oxfam but the other Samburu who had done most to keep the starving from slipping away. Before the food relief arrived, people who were down to their last few animals gave what they could to those who had nothing, and in some cases the eventual victims of the famine were not the first people to have lost their stock but the people they called on for help. The Samburu proverb 'Only the hyena eats alone' suggests that humans who do not share their food are no better than disgusting animals. People must keep their hungry guests alive even if they have to go hungry themselves.

Rosemary disliked food relief because it carried the danger, if badly handled, of undermining people's mutual reliance. It was, of course, no substitute for sorting out their fundamental problems. While their land continued to disappear and while the Pokot could raid them with impunity, no amount of donated grain could ensure the survival of the Samburu. Foreign nations which, through conservation, wheat schemes or sales of arms, contribute to the decline of the nomads, have little cause to congratulate themselves when they save them from starvation with donated grain.

In Baragoi, at night, the main street surged with shouting, jostling Samburu. The local MP, Peter Lengees, was standing on the raised verandah of a shop with fists full of money, handing it out to anyone who got close enough. The dreadlocks of the moran and shaven heads of the Samburu women shone in the paraffin lamps, the women's bodies ghosted through the tumult in translucent robes. There was supposed to have been a vote that day to select the ruling party's candidate and therefore – as no opposition was tolerated in Baragoi – the next MP. Mr Lengees had been confident of winning, but his officials made the mistake of announcing the result before the votes were cast. The constituents had then refused to vote and the election was postponed until the following day. Now he was working hard to regain his popularity.

When he had used up all the money in his briefcase, Mr Lengees moved to the Morning Star Hotel and sat in a huddle with local businessmen and councillors, speaking in whispers. Other men in safari suits surreptitiously edged their chairs nearer and nearer to his group, all the time looking the other way but leaning back to hear what was being said.

Mr Lengees's attempt to save the population the trouble of voting had upset the people of Baragoi. His term in office had been marked by the collapse of the telephone lines, the failure of the water supply, the continued absence of electricity and sewerage and the abuse of civilians by soldiers and police. Though glad to take advantage of his sudden munificence, the people were demanding that next day's ballot should be secret and that the MP should stop bussing-in unregistered voters from other constituencies.

The following morning the townspeople re-assembled in a field overlooking the empty river. Mr Lengees had agreed that only registered constituents should be allowed to vote, but he had insisted that there should be not a secret ballot but a queuing system. The voters should line up behind their chosen candidate in full view of several hundred onlookers and police. The literate townspeople kept away, standing behind the patrolling policemen at the top of the field. The only people voting were Samburu in traditional dress. The election was delayed by three hours, as the voters drifted in from the savannahs, by which time the only candidate not to have left for Nairobi to complain about the voting system was Mr Lengees. The tribespeople dutifully lined up behind him and, after a cursory and entirely superfluous count, he was pronounced the winning candidate.

There was one more place I wanted to visit in Samburu district, to see what was happening, not to the local people, but to the Turkana who were coming in to join them, after the government had failed to do anything about the famine in their district. They had walked for up to two weeks to reach Samburu, and those who survived the journey had been arriving in the village of Nachola, about ten miles west of Baragoi.

We travelled to Nachola in the back of a grain lorry Oxfam had commissioned. As we drove, I noticed something I had not seen since we had arrived in Samburu district: a thunderhead on the horizon. I craned over the top of the cab and saw another and, behind it, as if lining up to take its turn, another. The wind began to rise, and the first cloud swept towards us like a vast and darkening destroying angel. As it rushed across the sun, its shadow smoothed out the wrinkles of the land. The truck drove into the famine relief centre, and for a moment everything was hushed. Then, as Ledumen, the prophet of the holy mountain had predicted, the rain began to fall. It rustled as it approached the lorry, slapping down the dust, catching and pinning the dead leaves that leapt up ahead of it. The men with me in the back of the truck watched it racing towards them, and I saw that one of them was crying. They did not move. With their eyes closed and their faces lifted to the heavens, they let the water rush over them. For a minute or two afterwards all that could be heard was the dripping of the bare acacia trees. Then the men jumped down from the truck, shouting and whistling, and started pulling out the sacks of wheat.

From under the dripping eaves of the storeroom and the school the Turkana came out. I have never seen a group of people as close to death as these fugitives were. They shuffled across the stony ground on legs like braided rope, with knots for knees and ankles. Children as frail and silent as baby rabbits – they tried to cry but when they opened their mouths they made no sound – lolled from breasts that had shrunk to no more than nipples set in pads of skin. The women and men shuffled over the wet ground and squatted, their hands over their eyes, the knots of skin drawn tight in their cheeks. An old man with cataracts tottered blindly among the sitting people, twisting his head to the sky to catch what was being said. His legs buckled. On all fours, groping with hands and feet, he found a place to sit. In silence they waited for the grain distribution to begin.

These people had stayed in their own lands for as long as they could, watching their animals and then their relatives fade and die on the shrivelled pastures. They had kept themselves alive on berries and roots. When these ran out, they realized that they had no choice but to travel east, towards the distribution points in Samburu district. The only route was across the Suguta Valley, the hottest and driest place in Kenya, a one-hundred-mile gorge of cactus and broken rock where no rain had fallen for seven years. There were no wells, no rivers, no dams. They loaded their donkeys with water for a walk which only the Turkana could have survived.

Most of the people I tried to speak to simply shook their heads and said nothing; but after several attempts I found someone who could tell me about her journey. She was a shrivelled woman, wrinkled more by famine than by age, who had arrived in Nachola the previous day.

'We walked for ten days and ten nights, without food,' she told me. 'At first we could drink a little water in the morning and in the evening; but after a few days the donkeys died. After that there was no water. People began to die. All along the valley we passed dead bodies, and I thought that I would soon be lying there too, for other people to pass. It was God who led me out of there.

'We came because of hunger. There was no food where we came from. We saw our children dying one by one. When my own child died I couldn't stay any longer.' She leant back and sighed. 'Starvation is worse than anything else on earth.'

Two thousand six hundred Turkana had arrived in Samburu district, and still they came. Even as we sat in Nachola I saw a ragged group stumbling out of the west: three women and a man, black stick figures against the grey hills. One of the women fell, the others stopped to pull her up and they carried on moving towards us. I tried to imagine what these people had seen and felt, but my mind went blank. They had walked through the valley of the shadow of death and emerged as little more than ghosts.

Pillar after pillar of rain now swept across the land, and the refugees staggered to their feet and huddled once more under the eaves of the houses, where the water roared like falling gravel on the roofs. Amid the tumult, after the stumbling and the despair, the Turkana found the strength to sing.

When the rain stopped we drove back to Baragoi, across a land now sparkling with trapped water and sudden streams. Passing through the saltbush, their hides burning white and ginger in the new sun, were the flocks of the Samburu herders, whose soothsayers had urged them to return to the plains of Baragoi. As we drove I watched a rainbow slowly materialize above them. It arched from the western hills to the mountains in the east, the palette for the bright new colours now glowing on the plains. The Lord had set his bow in the heavens, but it carried no promises: for the famine to destroy all flesh was the work not of God but of man.

CHAPTER EIGHT

Bandit Country

There is a place in the red semi-deserts of north-eastern Kenya where the wells are so numerous and so deep that, the nomads say, 10,000 camels can drink together and be sated. These wells have for so long been important to the wildlife of the region that, even though they are now in the midst of a town and surrounded by roads and houses, giraffes still boldly stalk along the streets, past the pick-ups and the donkey carts, ignoring the bustle of men and women, and gather with the camels around the water, towering over them like construction cranes above a knot of shaggy houses.

But these wells, and the town of Wajir which surrounds them, are the focus for more than just thirsty animals. Over the last ten years they have been the scene of a series of beatings, restrictions and massacres, which at times has amounted to something approaching an attempt at extermination. For the Somali nomads who pass through here are seen by some people in the government as little more than wandering vermin, to be snuffed out, like the Gypsies of Europe or the Kurds of Iraq, before they infect the rest of the country with their evil ways. While other nomads in Kenya may find their lands or their animals coveted, the Somalis know that there are men in Nairobi who want their lives. In 1980 G. G. Kariuki, the Kenyan Minister of State for Internal Security, stated, according to the papers, 'The only good Somali is a dead one.'

The Somalis are hated because they are successful. While the British stopped the other nomads of Kenya in their tracks, confining them to particular districts, keeping them out of the way of other people, the Somalis kept moving. Moving south, they entered the lands now known as Kenya in the second half of the nineteenth century. On horseback, armed with swords and poisoned arrows, they met little resistance. Today they seem to have reached the limit of their expansion. In the south they roam along the coast near Lamu; in the west they are pressing on the borders of the Boran and Samburu territories. Overall, they cover about one-fifth of Kenya. They are still regarded as a threat by other nomads, by settled farmers and by the government. But this alone does not account for their unpopularity.

Throughout Kenya the nomads deeply resented the restrictions that the British and Kenyan governments imposed on them. They resisted by whatever means seemed most effective. The Turkana skirmished and, for a while, won themselves a degree of independence from the Empire. The Maasai, almost destroyed by smallpox and rinderpest, used passive resistance, agreeing to everything the British demanded, then simply failing to do it. The Samburu cursed their collaborators. But the Kenyan Somalis, supported by Somalia, launched a full-scale war. They had campaigned, before Independence, for their lands to be joined to Somalia. There, they believed (without, as it turned out, much justification), their nomadic traditions, their religion and culture would be respected. For a while it seemed that the British were inclined to wash their hands of them and grant them what they wanted: the lands they occupied were, after all, of no use to anyone but nomads. But as men in suits in smoky rooms in London made their final decisions about the lines on the map of Africa, it became clear to the Kenyan Somalis that they were still to be governed by settled peoples who resented and misunderstood them. They armed themselves and took to the bush.

They fought the Kenyan government for three years, with astonishing success. A few thousand men, armed only with old rifles, but with a consummate knowledge of the terrain, managed to fight the army to a standstill. At a conference in Tanzania in 1967, Somalia and Kenya agreed to resolve their differences. The Kenyan Somalis agreed to return to their herds and live peacefully. But they were never forgiven. They had humiliated the Independent government from the moment it took power. In February 1993 we travelled to Wajir, to find out more about a particular massacre, about what appeared to be active discrimination against the Somalis and about allegations of officially sanctioned banditry in their lands.

In most Kenyan cities the expensive houses are of brick and plaster, with tiled roofs. The paupers' shacks are made of corrugated iron, flattened refuse, wattle and daub and thatch. But in Wajir the big houses have flat roofs, and are plastered yellow, white or pink, and the huts are tiny tepees of woven mats on a frame of sticks. The men are dressed in sarongs and loose turbans. The women wear long robes which swirl round their ankles and keffiyehs on their heads, but no veils. Arab music drifts out of the kiosks selling milk, dates, tea and the narcotic stems of the *miraa* plant. Apart from the District Commissioner's Land Rover, a few beaten-up jeeps and a fleet of white pick-ups owned by UNICEF and the other aid agencies that have camped in the town, the only vehicles are donkey carts. Chickens scuttle around one's feet but there are no dogs. It seemed to me, wandering around this isolated city, that I was not in Kenya at all but somewhere on the Arabian peninsula.

Among the women I saw were some who would have captivated the critics at any fashion show. They were tall, straight and slim, and walked with self-possession, lightness and an inaccessible grace. They had high foreheads, large eyes with long lashes, slim wrists and ankles, small jaws, prominent teeth and soft curly hair. Many of the men were also graceful and lithe, with full beards, large, expressive eyes and fine noses, but the delicacy of the Somali figure seemed to suit the women better.

There are as many different theories about where the Somalis came from as there are regions in which they could possibly have arisen. Somalis I have spoken to variously claim that the land of their forebears was Egypt, Yemen, Palestine, Persia, Pakistan, the Philippines and, according to one erudite and insistent man, Great Britain. Anthropologists argue about whether they came from Ethiopia, Eritrea or Djibouti. In truth, like every people, they probably came from many different places, mixed with each other and assimilated other tribes on their travels. While the features I have described are common, they are by no means universal: some Somalis I saw could have passed for European Gypsies; others for central Africans.

I walked to the wells and found there not ten thousand but a few dozen camels, some threadbare donkeys and a group of mangy cows. It was now February, and the drought which had afflicted all of northern Kenya had come to a spectacular end two months before, with storms of the sort I had seen in Samburu district in every part of the country but the central Turkana lands. Around Wajir the grass had grown, died and faded, and the air had again become still, dry and chokingly hot. But, however much rain fell, it would take the Somalis years to rebuild the herds they had lost through drought and banditry.

I watched a young woman drawing water, the faint wind from the savannahs ruffling her long robes, nuzzled by the donkeys and goats crowding a dry trough. She looked away and smiled in embarrassment when I spoke to her, but her movements were not constrained by self-consciousness. She dropped the bucket and hauled it up again with smooth strokes. Her long round arms were marred only by a broad shiny scar on her shoulder, which looked like the bite of a lion. Except that her pitcher was a plastic jerrycan, she could have been one of the figures engraved in my old leather Bible: Rebekah before the servant of Abraham.

At another well, two old men were watering their camels. They were bare-chested, with shaven skulls and pointed beards, lean and unsmiling, watching us askance. They filled their trough swiftly and suspiciously, stopping suddenly to scan the sparse bush beyond the houses, darting glances at anyone approaching or leaving the wells. In his belt each man wore a short dagger in a sheath. Bound to their arms were strings of leather pouches containing Qur'anic prayers, each one marking a period of sickness. Their feet were as hard and gnarled as roots. The friend accompanying us told Adrian to put away his cameras: people had been stoned at the wells for less. The two men, with a last swift glare at us, the houses and the trees, untied their camels and led them away at a trot, glanced to the left and right, then slipped into the bush.

At night I watched the giraffes stride in, past the radio mast and the Bush House restaurant, to finish what water the domestic stock had left in the troughs. In a borrowed car, we drove out to meet someone on the edge of town and, returning, saw a vast male giraffe standing beside the road, waiting for us to pass. We drew up underneath it: we were so close that all I could see was a wall of crazy paving. Adrian snapped his fingers. The giraffe bent down and gazed at us through the windscreen with puzzlement in its eyes, then slowly backed away, skirted the car and walked on.

In the shade of a windbreak of sacks and green branches, Daudi, an old man with bright eyes and gentle movements, sat barefoot on a palm mat in the middle of the day, surrounded by his family. Spots of sunlight, which had slipped through the windbreak, bounced across the mat when the wind blew. Daudi's grandchildren crawled around his feet or tugged at his sarong to try to get him to play with them. He told me why he had gone to war with the government.

Before their spheres of interest in East Africa were any more than uncertain shadows on a questionable map, the British and Italian governments divided them along lines of latitude and longitude. In 1891 the Kenyan–Somali frontier was established, running straight through the lands of the Somali people. Even to those Somalis who had heard of the country to which they were supposed to belong, the lines were at first of no significance: the nomads moved according to their clan boundaries, and paid no heed to what the colonists said. When, decades later, officials started trying to change their lives, they did their best to ignore them.

As Independence approached the Somalis became uneasy. There were rumours, some of them well-founded, that the Independent Kenyan government would try to take their lands and distribute the wettest places to farmers. Already there had been confiscations of animals in the name of grazing control. A survey among the inhabitants of the north-east showed that the majority wanted their lands to be joined to Somalia. But the British declared that the people were too ill-educated to decide for themselves, and the region would have to remain part of Kenya. In 1963 several thousand Kenyan Somalis, as well as nomads of the Rendille and Boran tribes, travelled to Somalia to pick up guns. For Daudi there was simply no other way of resolving his people's differences with the government.

'We were herders and they were farmers. They didn't respect our traditions. They told us "You have no land. The land belongs to Kenya". They took our animals and never gave them back. We never wanted to be part of Kenya. Our culture and way of life are totally different. We are different people and we just wanted to be left alone. The Kenyans never understood us.

'I went to Somalia and got a gun and fought all the way to Marsabit. I fought for three years. It was very hard, but we had will and courage and good tactics. They had lorries and heavy armour, but we would ambush their convoys on foot. We gave them no time to get out of their lorries. Many times we destroyed them. I cannot count the number of men I killed, but they were many. They also killed many of us.'

When the fighting came to an end, the rebels were pardoned and went back to their families. But, Daudi claimed, the government still showed no signs of understanding the Somalis and their needs.

'When we came out of the bush, our names were already with the government, with Special Branch. So we surrendered our arms and told them we wanted to be peaceful citizens. And so we are. But the problem is still there. The government appointed people to govern us who were not of our background and culture. They have disrupted our lives.'

He leant across, picked up one of his grandchildren and bounced her on his knee. He put her down and she crawled away across the mat, chasing a dancing leaf.

'These men, these farmers, they have all the money in Kenya. They cannot understand our problems. How can a satisfied man know what it means to be hungry?'

As I travelled around the town of Wajir, holding a series of quiet meetings with Somalis, it became clear that the people and the government had still not overcome their differences. I heard of several cases of killings, beatings, mass punishments and government-approved discrimination. But by far the worst of these allegations concerned the events at an airstrip a few miles from the town, in February 1984.

At the wells in Wajir I met Abdullahi, a stooped and wheezing old man with a sucked-in mouth, who was watering his two goats. He agreed to come and talk to me. In the compound of a friend's house, when the onlookers had drifted away, I asked Abdullahi what had happened to him. He had been walking his herd out to the pastures, he told me, when an army truck pulled up beside him as if to get directions. He was asked if he were a member of the Degodia clan. He said he was. He was told to step round to the back of the truck. Two soldiers seized him and pulled him in. There he found several other men of his clan, none of whom had any idea of what was happening.

'They drove us out to the Wagalla airstrip. When we got there I saw there were thousands of men inside a wire fence. We were told to take off our clothes and lie on the sand. We were not allowed to get up. We lay there for three days and three nights. We were given no water or food. A water tanker came up to the fence and the soldiers drank from it. We watched them spilling the water over the ground. But we were allowed none.

'I drank my own urine. Some people died of thirst. The soldiers poured petrol on the ground, and many people were overcome by the fumes. On the third day we could stand it no longer, and some of the men made a run for the fence. The soldiers opened fire. Anyone on his feet was shot, as well as many people still lying on the ground. They killed hundreds. I was hit again and again with the butt of a gun. My ribs were broken and I lost all my teeth.'

Abdullahi opened his mouth, and I saw that his gums were as bare as the beak of a tortoise.

'I was convinced I would die. But I never lost consciousness. I lay there and pretended I was dead. An Italian missionary came and picked me up and brought me back to town in her car. It was thanks to her that I survived. Most died.

Eleven of my relatives died there, including my brothers and some of my cousins.'

In 1984 some of the men of the Degodia and Ajuran clans had been quarrelling over water and grazing rights. The problem was not a serious one, but at the beginning of February several people of the Ajuran were found murdered in the bush. No one knew whether the culprits were bandits, other Ajuran or their enemies among the Degodia, but the authorities decided that the Somalis were becoming wayward once more and needed to be taught a lesson. No one knows where the order came from to round up the Degodia men and take them to the airstrip or whether or not the soldiers were authorized to kill their captives, but the cruelty with which they were treated suggested that old scores were being settled. The people I met felt that the government had found the excuse it needed to exact a belated mass punishment for the civil war.

When the men of the Degodia clan had been rounded up and taken to the airstrip, their houses were burnt. The women and children fled; in some villages those that were caught were beaten and raped. Old and disabled people who could not get out of their huts in time were burnt to death. No one knows how many people, in the villages or at the airstrip, were killed, for people were rounded up from all over the district; but the number seems to have been at least 1200 and was possibly as high as 3000. On the outskirts of Wajir I met a Somali man who, like the Italian missionary, had seen the army trucks moving to and from the Wagalla airstrip and on the third day had driven out there with a friend to see what was happening. He bluffed his way through the army roadblock and got to the fence.

'The airstrip was surrounded by police and soldiers. They were the only people with clothes on. Naked men lay on the sand, some alive, some dead, some dying of wounds or dehydration. There were piles of bodies, where the soldiers had started clearing up.

'The soldiers chased us off, so we drove into the bush and started picking up people who had managed to escape while the soldiers were shooting. They were in a terrible state. Some died in the car on the way to hospital.

'When we got back to Wajir, we heard that the army had loaded some of the survivors and the dead at the airstrip into lorries and taken them in different directions for sixty or seventy kilometres. We couldn't get through the roadblocks, so we drove through the bush, looking for them. The first people we found were dead. We tried to revive the survivors with water, but many of them died where they were. Some were covered in burns, as the men's clothes had been used to try to burn them alive. It was the most terrible thing I have ever seen.

'The following night, as we were returning from another search for survivors, we saw a military convoy, travelling north. It was dark, and all we could see were men sitting on top of the lorries wearing masks. As the lorries passed us I smelt the most terrible smell. We discovered later that they were carrying away the remaining dead bodies to dispose of them in the bush. We found one of these places a few days later. The corpses had just been dumped near the road. We buried fifty of them, then we gave up. We couldn't carry on.'

The Kenyan government denied that any abuses of human rights had taken place. It announced that fifty-eight people had been killed in the cross-fire during a fight with bandits. Local officials were transferred; most have since been promoted. The District Commissioner told the people who complained to him that if they did not like it they should go to Somalia, as they were not wanted in Wajir. The government has consistently refused to discuss the possibility of compensating the families of the dead.

The Somalis I spoke to still feel persecuted. Unlike any other Kenyan citizens, they are required to carry two cards: their Kenyan identity card and another one, issued by the Special Somali Registration Unit. Its purpose, the government says, is to screen out illegal aliens, as Somalis continue to cross the lines the colonial powers drew across the map, either as migrating herders or as refugees. But the people of the north-east see it as a means of identifying them as potential enemies of the state. If Somalis try to leave or re-enter the country by air, they are taken into a room at Nairobi's Kenyatta Airport and interrogated, sometimes for two or three hours.

*

Banditry in the pastures of Wajir district had now become so bad that many people had crowded into villages close to the defended towns. This, of course, was disastrous for nomadic people trying to rebuild their herds after a drought: packed together in a tiny corner of the land, the nomads' animals continued to go hungry. Clearly, though, whatever lay beyond the pale of the district's towns was worse than what lay within. To find out from the fugitives what they were escaping, we left Wajir for the nearby village of El Adow, just half an hour's drive away.

The whole village was built of the little thatched tepees I had seen in Wajir: sticks covered by heavy mats woven from dried grass or the fibrous leaves of the doum tree. Unlike the huts of the other nomads I had visited, these are transportable. The mats are loaded on to camels or donkeys, making a saddle which cushions the animal's back when the family's possessions are piled on top. When we arrived, women with swift fingers and shrill voices were weaving more of these mats under a tree: the murmur of conversation would surge into keening laughter or the high-pitched shouts of a mock quarrel. They fell silent when I came forward to introduce myself and became absorbed in their work, so I left them alone and their gossip resumed.

I had been told, before we travelled to El Adow, that we would be looked after by the local headmaster, so when we arrived I wandered around the village asking where he was. I was told he was away for a while, but that I could wait outside the school for him. I was led to a tiny tin shed, of the sort used for storing garden tools, which had 'Headmaster's Office' stencilled on the door. Outside the Kenyan flag flew from a tall pole. In the shade of a tree which overhung the hut the sand had been trampled flat, and the brake drum of a lorry hung from one of the branches. Otherwise there was nothing to suggest that this was a school in anything but name. I sat on the sand beneath the tree and waited.

After half an hour the most extraordinary-looking man arrived. He paced with long, jerky strides around the beaten sand in front of me, muttering into his beard, then sat down a few yards away, chewing his moustache and talking to himself. He wore a check shirt, clean buff trousers and open-toed sandals. Behind his glasses, which were tilted at a crazy angle across his face, were enormous bulging eyes. When he reached, in deep, guttural Somali, what seemed to be the critical points in the monologue with which he was entertaining his beard, his eyes rolled up, showing the whites, and he struck the air with his hand. I watched him, dumbfounded for a few seconds, then cleared my throat. He started, looked round, pushed his glasses up his nose and double took.

'Goodness gracious, my dear sir, I had no idea.'

I introduced myself and apologized for startling him.

'Sir, apologies must be on my part. Please, allow me to introduce myself. I am Mohammed Koriow, the headmaster of this establishment. Indeed, sir, I am privileged to be the only master.'

He swept his hand magnificently towards his office. 'Any time is tea time. Would you care to partake of some?'

I said I would be delighted. I sat down on the mattress Mohammed pulled out of his office, while he found one of his pupils and sent him off to brew some tea. He returned and sat down beside me.

'I sincerely hope that this tea will be of satisfaction to you. We are accustomed to it here, but it may not be greatly to your taste.'

I assured him that I looked forward to it.

'Thank you, my dear sir. After all, what is sauce for the goose is sauce for the gander.'

I wondered if he had ever seen a goose.

As soon as we had taken our tea, Mohammed leapt up and once more began pacing up and down the trodden sand, chewing his moustache, muttering, rolling his eyes and waving his arms around. After several turns around the arena, he spun on his heel and stopped in front of me. 'You will observe sir, that I am in a state of some disquiet.'

I admitted that I had noticed it.

'I am suffering from the withdrawal of my customary narcotic, sir, and this tends to induce the most uncomfortable

189

effects. For the second time this week the miraa plane is late.'

Miraa, the plant stems chewed throughout the Somali regions, but grown only in the wet highlands of Kenya, Somalia and the Yemen, contains amphetamines and is said by many Somalis to be the lifeblood of their land. Just as Andean Indians chew coca, many Somalis chew miraa to keep them going on their travels across the desert. Mohammed told me that when the miraa did not arrive he became restless and sexually inactive.

'But when it comes, then, goodness gracious sir, I become a carnivore, an animal.'

I was not convinced that I wanted to witness this. But a few minutes later a boy came running across the desert with a bundle of newspaper. Mohammed gave him some money and opened the bundle: it was full of thin red stems, like miniature rhubarb. Though his hands were trembling, he paused and elaborately offered it to me. Then, pinching a couple of stems as if taking snuff, he placed them delicately in his mouth. The change was extraordinary. As soon as he began to chew, his face relaxed, his eyes settled down, he stopped twitching. The miraa did nothing for me. It broke up into pithy fragments in my mouth, tasted bitter and made my tongue dry. Mohammed said it had to be taken several times before its effects could be felt.

We sat talking about his school for a few minutes, then he leapt up. I imagined, for an alarming moment, that he was about to start pacing again. But instead he strode to his hut and opened the door. 'My dear sir, you will excuse me, but we are just in time to catch that excellent refrain, the Lillibullero.'

He brought out a short-wave radio and for the next hour, nodding his head and tapping his foot with approval, listened to the BBC's Newshour. When it finished he sighed, as if some beautiful music had just come to an end, shook his head and turned off the radio. Then he returned to his hut and brought out a piece of sacking. A few minutes later, two other men arrived, also holding bits of sack. They washed, then laid out their rags on the ground. Barefooted, they stood with their palms raised to the sky while Mohammed recited a prayer.

Then, muttering, they bowed, knelt on the sacking, and touched their foreheads to the ground.

They prayed for twenty minutes, bowing and lightly chanting in Arabic, grave, absorbed and dignified. It seemed to me that Islam lived in Wajir district in a way that Christianity has ceased to live in Europe. Here, in the drylands, where women still walked in long robes to the wells and men drove their animals beneath an overarching sky, this nomad's creed had no need to be forced: it spilt, it seemed, from those men's lips, as if the desert itself were speaking. It appeared to me that Christianity, the religion of settled nomads, of the fugitive and the persecuted in the parched Middle East, might never have been truly understood in Western Europe, among the farms and cities of that cold, wet, colonizing corner of the world. Without an overriding principal stretching across our lands like the bleached desert sky, we are, for all our protestations, Godless. Our houses of God have become little more than shrines to a forgotten place and time we have, in all but name, forgotten, separated by a labyrinth of houses, fields and fences.

When he had prayed, Mohammed explained to me that the Somalis are Sunni Moslems, and are respected throughout the Arab world for their devotion. Although he had not made the great pilgrimage, he was sometimes addressed as 'Hadjow' – he who has completed the *Hadj* to Mecca – as a mark of respect for his dedication to God. He told me that Islam had been terribly misunderstood by the Western world. The Qur'an, he said, taught that everyone should be treated as a brother, that the poor should be cared for, that peace must be sought above all things. The Moslems who were fighting each other, in Somalia, and lately in the Gulf States, were doing so in defiance of the Qur'an, and God was punishing them with calamities. Allah, he told me, was everywhere, and neglected no one who came to Him with a clean heart, turned up his hands to Heaven and asked Him to answer his prayers. He was a forgiving God, a just God and a peaceful God. The rise of fundamentalism and the intolerance we perceived were, he claimed, partly the result of attempts to impose foreign systems upon Moslems, and to introduce them to the consumer culture they knew was ungodly.

In Wajir I had met a Somali woman, Aisha Ahmed, who was using the Qur'an to teach other women that they were entitled to education, to inheritance and to democratic rights, that they did not have to wear veils and should not be married without their consent. These rights and many others, she told me, were enshrined in the Qur'an: when the men ignored them they did so on cultural grounds and not, as they claimed, religious ones. Her teachings made the men of Wajir furious, as the Qur'an, whose learning they had monopolized, was now being justly used against them: they could see that their excessive power over the women was ill-founded. Aisha told me that though it is true that Somali men are generally sexist and demanding, often beat their wives and give them the most arduous and demeaning tasks, Somali women are no worse off than most other Kenyan women, who are ill-treated everywhere. In some respects they are more fortunate, she said, as there are formal councils and an Islamic court to which they can appeal if they are treated badly.

As the sun went down, crowned plovers started swooping and yelping over the dried grass around the village. Miles away, across the savannah, moving down the tracks converging on El Adow, were clouds of red dust. Long before they arrived I heard the clatter of bells and the hoarse cries of sheep and goats calling to their offspring in the village pens. A full moon rose behind the doum palms, and a fork-tailed drongo sang from a tree above Mohammed's office. In the moonlight, Mohammed and his friends laid out their mats once more and prayed, accompanied by the music of the settling goats, the clink of slow bells and water buckets, and the long fluid unburdening of the drongo.

The moon was so bright that the birds sang all night. They were joined in their clamour by the bellowing of donkeys: stallions on heat, chasing each other back and forth around the village. At dawn I felt fingers massaging my scalp and started awake. No one was there. I leapt up with a shout and a toad fell out of my hair and hopped under the office. Women were leaving their huts with pails and jerrycans; I could hear the creak of the hand-pump and the murmur of prayers. An old man sat beneath the rising sun with a prayer board and recited his devotions in the dry worn voice with which the wind rustled over the desert.

When Mohammed had prayed and taken tea, he struck the brake drum hanging from the tree with a metal stick: it rang like a clear bell. Scores of children soon appeared, carrying their exercise books in plastic bags. They lined up and said their prayers, then divided around a partition of sticks. Mohammed taught the first class for a few minutes, told the children to recite something, darted round the fence, taught the second class for a few minutes, set an exercise, then, his glasses slipping down his nose, papers flying in his wake, dashed back to the first class. He kept up this exhausting routine all morning: I was beginning to see why he needed his miraa. As the heat rose I walked out into the savannahs.

February is the hottest time of the year in Wajir. The heat of mid-morning compressed the sounds of the village and laid them out flat on the savannahs. Around El Adow the land glared orange, trampled bare by animals and human feet. Beyond it were meadows of combed peroxide grass. I wandered through a grove of twisted trees, whose exposed roots were polished by the hooves of village livestock, and startled some yellow-billed hornbills and a couple of dikdik antelopes. In the blue-green shade in the middle of the grove I came across two men with their herds, talking in angry whispers and waving their sticks.

El Adow had been founded during the famine of 1984. That year had been a bad one throughout northern Kenya, but in Wajir district the effects of the drought were exacerbated by the absence of many of the elders and herders of the slaughtered Degodia clan, whose dependants now turned to others for survival. Abdur, an old man whose herd had been reduced to a few sheep and goats, settled here by himself, as he needed to be close to the markets and the food relief in Wajir. For thirty days he had dug through rock with a pickaxe, until, at twenty-five feet, he found water. Other people began to settle around his well; by 1991 there were seventy-five families in the village. The drought, the banditry and the gathering troubles in Somalia began to drive people out of the bush. By the time we arrived there refugees both from Somalia and the remote parts of Wajir district had swollen the population to 275 households.

No one will be surprised to learn that tens of thousands of people had fled across the border from Somalia. Everyone has seen the bones of that country, laid bare on television by the vicious anarchy with which the cruel dictatorship of Siad Barre was replaced. Siad Barre had governed his country by setting one clan against another. The Soviet Union and the United States, in turn, had helped him by stuffing the country's armouries with the most lethal modern weapons. When Siad Barre left, the conflicts between the clans he had helped to provoke exploded and, with the help of the weapons so generously supplied by Somalia's absent friends, they started to massacre each other. For many people in the country, the only possibility of remaining alive was to flee across the border to Kenya.

While this is scarcely remarkable, what is, perhaps, more surprising is the extent to which the Kenyan government is responsible for the continuing massacres and pillage on both sides of the border. The government is deeply implicated in the banditry destroying both the innocent fugitives of the terror in Somalia and the nomads born and brought up in Kenya. In crossing the wild lands to get to El Adow, some of the refugees I met had passed through horrors as frightful as those reported by the journalists in Mogadishu.

Fatuma Mohammed was a tiny old woman, as shrivelled as a mummy, who lived in a thorn shelter beside Mohammed's office. She had the voice of a lost seabird, and unhappy lines carved into the skin around her mouth. Slowly, sentence by sentence, prompted by Mohammed or me when she faltered and stopped, she told me her story. She and her husband had lived in Lower Juba Province, with their five children and a large herd. Over the years they had suffered several prolonged droughts, but, as there were good dry season pastures, they had survived them all. When Somalia fell apart, the grazing lands they had used became too dangerous to visit. When drought struck, their herds collapsed. Fatuma's husband died, followed by three of her children. With her remaining two sons, she drove her few animals across the border into Kenya.

Fatuma had imagined that she would have to travel for no more than a fortnight before she reached Wajir or another town where famine relief might be available: she knew the towns were not far away, and thought she could walk straight to them. But as soon as she crossed the border she found that the land was crawling with bandits. She had to skirt the best grazing lands, the wells which might have kept her animals alive, the direct paths that led to safety. In the worst areas she hid in the scrub by day and travelled only at night. Twice she saw men with automatic weapons stalk past the bushes where she and her animals had hidden: she knew that if she were seen she would be killed. She walked for thirty days. Three weeks after leaving Somalia, one of her two remaining sons died. One day before she reached El Adow, her last child was bitten by a snake and died within an hour. She did not break down. Propelled by anger, grief and fear, she almost ran the final, hazardous leg of the journey, driving her one remaining animal, an old camel she had suckled by hand when it was orphaned many years before. At El Adow the camel staggered to the well, drank, keeled over and died on the spot. Fatuma collapsed. She cried for two days. Even now, two months after her arrival, she cried herself to sleep every night.

Others in El Adow had suffered more directly from banditry: they had been held up in the savannahs and forced to hand over their animals and possessions, or had fled while their relatives were shot. The bandits were everywhere. Wajir and the surrounding villages were effectively under siege. All roads into the district were closed: even army convoys were now being attacked. Most of the shops in Wajir were empty; schools had closed because the teachers had been unable to return from their holidays; the only food reaching the district was being flown in by the aid agencies in troop transporters. El Adow was safe partly because the bandits were cowardly and seldom visited places where they might be engaged by troops or home guards, and partly because it simply had nothing to offer them. Bandits had raided it a year ago, tied up the inhabitants, driven away their four cows, stolen the village store's cash box and, outside the village, prised it open, only to discover that there was nothing inside. Now, if they came at all, it was only for a drink of water. But, though there were many kinds of bandits in Wajir district, it was becoming clear to the Somalis that not all of them were ordinary civilians who found it easier to make a living from the pack and prime trails than from herding.

It was true that automatic rifles could be bought for as little as two goats on the Somali border (a cash value of around £10), so that banditry was a business in which almost anyone could invest. But all over Wajir district one name cropped up again and again: Morgan. General Mohammed Siad Hersi Morgan, Siad Barre's son-in-law, was one of the warlords squabbling over Somalia's corpse. According to local people, his headquarters were now in the Kenyan town of Garissa, where he was building up his armed strength before launching attacks on his rivals in Somalia. He raised funds for his campaign from two sources: the Kenyan government and, through banditry, the people of the north-east.

President Moi, apparently finding in Siad Barre a soul mate, had supported the dictator during the last years of his murderous regime. When Siad Barre fled he was housed, at the government's expense, in the best suite of Nairobi's Norfolk Hotel for three months. Morgan, bereft of his benefactor, might well have perished, were it not for the help he received from the Kenyan army. Morgan's position suited the government well. He had no power base in Somalia, so he would do as the Kenyans told him. If he came to power he would remain little more than a Kenyan puppet. If, some observers speculated, President Moi lost his election and found himself with no option but to rely on armed force to retain power, Morgan would come to his assistance. The Kenyan army assassinated Morgan's nearest rival in the region, trained and re-armed his men and escorted them to the Somali border. Supported by Kenyan helicopters and convoys, Morgan launched his re-invasion.

Despite massacring thousands of Somalis, he strangely failed to win much popular support in Somalia. He continued to rely upon Kenya for weapons and sanctuary. He was allowed to come and go as he pleased and to use whatever means he chose to raise revenue. Kenyan district officers began to complain that the guns Morgan had been given by the army were being employed to shoot the Kenyan policemen guarding the food convoys. So at the end of 1992 the government stopped supplying Morgan with weapons, but continued to provide him with fuel. This seems to have made the situation worse. Still mobile, still unregulated, but worried about their arms supply, Morgan's troops now redoubled their attacks on Kenyan police and soldiers, to steal both the merchandise they were guarding and their guns.

The freedom with which Morgan operated in Wajir district was catastrophic for the nomads. His soldiers stole everything they could lay hands on and killed anyone they caught. All the best grazing lands were too dangerous to visit: the herders were confined to the over-used pastures around the settlements. No rain had fallen in Wajir district in 1990 or 1991. The heavy rains at the end of 1992, far from bringing immediate relief to the nomads, had killed many of their animals: weakened by famine and disease, they had contracted pneumonia when they got wet. Now the Somalis desperately needed to return to their best grazing lands to start rebuilding their herds, but Morgan and his rabble made this impossible.

Instead, the fugitives had been relying first upon the local people and, later, when the charities moved in, upon foreign aid. Mohammed and the other people of El Adow were alarmed and a little suspicious when the refugees started converging on their village. Their own herds were already weakened by the drought: they were worried that the pastures round the village would become even more degraded and that the extra people might attract bandits to the village. But, as Mohammed explained, they realized that the immigrants had no other means of survival. As Moslems and Somalis they were to be welcomed. Anyone who rejected them was a man without honour.

The villagers formed a relief committee – Mohammed was the secretary – and set up, at their own expense, a feeding centre for people who could not look after themselves. They dug new wells for the refugees and Mohammed wrote to the government requesting food aid. The reply he received claimed that the government had no fuel for its vehicles; if the villagers sent some money for petrol to the undersigned, he might be able to help. This, Mohammed told me, was 'the work of a blackguard'. When at last Oxfam, World Vision and the African Moslem Agency turned up, the government chiefs tried to elbow them aside and take over the food distribution themselves. The local people believed that they wanted to take charge solely in order to loot the supplies. They successfully beseeched the charities not to yield to the chiefs' demands.

Though the foreign charities were now well-established in El Adow and the other settlements, the malnutrition rate was rising again. There had been epidemics of measles; now a new strain of malaria, that began with a mild headache and ended in death within twelve hours, was killing scores of people around Wajir: El Adow was the only village I visited where there were no fresh graves. But, alarmingly, the government was now planning to repatriate all the refugees in northern Kenya, even though it was clear that many had no safe homes to return to. The justification was that the Somali immigrants were engaged in banditry.

The sheep came back across the savannahs, bleating to their lambs inside the corrals. The women knelt on the ground to milk them. The hand-pump wheezed and namaqua doves fluttered down to drink the water that spilt from the pitchers. The drongo that lived in Mohammed's tree chased a pied crow out of the village and away across the desert. His lessons ended, Mohammed blew his whistle and lowered the Kenyan flag outside his office. It came down with the day, on a land laid waste by its government.

CHAPTER NINE

Moses
in the Wilderness

Woe to the bloody city! it is all full of lies and robbery; the prey departeth not.

Nahum 3:1

On the steps of the Alakara Hotel in Kitale, a city in Kenya's north-western highlands, was a short, plump, red-faced white man with brown hair and blue eyes. I was a little suspicious of other mzungus in Kenya and, perhaps through some strange inverted racism, kept away from them. Having been brought up, like me, not to talk to strangers, other white people seemed also to keep their distance. Whenever I met a European in Africa, we tended to circle each other warily, like jealous dogs, and pass on without speaking. What mzungus miss by such evasions, at home or abroad, I do not know, but wherever I travel I am reminded that Europeans, myself included, are perhaps the most anti-social of all the world's people. So when he came down the steps towards me, said 'Hello' and stuck out his hand, I knew that he was either a remarkable man or a lunatic.

He had a Glasgow accent and he was sweating. When he told me that he was working on a project to help Turkana street children, I unloaded my bags and sat down in the hotel restaurant to listen to the first instalment of a story which, over the course of three days, we slowly pieced together. Until the age of twenty-three, Brian Nugent had belonged to a Glaswegian razor gang working in Manchester. He spent his youth extracting protection money and beating people up, with occasional brutal spells in jail. It was in Strangeways Prison's Top Security Wing that he converted to Christianity, and vowed to spend the rest of his life atoning for the sins of his youth. Now, at fifty, he was an elder of the Church of Scotland, with a degree in English Literature and Medieval History from the University of Glasgow. He was direct, alarmingly honest, with old-fashioned courtesies and a tough, hard-bitten humility which I found appealing. He ran a junk shop in the Gorbals, where he spent his spare hours counselling local people who had fallen on hard times. But it was here, just where I had encountered him, on the steps of the Alakara Hotel, that his life had taken another dramatic turn.

Having turned his junk shop into a profitable business, he had taken a holiday in northern Kenya, eighteen months before I met him. He had travelled up the eastern side of Lake Turkana and into Marsabit, crossing the drylands of the Gabbra and Boran. On the way back to Nairobi, he had stopped for a night in Kitale. He had been unable to sleep, and at two o'clock in the morning had wandered out onto the steps. He was amazed to see that the streets were full of children, running around, playing, fighting, crying. He asked the night-watchman whose children these were.

'No one's,' the man replied.

'Where do they live?'

'Nowhere.'

He was astonished: some of those children were as young as three and four. He could not believe that no one was looking after them. The following day he visited one of Kitale's churches and spoke to the vicar and the lay workers. He was told that nothing was being done for these children because no one had any money to spend on them. Brian took out the remainder of his holiday money and the stack of notes he had put by to spend on sapphires and, on the spot, started the Kitale Orphans Trust. Perhaps God really was looking over his shoulder, because the people he gave it to were as determined and as incorruptible as himself. Within a week, a project had begun to feed and clothe the children and treat their diseases. Now, eighteen months later, those who were not too brutalized or too disruptive were being offered the chance of education, skills training and a home. Brian returned to Kitale every six months to see how the project was going. In Scotland he now spent all his spare time raising money for it. His junk shop was neglected, his social life had evaporated, but he was an entirely happy man.

For the nomads of East Africa who lose either their lands or their animals, there is only one place to go: the cities. When traditional life comes to an end, only a few of the local people have the means to stay in the savannahs. The commercial ranches need just a handful of herders. The wheat farms bring nearly all their labour in from the agricultural areas. Even the parks and reserves can each employ only a few hundred people. Nomadic herding is the only reliable livelihood for the three or four million people who live in the Kenyan savannahs.

In the cities there are only jobs for people with qualifications and connections, and then only for some. But, where so many people are crammed together, without the resources to be self-sufficient, and where the poor walk beside the stupendously rich, there are, for those wily and swift enough to seize them, other opportunities. For those who can reach a car before the owner gets out and offer to guard it, for those who know where to find waste paper and to whom they should sell it, for those sharp and persistent enough to make a margin by polishing shoes, for people sufficiently charming or deformed to beg, pretty enough to sell their bodies, fast and daring enough to steal, there is a living to be scraped from the streets. These under-employed scavengers are the trash people of East Africa, filling its corrugated iron dustbins, treated by the rich, the police and the government like the rubbish in which they live and on which they have to survive. But while, in the countryside, they would have starved to death, in the cities there is just enough to keep them and their families alive. It is this which draws the dispossessed nomads out of the savannahs.

Although Kitale is 150 miles from Turkana district, wet, cold, 6000 feet above sea level, and in an entirely different social and ecological zone, as many as 10,000 Turkana have made their homes there. Nearly all of them lost their herds

201

through raiding and were faced with no future in Turkana district but death by starvation. They walked, stowed away on trucks, or used all the money they possessed to buy a seat on a bus, travelling to where life could be sustained at the most appalling cost.

Most of the Turkana children in Kitale lived in the slums with their parents or aunts and uncles. Their houses were Turkana huts made of sticks and polythene, cardboard, beaten-out tins and sacking. On arriving in Kitale, some of these children found that their parents had changed completely. Having lost their animals, their land, their pride and their identity, they now drank (when they could afford it) maize beer and methanol spiked with petrol. They robbed, gambled, fought, burnt down each other's houses and beat their sons and daughters whenever they could catch them. But at least these children had homes, and some of them were even lucky enough to go to school.

But there were 120 Turkana boys and girls in Kitale who had no homes. Some had travelled to the cities with their families and had since lost their mothers and fathers, through disease, fights or imprisonment. Others had been sent away from Turkana district by their starving parents, who did not have the money to move the whole family, but realized that the only chance any of them had was to get on a bus to another region. Some of those men and women had since died, others had lost touch with their children. There were other boys and girls – just a few – who found conditions in the Turkana slums in Kitale so frightful that they preferred to live apart from their parents.

The next day Brian took us to meet the children with whom the project was working. We walked down broad avenues, shaded by eucalyptus trees and brightened by flags and triumphal arches of painted metal. Here, behind steel grilles, were shop windows crammed with televisions and hi-fis, suits and silk dresses, footballs, bicycles and imported fruit. There was a new Barclays Bank, gleaming with ceramic tiles and polished wood, into which strolled prosperous men and women with briefcases and handbags. Mercedes and

Landcruisers jolted along the bumpy streets. A squadron of men in blue and red Securicor uniforms paraded up and down in front of their offices to the music of a brass band. Men hanging out of the backs of minibuses, painted with the trademarks 'Injury Time', 'Last Warning' or 'The Vulture is a Patient Bird', waved and whistled to us.

We walked through the gates of the big plaster-fronted market built by the British into a tumult of bright colours, delightful and nauseating smells, shouting and laughter. Here, big women with white teeth and pink tongues, in wrap-arounds of blue and purple, yellow and black, green and orange, jostled, haggled, slapped hands and gossiped. On the wooden stalls were piles of bananas, mangoes, pineapples, papayas, coconuts, oranges, watermelons, plums, carrots, coriander, turnips, cabbages and tomatoes. Among the fruit sellers and the shoppers were Kikuyus, Luhyas, Nandi and Bukusu, but most of them were Pokot. Dispossessed by Pokot raiding, the Turkana had been forced to flee to a city within their enemies' land, as this was the only one they could afford to reach. The hatred with which they were regarded appeared to have compounded their dissipation.

As we walked down through the market, the atmosphere of busy prosperity began to thin. By the time we reached the bottom, the crowds, the clamour of voices, the piles of fruit and the clink and rustle of money had given way to lines of empty stalls, a rubbish heap that smelt of vomit, black sludge and barbed wire. It was here that the destitute children, who came out onto the streets at night, hid and tried to sleep by day.

The project workers had already arrived, and some of the children had woken up and come out from under the raised floor of the market to see them, to play and to gamble. In front of us was what seemed to be the entire human experience, compressed and miniaturized in a tiny arena of mud and broken wood. Twenty or thirty boys and girls sat on the ground or wandered about. When we arrived the older boys, eleven- and twelve-year-olds, were helping the younger children to dress or giving them piggybacks; one even trimmed another's hair. A moment later the same boys caught sight of a five-year-old who had found half a loaf of bread. He ran off, but they cornered him against a stall, snatched the bread from his hands, then knocked him down and kicked him while he curled up into a ball, wailing and screaming. Just as suddenly, they left him alone and sat down to eat the bread. He got to his feet and was picked up and hugged by a girl of twelve.

A huddle of nine- or ten-year-olds squatted on the ground with little piles of coins they had begged and took turns to throw down four white maize seeds, calling their bets, snapping their fingers and hissing through their teeth. Depending on whether the seeds fell shoot-up or shoot-down their piles of coins would rise and fall. One boy seemed to be winning most of the money. As I watched, he threw down the seeds and snatched up the pile of bets the moment they landed. Someone shouted 'Cheat!' and all the other boys landed on top of him, pummelling and kicking him, and snatched his money. He staggered up, smiling and calling names. A few children had drifted over to the stinking rubbish heap where they picked through mango skins, rotting fruit, pieces of chewed sugar cane, dead rats and chicken feathers for anything worth eating. If they found something they put it straight into their mouths, before anyone else could take it from them. Leaning against a swaying barbed-wire fence, a seven-year-old sniffed petrol from a plastic bag.

They were filthy, ragged, scabrous children, with shiny scars and dull circles of ringworm on their heads, boisterous, energetic and clever. They ranged from two years old to fourteen, and the highest authority they knew was the boy with the hardest fists. Some of the younger ones were sweet and trusting; but I soon saw that the brilliant, engaging smiles of the others were no innocent charms, but part of their survival kit. Their lives depended upon the generosity of passers-by and the restraint of the police.

Brian introduced me to Daniel Juma, the lay worker in charge of the project. I shook his hand and was immediately captivated. He had been crippled by childhood polio. His back was bunched up and twisted, his broken chest rose and fell visibly when he breathed. He was no more than four feet tall and his head looked almost too big for his body to support. Yet there was something about him so still, so gently authoritative, that I would, without questioning, have done whatever he asked. I watched with astonishment as he quietly called out a name or beckoned to someone, and the mean, brutalized boys would stop what they were doing, come over to him and ask if they could help. Daniel not only walked in comfort through that lions' den: he had the lions on their backs with their paws in the air.

Daniel told me that the purpose of his project was ostensibly to clothe, feed and eventually educate the children, but what they really needed was love and attention. They needed to feel that not everyone in the world hated them, that there were some people who wanted them to prosper. Some of the older boys had been on the streets too long. They were defensive, violent and careless of their own lives and other people's. It was almost impossible to reach them. But the younger children responded with pitiful elation to the slightest attention, clinging to Daniel's hands and Brian's legs. If they were spoken to, they would grin with embarrassed delight, twisting one leg around the other, with lowered heads, flashing white teeth and bright, raised eyes.

I peered under the floor of the market, where the children slept. The wooden planks were raised about two feet off the ground. When my eyes had become accustomed to the darkness, I saw that much of the intervening space was filled with flies. On the black mud, littered with the fruit skins and offal which had fallen through the slats, lay the dirty rags on which some of the children slept. Daniel said that there had been a rat hunt the previous week: they had flushed seven hundred from under the market floor.

Daniel's task that morning was to treat the children for scabies. Several of them were covered in small dark bumps. Some of them had scratched themselves until they bled, and in places their skin was stretched shiny by pus. Scabies is caused by tiny mites which burrow under the skin and can only be cured by smearing the body with a mild poison. Daniel and Brian explained to the children what they intended to do and why, recruited a couple of girls to help, and got them to undress, wash and spread the lotion over their bodies. Their clothes were taken and thrown into a pit latrine to prevent other children from putting them on. The boys and girls were given new clothes which Brian had bought with money from Scotland. They were delighted with the change, and ran around afterwards, jumping in the air and laughing.

Brian told me that disease was one of the children's biggest problems. They were not used to the wet and the cold of Kitale, and had arrived from Turkana district with the clothes they wore in the desert. Some of them had lung infections, almost all of them had diarrhoea. One boy, of about nine years old, caught every disease the other children contracted and could not put on weight. Brian suspected he had AIDS. One little girl had a wide red gash on her calf. She had been attacked by a mad woman who lived around the market, who had struck her with a machete. Had she not been treated she would certainly have died of septicaemia.

As they worked, Daniel and Brian told me how the children survived. In the streets lay all their opportunities and all their perils. They raided the litter bins, begged, picked pockets and stole food from the stalls. The older girls sold their bodies. They hung around the fish-and-chip shops with pitiful faces, crying 'Chippies, please, give me chippies' until the customers softened and bought them a bag of chips, which they fell upon like wolves. Though the older children often beat the younger ones, they also fed them, and the two- and three-year-olds I had seen were looked after by the teenage girls as if they were their own.

Talking to people in Kitale, I discovered that the police hated the children. They were, they believed, the criminals of the future. They disfigured the streets and gave the city a bad name. They could be beaten up or imprisoned without consequence, and they were treated with all the viciousness that frustrated provincial officials could muster. The town council had promised for years to do something for them but had produced nothing but fine words. Any money set aside by the Social Services Department had long since disappeared into the pockets of local civil servants. These officials, I was told, detested the work the project was doing, as it showed up their own deficiencies. They took every opportunity to disrupt it.

Daniel had built a bare wooden shack just outside the market in which some of the children slept. But now that Brian had raised more money they would be able to rent a proper house on the outskirts of town, to accommodate the children who wanted to leave the streets. They would sponsor them through school and teach them carpentry, dressmaking, farming and animal husbandry. There was little chance that any of them could return to Turkana district so they had to find a way of supporting themselves in Kitale. Some of the children were overjoyed at the prospect of going to school; others preferred to remain on the streets. Once a day the project workers would cook a meal for all the children who came to them, and every few months they could give them a change of clothes.

The education and security offered by the Trust was the best hope these children had, their only possibility of a future other than theft, vagrancy, prostitution and early death. What it could not do, of course, was to solve the fundamental problems from which they and the rest of their tribe were suffering. It would try to pick up the pieces of their lives when they arrived in Kitale, but, while the raiding and the government's neglect of the Turkana's needs persisted, they would continue to come.

I spoke to John Kisitu, the ten-year-old who had been beaten up for cheating. He had only been in Kitale for four months, but he was already streetwise, charming, self-possessed and possibly beyond recall. He was loud and aggressive and shrugged off attempts to get close to him. But he was lucid when he told me about his life. He spoke excellent English and Swahili, as well as snatches of some of the local languages. He learnt fast and, I later found, had become one of the most successful of the beggars and gamblers. With his alacrity and adaptability he could, given the opportunity, have made a success of his life. As it was, he would almost certainly live and die without raising his head above the gutter.

He told me that he had been sent to Kitale by his parents

when their cattle had been stolen by the Pokot. He had climbed into the back of a lorry and hidden under some empty sacks. When he arrived in the town he slipped out and ran away before the lorry driver could catch him. He had an uncle living close by and sought him out, but the uncle had no home and was too poor to look after him. As he spoke, I watched John's face. It was rigid, clamped shut, as if to prevent anything that might be interpreted as gentleness from slipping out. He seemed so serious, so cynically aware of how people behaved, that I could not help feeling that he, at ten, knew more about life than I did at thirty.

At first, he told me, he had slept on the patios of shops. He had been beaten up by their watchmen, and had several times been hauled away by the police. Just a week ago they had taken him to the cells and beaten him with sticks, whacking him whenever he moved as if he were a rat. They called him a thief and asked him why he did not go home. He told them that the street was his home. Now he had moved into the shack built by the project, but still rummaged and begged on the streets to keep himself alive. He hated this town and would go anywhere where life was better, but there was nowhere he knew of. If he returned home he would die of starvation. I asked him if he were homesick.

'Yes,' he said woodenly. 'I miss my mother and father. I miss being in Turkana. I want to go back home. I want to see my family again.'

Then, to my astonishment, his faced relaxed and he started to cry. Perhaps I should not have let my own reaction register, or perhaps it would not have made any difference. As soon as he noticed my response, his face locked up again, he turned and sprinted off towards a clump of other children, picked up a stone, threw it at someone's legs and started to scuffle.

Ten minutes later, Daniel and Brian were treating the last of the scabies cases when a fat, dark, marvellously ugly woman in a scarlet twin-set and high heels, carrying a patent leather handbag, came striding down the market. She walked up to Daniel and stuck a finger in his face. I flinched. For a second she stood silent before him, her fat finger trembling, her face becoming darker and darker. The words, when they came, exploded from her mouth.

'Who are these people?'

She towered over Daniel, her legs splayed, her handbag swinging dangerously. Calmly, as if this happened to him every day, Daniel told her that we were friends from England who had come to see his project.

'Why have they not reported to the town clerk?'

'This is an independent project. It is not run by the council. They do not need to seek the council's permission to see it.'

Daniel's gentleness, his downcast eyes, his steady, unwavering voice, seemed to infuriate the indignant woman, who started making puffing noises, pursing her lips and inflating herself. At last she struck upon something to say.

'This is an illegal organization. The correct fees have not been paid. You are acting outside the law.'

I leant across to Brian. 'Who is this woman?' I whispered. Somehow she heard. She swung round, drew herself up, her bosom quivering, and raised her finger as if about to strike me down with it.

'I am not a woman!'

I stared at her in astonishment.

'I am a lady!' She seized her handbag in both hands and, elbows out, heels clattering, marched away through the market, colliding with and almost felling a man stooped under a bushel of green bananas.

The lady was, I discovered, a middle-ranking official on the town council. She had been persecuting Daniel and the project ever since it began. She had demanded money, tried to have him arrested, and made several official attempts to have his work stopped. She hated Daniel because he was doing what the council should have done; because he never gave her money; and because he was helping street children, and Turkana street children at that, to keep themselves alive in Kitale, as a menace to civilized society. A few minutes after the woman had left us, three tall men carrying sticks came down to the wooden shack and asked us to accompany them to the council offices.

We waited in a cavernous hall of polished wood, painted wooden shields and glowering colour photographs of the President. I could hear the hum of air-conditioning, the echoing footsteps in the corridors, laughter in a distant office. We sat around a conference table, in silence, for fifteen minutes. 'This is quite serious,' said Daniel.

The woman who had accosted us strode in beside a fat, unsmiling man in a silk Hawaiian shirt and introduced him as the location chief. (This later turned out to be untrue.) He asked us what our business was. The woman told him that it was to create a bad impression of Kenya. I watched him turning this intelligence over in his mind, as if trying to decide whether we could be charged for that. He seemed to conclude that it would not suffice. He ordered Daniel to hand over his charity licence.

'Aha! This is an illegal organization.'

'No, it is not.'

'It is called the Kitale Orphans Trust. But some of those children are not orphans. Therefore it is illegal.'

With patience and diplomacy, Daniel explained that the Trust had been approved by the town council when it issued the licence: if they thought the name was inaccurate they could have asked him to change it then. He had done all that the law demanded. The 'chief' turned and led us into the office of the town clerk. Behind a mahogany desk sat a slim, handsome man in an expensive blue suit, with a striped shirt and silk tie. He leant back in his chair, looking smooth and judicious. The woman remained on her feet. Jabbing her finger at us, she told the clerk that I had publicly insulted her by calling her a woman. That man – pointing to Adrian – was trying to destroy Kenya's image abroad by taking pictures of street children, and he (Daniel) was running an illegal organization. The clerk leant further back in his chair, twiddling his gold pen between his fingers, as if about to pronounce the wisdom of Solomon.

'You,' he told me, 'must apologize to this lady, for calling her a woman.'

This, gritting my teeth, I did.

'You,' he said to Adrian, 'must stop taking photographs.

And you, Mr Juma, must report to my office at nine o'clock sharp tomorrow morning to explain your motives.'

'And to mine,' said the chief.

'And to mine,' said the woman, with lofty finality.

I knew that all three would demand money from Daniel. I knew that Daniel, whatever it might cost him in time and exasperation, would not pay.

That night I stepped out of the Alakara Hotel and walked slowly down to the fish-and-chip shop. I stopped outside, watching the quiet bustle in the streets. I felt a hand, small and gritty, fit into mine. I looked down. It was John Kisitu's. He gazed up at me with his most pitiful false smile.

'Please sir, give me chippies. Chippies, please, chippies.'

The Kibera shanty town is the biggest unplanned settlement in East Africa. In a valley just two miles long and one mile wide live 400,000 people, yet none of the houses rises above one storey. Approaching Kibera, it looks as if someone has come to the rim of the valley with a wheelbarrow full of corrugated iron and tipped it over the edge. There is not a yard of vacant ground to be seen. The tin huts, tilted at crazy angles, spreading along twisting narrow paths, are built so close to the edges of the mud pits – sheer-sided quarries one hundred feet deep – that every few weeks some slide in when a bank collapses. Beyond the iron roofs, the web of illegal wires, the mud pits and the thousands upon thousands of people, rise the gleaming concrete towers of Nairobi.

Kibera is also one of the most notorious places on the continent. Its 400,000 people have no water supply, no sewerage, no roads and no official power lines. One in forty of its inhabitants has a job. I had heard that gangs of several hundred eight- and nine-year-olds roam the alleys, seizing adults too slow to get out of their way, stripping them naked, taking everything they possess, and dumping them, beaten and bleeding, into ditches flowing with rotten food and human excrement. Adult bandits hold up shops and mug passers-by in broad daylight. Protection rackets and *chang'aa* gangs – who try to monopolize the sale of moonshine and petrol – fight each other in the alleys with Kalashnikovs. In the yellow water at the bottom of the mud pits are said to lie the bodies of hundreds of people killed in these battles or murdered by burglars. I was told that, as a mzungu, I would not last an hour.

As soon as I walked down into the valley it was clear that, though some of the stories of Kibera's depravity may have been true, I was safer there than in the city centre. Everywhere we went, children swarmed about us, calling 'zungu, 'zungu', clinging to our hands and keeping with us until they felt they were too far from home, when they would let go and run back with big grins and bouncing steps. Every adult we passed greeted us. Watched by so many eyes, and surrounded by so many friendly smiles, I felt invulnerable. The alleys were filthy, ankle-deep in mud in places, strewn with dead animals and excrement; but the people were as clean and decent as they could afford to be: most of them looked more respectable than I did.

There were none of the packing-case and polythene houses I had seen in the slums in other parts of East Africa: all were built of corrugated iron, or iron, sticks and mud, and were clean and neat inside. Some had been cut open to make tiny shop fronts, from which vegetables, dried fish, soap powder, sugar and tea were sold. Women boiled cows' feet in tin tubs for soup; outside a tiny laundry a man pressed trousers with a charcoal-filled iron. Everyone appeared to know everyone else: people strolling along the alleys kept stopping to shake hands or gossip. They had, it seemed, partly filled the gaping hole of poverty with their wealth of spirit, and softened their hard lives with human kindness and reciprocity.

But there were some among these slum dwellers who did not fit in, and for them life was almost unimaginably cruel. None were more isolated than the two Turkana people I met outside their tin hut in the middle of the shanty town. Though they had been there for eight years, they still bore the mark of outsiders, of people thinking of the limitless savannah, as they gazed at the crowded grey horizon of metal sheets and wires. There were as many people in the two square miles of Kibera as there were in the whole of Turkana district.

Daudi and Margaret Limlim had been raided by the Pokot long before that tribe had started supplying the Kenya Meat Commission. In one night in 1985 Daudi's father was killed and all his animals were stolen. They could have fallen back on their extended families in Turkana district, but Daudi had a friend in Nairobi, who had written to tell him that he owned a successful business, was a rich man, and could find him a job the minute he arrived. Daudi was literate, spoke Swahili and some English, and it seemed to him that his energies would be rewarded in the city. He sold his possessions, borrowed from his friends and used the money to travel, with his wife and two of his four children, to Nairobi. After a year or two he would return, having made his fortune, buy a new herd and rejoin his family. He found his friend sleeping on the porch of the office block he was supposed to be guarding. He was a night-watchman, who earned the equivalent of £3 a month. He could not afford to rent a room, so he slept where he worked. He had not the faintest idea how Daudi could find a job.

Daudi was a slim, very dark man with scars on his forehead made by a shaman's knife and twitching muscles in his cheeks. As he spoke, his eyes darted around, and twice he looked over his shoulder and into his hut, as if afraid that someone might be breaking in. He had been attacked several times: without a network of people from his tribe to defend him he was easy prey. For the first two months in Nairobi, he, his wife and their children had slept on the porch with his friend. Every day he crossed the city, looking for work. He visited shops, building sites, news distributors, garages, security firms, government offices and markets. He found that for every formal job, however lowly, there were hundreds of applicants, and that the successful people were those with relatives or friends in the company. He gave up and started looking for casual labour.

He was employed for a few days plastering new houses with mud, and earned enough for a week's rent of a tin shack. Since then he had found about one day's work each week. With this he could pay the rent, but little else. Today the local blacksmith had given him a cast aluminium pot to polish. The work would take him two hours and he would be paid twelve pence. If he could persuade the man to give him two more, he could make enough to buy a kilo of flour and some milk for the children.

'But we don't eat every day. Everything costs money, even the water. We seldom have enough to buy flour. Normally I have only enough to buy a kilo of maize grain. That is what we live off, when we can afford it. I am used to being hungry, but the children find it very hard.

'I don't know what we can do. Sometimes I can search for two weeks without finding any work. Every day I am on the streets, going round to all the people I know, going to all the local businesses, begging for work. They are good people, and they would give me work if there was any, but there's none. I can't afford to send my children to school. They just hang around idly all day. I don't know what to do with them.'

Margaret had arrived in Nairobi speaking neither Swahili nor English. Eight years later, she spoke halting Swahili, and she still knew no one. Her arms were decorated with chains of scars, considered beautiful in Turkana district, but believed, in Nairobi, to be the mark of the savage. She told me she felt desperately lonely. She missed her family and her friends. All the things that had been so easy in Turkana district were almost impossible here. She called to her children, two of whom came nervously out of the shadows, a boy of nine and a girl, born since they arrived in the city, of six. The girl buried her face in Margaret's skirts. The boy watched us with big round eyes and wiped his nose on a filthy sleeve.

'They are both sick, as I can't feed them properly. They catch every disease there is because they're so weak. And there's no money to take them to hospital. I can't even afford the water to keep their clothes clean. Everything costs money here. In Turkana you never needed money. If you wanted to wash, you went down to the river. If you wanted food, you milked a goat or picked some fruit. If you were ill, the shaman would cure you. Here in the city, no one will help you.'

I asked Daudi if there were no other Turkana in Kibera.

'There are other Turkana. Quite a few. But we don't understand each other here. Our difficulties keep us apart. People might come to ask me for something, but I have nothing to give them. So how can we build up a friendship? When you meet another Turkana it is like meeting someone from another tribe. Everyone is desperate, so everyone just wants what he can get. Even when my friend died, no one would help me to bury him.

'I felt proud when I lived in Turkana. I had my own home, my own animals. No one told me what to do. I needed nothing. If I did not like one place I could just pick up my belongings and move somewhere else. I was surrounded by my family and my friends. Now I miss them so much that sometimes I cry. I have not seen my children since we left.'

'Could you not go back to Turkana?'

'If the money fell into my hands today, tomorrow I would be at the bus station. Every day I have been here I have wanted to go back, but to get my family to Turkana would cost 880 shillings [about £9]. I will never have that money. I could walk, but Margaret and my children cannot. If God does not help us, we will be here for the rest of our lives.'

All over Nairobi lived men and women like Daudi and Margaret, people of the Turkana, Samburu, Gabbra, Boran and Rendille tribes, who had come because they had lost their livelihood, then found themselves too far from their homes to return. As the lands of these nomads were seized and their herds were stolen, the trickle of people had turned into a flood. Every day hundreds of hopeful migrants stepped out of the county bus station. Every day tens of thousands of sedentary nomads wished they had never come.

Among them were some who had come through choice. In Nairobi I met people of nomadic tribes who could have stayed on their lands, but had heard fabulous stories about the city's wealth, and fantasized about fast cars, sophisticated women or beautiful clothes. A very few succeeded; most found themselves stranded in the slums. But the majority of people had moved because they had to, because they had lost the stock, the land or the mobility that nomadic herding requires. Even if these people could afford the bus fare, most had nothing to go back to. Daudi's dreams of making a living in Turkana district were now as unrealistic as his chances of making a fortune in Nairobi.

To people like Daudi and Margaret, moving to Nairobi means leaving themselves behind. Without their land they lose the physical coordinates that chart the progress of their lives. Without the land and the sky there is no God; without their tribe, their language and their laws there is no identity. Nairobi is a place in which they do not register. There is no network of friends and family to convince them that their existence is significant. There is no one to listen to their stories or songs, no one with whom to predict the weather from the stars; often, in that humid and smog-choked city, no stars. Here, amid the millions, they are no one, for the city is a no man's land.

But it is not just the nomads who suffer as a result of this migration. Before theft and dispossession forced them to move, these people were resilient, self-sufficient and productive. They kept themselves and their dependants alive, even in times of national catastrophe, and produced a small surplus of animals and hides. With the rest of the rural dispossessed, they now depend either on imported grain or on crops produced by Kenyan farmers from ever-diminishing pockets of land. As their choices become more and more limited, many of them are turning to crime to keep themselves alive. As the shanty towns grow and the Kenyan economy shrinks, the urban poor are becoming so desperate that there is now real danger of anarchy and bloody revolution.

The nomads, Kenyans are told, have to make way for development. But, as this book has shown, the type of development pursued in Kenya has not made the country richer. It has made a handful of men and women extremely wealthy: three particularly senior politicians, for example, are each reputed to have fortunes bigger than Kenya's national debt. It has made everyone else in the country poorer, as their land and resources are taken away from them for the benefit of the wealthy. Privatization, farming and conservation in the savannahs have not created wealth but concentrated it. The nomads' necessities are being turned into other peoples' luxuries.

But even today, amid the squalor of Nairobi and the desperation of its inhabitants, the story of the nomads is not an entirely bleak one. On the savannahs and in the slums are the first faint stirrings of hope.

I first met Moses Mpoke in the manyatta at Enkaroni, where I had watched that Maasai community's last graduation ceremony. He was a slight, eager, intense man of twenty-eight, with a small head, protruding teeth and a wispy moustache. Like the other Maasai, he wore a red check cloak and carried a staff of acacia wood. He spoke so fast that it was often hard to follow him, but when I watched him talking to the other junior elders, I saw that he was witty, confident and well-respected.

When the group ranch was divided up, he had used his good name in the community to secure seventy-six acres, a little more than the average, which included part of the valley of a small stream, kept moist in the dry season by groundwater. His father, who had owned a large herd, had been rich enough to send him to secondary school: Moses was one of the few at Enkaroni to have been fully educated. When he married, after his moranhood, he realized that his land was not sufficient to support him, his wife and his widowed mother. He travelled to Nairobi, where a cousin was working for the university. After a month of negotiations, the cousin found him a job as a filing clerk in the vice-chancellor's office. Moses worked there during the week and returned to Enkaroni at weekends. I was intrigued to see how he balanced the two halves of his life, so when he invited us to visit him in the office I immediately accepted.

Had he not straightened up, grinned and taken my hand I would have walked straight past him, for all I saw was a man in a suit and tie crouching beside a filing cabinet. Even when he had fetched us some tea, and sat down, talking about Enkaroni, I was still not fully convinced that this was the same man. He wore a neat, double-breasted pin-striped suit, a gilt pin in his tie, a handkerchief in his breast pocket and shiny black shoes. A furled black umbrella leant against his chair. He sat not as he had done on his stool in Enkaroni, with his legs stretched out and his hands on his thighs, but on the edge of his chair, leaning forwards, his hands on his knees. He spoke in an excited whisper, so rapidly that I could not understand a word he said.

Moses shared his office – an annexe to the vice-chancellor's room – with two well-dressed young women who sat behind a desk typing and answering the telephone. Twice while he was talking to us, one of the women asked Moses to get something for her. The nervous smile died on his face, he leapt up and scurried across the room to rummage in a cabinet. When the two women left for tea, Adrian asked Moses if he could take some photographs of him in the office. He asked him to sit behind the desk, pretending to answer the telephone. Moses had just sat down when the door to the vice-chancellor's office swung open. He bounced out of the chair as if he had been stung. In the doorway stood a thick-set man of sixty, with sideburns and a grey moustache, wearing a blazer with brass buttons and a silk college tie. 'Mpoke, what is the meaning of this?'

'Sir, I—'

'You do not have photographs taken in here without my permission, Mpoke.'

'Yes sir.'

'Is that clear?'

'Yes sir.'

'Get back to your work.'

'Yes sir.'

'And who are you?'

'I—'

'Well get out.' He turned on his heel and slammed the door to his office.

On the following Friday, after work, we met Moses outside the university and drove to his Nairobi home in the shanty town of Kawangware. Smaller and a little neater than Kibera, it was still intensely crowded. Moses lived with two friends from Enkaroni in a room in an iron dormitory, ten feet by ten. There were two single beds (two of the men slept in one bed), a table, a wardrobe, a portable gas stove and two chairs. There were six inches between the beds and the table for the men to dangle their legs. The walls were decorated with pictures cut from magazines – advertisements for cars, hairspray and clothes – and a map of Kenya. Moses put the stove on top of the table and brewed tea for us. He said something that made the other men laugh, leant forward and slapped me on the thigh. I recognized him for the man I had met in the savannahs.

He agreed that the room was crowded, but he felt safe and happy there. The two men were close friends from his age group and, when they had shut the door on Nairobi, it was, he said, as if they were back in one of the houses at Enkaroni. Living together meant that they could keep reminding each other that they were Maasai, as well as helping to reduce the costs of living in the city. I asked him if they ever quarrelled.

'We are age mates. Why should we quarrel? We have to stick together here and help each other. Wherever you meet a Purko Maasai, he will help you.'

The Maasai, Moses told me, were better off than the other nomads in Nairobi, because they were close to home and there were many other people of their tribe in the town. If they could afford it, they would go back to see their families at weekends, and there were always people coming back and forth with news from the community. Sticking together was the only way of coping with the city: without the other Maasai it would be a nightmare. This way, he told me, he could keep his family alive and keep his pride.

On the way back to Enkaroni, Moses asked us to pass through the suburb of Gigiri, to visit his elder brother, who had moved to Nairobi a few years before him. He had, he said, done well. We drove down asphalt streets, past gravel drives and hedges of hibiscus, stone gateposts looming white in the headlights. We pulled up at an enormous double gate. In the darkness beyond it was the vague glow of a colonnaded white house.

'Moses, when you said your brother had done well, I did not realize you meant this well.'

'Yes, he has done very well indeed. Ah, here he is.'

A man in a torn plastic coat and wellington boots, carrying a stout stick, came out of the shadows and shone a torch into the car. When he saw Moses his stern face broke into a grin. Moses jumped out and touched fingers with him. They talked happily for ten minutes before he returned to the car.

'Yes, he has done well, my brother. He has been a night-watchman for nine years, and still he is a happy man.'

At Kajiado we left the road and bumped down a stony track to the hospital. Moses's younger brother, who had been a moran in Toronkei's age group when I had last visited Enkaroni two months before, had been admitted to hospital with malaria. By the time we got there, however, he had been discharged and had returned home. Moses paid the doctor for the chloroquine.

'A very powerful drug,' he said. 'Without it my brother would have died.'

'What type of malaria was it?'

'*Plasmodium falciparum*, a bad variety. He caught it because he stole three goats from a man, and the man bewitched him. I had to go to the prophet to get some special fruits, to undo the witchcraft.'

I stared at Moses: I thought he was pulling my leg. But he looked earnest and thoughtful. Surely, I asked him, it was the chloroquine that cured the malaria. Yes, he said, the chloro-quine and the magic fruits.

I had forgotten how fresh the air in Maasailand was. I stood outside Moses's compound sucking in the scents of the sav-annah: the perfumed resin of the acacia trees; the bitter tang of trampled herbs; the warm, comforting odours of cow-dung and woodsmoke. Moses's nephews and nieces came out of the houses and dipped their heads so that we could lay our hands on their hair, then stepped back, giggled, and ran indoors. His mother, an ancient lady with grey stubble on her head and layers and layers of bead necklaces, smiled shyly and extended a long firm arm to shake my hand.

We stepped into the darkness of his house. Feeling my way around the partitions, my hand ran over the backs of the calves brought in for the night to be close to the Maasai, to grow up with no fear of the humans who would depend on them. The house was packed. Moses's wife, aunts, mother, sister-in-law, nephews and nieces sat around the fire, stoking the flames and making tea. On a couch of sticks and cow hides was a sedate party of junior elders, in red and blue cloaks. It was not until he stood up and smiled that I recognized Toronkei. He seemed demure, contented, confident: he was a man already, and told me of his plans to find a job and build up his herd. He had stayed with Moses's brother in the hospital, holding his hand for six days as he lay in bed, carrying him to the lavatory.

Moses, in his suit, holding his umbrella, disappeared behind one of the dung partitions and came out a few minutes later in his red cloak and sandals, a stick in his hand. The other junior elders made room for him on the couch, and he was immediately lost among them. When we had taken tea, I drew a stool up to the foot of the couch and asked Moses if he preferred this house to the one in Nairobi.

'In Nairobi my room is cleaner and there's no smoke. The bed is more comfortable than it is here. But I prefer being here. I feel safe. People do not come round to your house in the night here and break in. My friends are always visiting me, you can never be lonely for a moment. And I am glad to be with my family. The best thing would be to have a brick house, here in Enkaroni. Then I would have the best of both worlds.'

'So which is the real Moses Mpoke, the man in the cloak or the man in the suit?'

'This is the real Moses Mpoke, but the other one is also me. In the week I can live in the city and be comfortable; at weekends I can live here and be comfortable. The city has not stopped me from being a Maasai.'

I remembered what Moses had told me about his brother's malaria. He could believe simultaneously in both the Western way of treating the disease and the Maasai way: the one did not have to exclude the other. It was possible to live with a foot in each world, and to use the money and experience of the city to make life in the savannahs more secure.

Moses told me that he had been saving money ever since he moved to Nairobi, to set himself up as a cattle trader. In two months' time he would have the £300 he needed: in a week from today he would be handing in his notice. He would give up his room in Nairobi and move back here permanently, buying cattle from the other Maasai and hiring herders to drive them to the markets outside Nairobi. The trade would not make him rich, but would produce enough to feed his family and keep him among the cattle and the people with whom he felt at home.

I stepped out of Moses's house into the light of a full moon. My shadow was crisp on the ground. I could see the twigs and leaves of the acacias, silhouetted against the glowing sky, and the colours of the restless cattle shifting from foot to foot in the corral. I could hear the occasional clink of a cowbell, the barking of dogs and, far across the savannah, the strange, piping call of a hyena. From the house I heard Moses's voice and the laughter of the other junior elders. Moses was leading himself out of the wilderness of the city and back to the land of his forebears. Where he went, others were beginning to follow. In Narok district some of the Maasai were now putting their divided land back together again, and buying degraded fields abandoned by the wheat farmers, in the hope that they would gradually regenerate as pastures. Across Maasailand, new organizations were forming to contest the theft of their land and – for the first time in Maasai history – making common cause with the other nomads of Kenya and Tanzania. In the cities some Maasai were making the money they would need to keep themselves alive in the savannahs. The nomads, always tough and adaptable, were finding ways of responding to the demands of the outside world without compromising their identity.

These, of course, were only partial solutions. Moses and others like him were still faced with the problems of being confined to one spot. He was luckier than most Maasai, as his education and contacts had allowed him to find a job and his farm was big enough and wet enough to support his cattle: only a few could do as he had done. But what Moses shows is that the troubles of the nomads need not be terminal. There are ways in which many of them (population growth means that there is not room for all) can recover both their lands and their self-esteem. Now that foreign aid to Kenya has been resumed, one of the best uses to which it could be put is to help the nomads who are trying to protect or reclaim their birthright. They need, first of all, to feel secure in their lands, to know that neither misguided development schemes nor greedy politicians will take them away. They need help in reclaiming their stolen lands and, where they want it, in rebuilding the sort of communality which prevents a few individuals from taking everything for themselves. They need more schools and more job training, so that those whom the savannahs cannot support have other means of making a living. With this help they can prosper once more, and rebuild the lives that suit both them and the countries they inhabit.

By the time I awoke, the women of the compound were already milking the cows. I walked out into the sunshine, stopping and blinking for a few seconds, and watched as Moses wandered around his cattle, running his hands down their legs, checking their ears and the folds of their dewlaps for ticks. The cattle stamped and snorted, impatient to move into the pastures. The women finished their milking. Moses's mother squirted a few drops from the last udder into the lid of her gourd and flicked it over the backs of the cattle. Then the gate was opened. Ears raised, bells clinking, they trotted out onto the savannah.

In a tree a few hundred yards from the houses, a harrier hawk was robbing a colony of weaver birds. It hung upside down from a branch, flapping its wings as it pulled a nest to pieces with its beak. The tiny weaver birds dived and screeched at the hawk, landed on its back and tugged at its feathers. It broke through the straw basket, pulled out a fledgling and flew off over the scrub, the little birds mobbing it until it disappeared among the trees. Moses followed it with his eyes.

'This is the best time of the year. The rain has fallen and the grass is high. The cows can graze peacefully: they don't have to go far to find grass. At midday they'll get thirsty and take themselves slowly down to the river. They'll drink some water then graze their way back home. It is the same every day.'

The cattle buried their heads in the grass and Moses began to whistle, trilling and piping, blowing a brisk tune into the wind and across the heads of his cows. This, he told me, showed the animals that they were safe, that they need not raise their heads for fear of predators, as he was there. But I could see that he also whistled for the delight of being in the savannahs, of walking, in his cloak and sandals, through the long grass and the flowers brought out by the rain.

The cows pushed through the grass, rasping and crunching, and Moses, still whistling, retreated in front of them. I stayed where I was, close to the Land Rover that would take me back to Nairobi – back to the airport from which I would fly home – gazing on a scene that looked as old as the Creation. Moses raised his hand, then turned, pulled his cloak around his shoulders, and led his cows away over the savannah.